Abortion:
The Moral Issues

ABORTION
The Moral Issues

Edited by
Edward Batchelor Jr.

The Pilgrim Press
New York

Biblical quotations unless otherwise indicated are from the *Revised
Standard Version* of the Bible, copyright 1946, 1952, and © 1971 by the
Division of Christian Education, National Council of Churches, and are
used by permission. Quotations marked kjv are from the *King James
Version* of the Bible.

Library of Congress Cataloging in Publication Data
Main entry under title:

Abortion, the moral issues.

   Bibliography: p. 243
   1. Abortion—Moral and ethical aspects—Addresses,
essays, lectures. 2. Abortion—Religious aspects—
Christianity—Addresses, essays, lectures.
I. Batchelor, Edward, 1930–
HQ767.3.A256   363.4'6   82–7505
ISBN 0–8298–0611–3   AACR2
ISBN 0–8298–0612–1 (pbk.)

The Pilgrim Press, 132 West 31 Street, New York, New York 10001

Contents

Preface

W<small>HAT IS THE TASK OF THE MORALIST</small>? In 1755, Alphonsus di Ligouri wrote that we must know more than the general principles; they are few and known to all. He asserts, "The greatest difficulty . . . is the correct application of the principles to particular cases, applying them in different ways according to different circumstances [*Dissertatio,* c.4, n.122]."

The issues of abortion and homosexuality have been vigorously debated in religious and public forums over the past twenty years. Such debate undoubtedly will continue for many years. One reason for unhelpful results in the past is that we have disregarded di Ligouri's warning that the ethicist must know more than general principles.

The question of the morality of abortion is a case in point. We know the general principles: protecting and preserving innocent human life is an ethical value in the society; the *direct* termination of a pregnancy eliminates a potential or actual human life; therefore, such an intervention is always morally wrong.

Or is it? In "the correct application of the principles to particular cases," we discover deep and agonizing moral dilemmas to which there are no facile or simple answers. For example:

—Is abortion a religious issue at all?
—If so, how can the religious ethicist clarify the moral question?
—Is preserving and protecting innocent human life an absolute value?
—Are the rights of the mother or the embryo foremost?
—Is an unborn child a human being with full rights?
—If so, at which stage of its development?
—What is the proper place and function of religious, judicial, and legislative institutions in public policy decision-making?

Abortion: The Moral Issues, as with the volume I edited previously, *Homosexuality and Ethics,* does not attempt to furnish easy answers to complex moral questions. Rather, it surveys the present debate with writings of leading religious ethicists in order to provide the reader with necessary resources for reflection and response.

I thank the following persons for their help: the Rev. Robert Hare, pastor, Scarborough Presbyterian Church, Scarborough, New York, who furnished copies of the papers read at the October 9, 1980 Symposium on the Theology of Pro-Choice in the Abortion Decision, sponsored by Religious Leaders for a Free Choice, and the Religious Coalition on Abortion Rights; Dr. John Hurling, chief librarian at Brooklyn College, City University of New York, Brooklyn, New York, whose assistance and cooperation were invaluable in obtaining research privileges in various New York City libraries.

Both volumes in this series developed out of my experiences as a chaplain and lecturer in religious ethics at a campus of the City University of New York. I dedicate this volume with gratitude and affection to my past and present students—fellow learners in the difficult but rewarding task of moral problem-solving, sine qua non.

EDWARD BATCHELOR JR.
New York City

Part I

The Voice of Women

Lisa H. Newton
Margaret Mead
Sarah Ragle Weddington

The Irrelevance of Religion in the Abortion Debate

Lisa H. Newton

THE JUSTIFIABILITY OF ABORTION is in no way a religious issue, but an ethical, legal, and—regrettably—a political issue. It is an ethical issue because it involves an agonizing conflict between deeply felt moral values. It is a legal issue because it challenges the coherence of that notion of "legal personality," or personhood, on which our constitutional rights and duties are based. And it is a political issue because some have chosen to make it a test of strength and political influence in state and federal courts and legislatures. Simply because the groups who have made the issue an occasion for a test of political strength are loosely gathered, often enough, under religious banners has nothing to do with the philosophical status of the issue of abortion.

What is a "religious ethical issue," as opposed to an "ethical issue" that has no religious character? If we define "the ethical," very roughly, as "concerning norms (or prescriptions) for human conduct," then "the religious ethical" must mean "concerning God-given

Reprinted with permission from August 1978 issue of *Hastings Center Report* of the Hastings Center. ©Institute of Society, Ethics and the Life Sciences, 360 Broadway, Hastings-on-Hudson, NY 10706.

LISA H. NEWTON is professor of philosophy, Fairfield University, Fairfield, Connecticut.

norms for human conduct." The distinction between an "ethical" issue and a "religious ethical" issue is that the latter includes an essential appeal to the will of God and the former does not. In adopting that statement as the first premise of this discussion on the ethical status of abortion, the following questions are begged. Can there really be norms for human conduct, that is, is ethics possible? Is there any God to give norms, that is, is theistic religion possible? Can there be nontheistic religions? Is the idea of "the religious" exhausted in the concept of God's will? And can anything "ethical" exist apart from some appeal to religion? (One question is neatly skipped over, whether "the ethical" concerns only norms pertaining to conduct vis-à-vis others, as opposed to purely self-regarding conduct, if such there be. One of the peculiarities of the abortion issue is that no specification on this matter may appear in our assumptions; whether the fetus is "another person," to whom we might conceivably have duties, is precisely the issue in dispute.)

We adopt, then, the assumptions most likely held by the man and woman in the street and the jury in the courtroom: that there are ethical duties that are religious, in that God (ultimately) has commanded them; that there are ethical duties that are secular, in that they are based on considerations of human rights and welfare. While there is an enormous area of overlap, in that God has commanded much that is necessary for human welfare (for example, in the decalogue and in the Sermon on the Mount), there remains a clear distinction between them, deriving from their differing sources of authority or justification. Religious ethical issues are settled by appeals to the will of God; secular ethical issues are settled by appeals to human justice, common rights and duties, and the happiness of the greatest number in the long run.

What appeal is appropriate in the abortion dispute? Surely not an appeal to the revealed will of God, for nowhere in the Bible (or elsewhere, to my knowledge) was God's will on abortion revealed. Aristotle, granted almost the same status as Revelation for certain purposes, actually recommended abortion in some cases, and not just to preserve the life of the mother. The belief that the fetus is a fully independent human being has evolved only slowly, in certain religious traditions (Orthodox Judaism, Anglicanism, Roman Catholicism), traditions that otherwise have many differences. There simply is no religious root for this belief, which might be reached by anyone meditating on the implications of the available data on prenatal growth and development. And on this belief alone the prohibition of elective abortion is based: everyone—religious or not—with whom we would willingly discuss ethics agrees that full human beings—persons

—have a prima facie moral right to life, a right that will be protected by law in any civilized society.

When the dispute about the ethical issue of abortion is joined, the appeals are to scientific evidence of fetal activity; to legal and moral conceptions of "the person"; to property rights, rights of privacy, the right to life, and the right to liberty; to parental duties, duties of care and compassion; to the state's interest in future life; and even, unfortunately, to the taxpayer's interest in smaller welfare rolls. All these appeals are familiar from a host of ethical issues; God's voice is simply absent from this very human debate. The ethical content of this issue is painful and deeply divisive, for whichever way the evidence persuades each of us, we must see terrible, inhuman violations of human rights being countenanced by those who are persuaded to the opposite conclusion. But no religious appeal at all is needed to condemn the wanton slaughter of infants, if that's how we see abortion, or the callous stifling of the human potential of unwillingly pregnant women, if that's how we see its prohibition. Secular ethics is well enough equipped to fight this battle.

Then what is the "religious" component in the abortion issue, such that McRae et al. can contend that the Hyde Amendment is a violation of First Amendment separation of church and state, specifically of the "religious neutrality" of medical services intended by the Social Security Act? The component is not far to seek; it obtrudes on our consciousness every time the abortion issue is raised. It is the overwhelming presence of the Catholic Church, marching on Washington under right-to-life banners. Granted that the Church, in its proper teaching role, teaches the immorality of abortion; granted that individual Catholics and pastors, in their proper role as American citizens, have supported legislation designed to limit the performance of abortions in the United States; the two facts may not, should not, and by our Constitution, cannot have anything to do with each other. All citizens have the right to seek the enactment of law in conformity with their ethical convictions, however these convictions evolved in their own consciences, and any religious institution is surely free to address the conscience of each of its members; but the direct participation of such an institution in the political process can only confuse that process.

Whatever error permitted the Church's name, personnel, and monetary resources to be used in political power-seeking and legislative battling, is matched by the error committed by McRae and her courtroom allies in confusing legislative influence with the effect of legislation. There is no discrimination against non-Catholics in the Hyde Amendment. A law is discriminatory if its effect is to disadvantage an identifiable class of persons; it is not discriminatory simply because an identifiable class of persons influenced its passage. For all I know, our housing codes may have been written entirely by practicing Buddhists; more likely, our laws regulating alcoholic beverages may have been written from beginning to end by convinced Methodists. (How odd to see *them* party to a suit alleging "undue influence of religion on legislation"! If McRae's suit succeeds, every parched Catholic trying to survive in a bone-dry Methodist town should immediately launch a class-action suit relying on it.) To determine whether a law is discriminatory in effect, its principle and provisions alone are relevant; no import can be attached to the religious affiliation of the legislator who argued for it, of his legal counsel, of the lobbyist who, according to testimony, "leaned forward and slipped papers" to that counsel, or of any organization providing him with financial support. At least insofar as the religious discrimination issue is concerned, McRae et al.'s suit is fundamentally in error.

Perhaps in some eternal framework, these serious errors of constitutional interpretation cancel each other out, and we will be free to enjoy the residual humor. But the immediate result of the abortion donnybrook is nothing but evil: the judicial process is confused with emotional claims and counterclaims on legally irrelevant material; the legislative process is confused by the embarrassing presence of parties whose participation can never be legitimate and can only polarize the citizenry; Christianity is demeaned by official association with hate-filled rhetoric; and the human beings at the bottom of this all —pregnant women and their unborn children—are forgotten in the confusion. Abortion is a genuine issue, one with powerful ethical problems and implications; the sooner we get the word religion out of the dispute, the better it will be for all concerned.

2

Rights to Life

Margaret Mead

THE TREMENDOUS CONTROVERSY that is shaking the country over the abortion issue is compounded of half a dozen issues—hardly ever clearly stated together—each of which contaminates the others. Possibly by placing them together in one short statement we may reduce this tendency to reach unexamined conclusions.

A number of issues are involved. First, the question of whether it is ever right to kill, which includes the questions of capital punishment and of war. Anyone who is prepared to rest the abortion issue on the commandment "thou shalt not kill" has to examine also his or her stand on capital punishment—a willingness to condemn to death a citizen of one's own country—and on war—a willingness to kill, or to send personnel or bombs to kill, the citizens of other countries. If the answer is affirmative on either of these two issues, a stand that it is wrong to take the life of a conceived child becomes merely a matter of preference and not a matter of obedience to the ethic that the children of God should not murder one another.

Second, the question of the right to life of those who for some reason are judged defective: the feeble-minded, the crippled, the sufferer from birth defects or mutilations from accident, and the aged who have lost the power to contribute or participate—even by consciousness—in society. This question hinges on the existence of some sort of hierarchy of rights and on the assumption that those who

---

Reprinted with permission from the January 8, 1973 issue of *Christianity and Crisis*. © 1973 by Christianity and Crisis, Inc.

MARGARET MEAD (1901-78) was curator emeritus at the American Museum of Natural History, New York City, and adjunct professor of anthropology at Columbia University, New York, NY.

are least able have the fewest rights—or no rights at all. Among this group of the less blessed we find the conceived but unborn child who is diagnosed before birth as being defective, or for whom there is a reasonable prediction of defect—as with the child of a mother who has had German measles or who has taken a drug subsequently found to produce birth defects.

Third, the issue of the right of an individual to control his or her own body, to refuse a mutilating operation, and in the case of a woman, to refuse an abortion. The question of a man's control over a child of which he is believed to be the father—a belief that is always inferential—raises still further questions. If, as we at present think, the father's contribution of genes is as great as the mother's, does this give him a right over every conception into which one of his sperm has entered?

Human societies have settled these questions of paternity by fiat, legalisms, and fascinating rationalizations. For example, a legal case where a child born by artificial insemination from a donor (not the husband) was nonetheless declared to be the child of the woman's husband—who therefore could claim visitation rights after a divorce, because he, as a legal entity, had accepted the child as his.

Within this issue of a right over one's own body, including its genetic potential, comes the whole question as to whether society should ever have the right to deny or command an abortion, and whether this is not a matter for the individual woman, and possibly her partner, to decide. In a recent decision in Canada, the husband joined with the fetus in a suit to enjoin the wife and future mother from having an abortion. In connection with this right comes also the question of one's right to donate eyes to an eye bank or one's body for an autopsy—of whether in fact one's body belongs to oneself after death or is part of the legacy left to one's heirs.

Who Has the Power of Life and Death?

Fourth, the question of the right over not only one's body, but over one's life itself; this includes the right to commit suicide and the right to provide—through a living will—for the conditions under which one's life may be artificially prolonged, in spite of suffering, distortion of personality, imposition on others and society at large, etc. Should this living will be a will that a physician is not only permitted but obligated to respect, just as with the wishes of a fully competent patient?

Within the question of suicide (especially the suicide of one who feels her or his life is in some way a burden to others) is the question of sovereignty. Many societies conceive of the individual life as the *property* of the body politic, the property of the sovereign or state. In this case, the individual whose life it is has no final right. This same position can be taken about God—treating God as an absolute monarch in the European style of the Middle Ages, e.g., in the statement of Pope Paul VI, in October 1971, that euthanasia "without the patient's consent is murder and with the patient's consent is suicide—what is morally a crime cannot, under any pretext, become legal."

The fifth issue is that of competence. When are individuals competent to speak in their own right, and when must surrogates—parents, children, relatives, an advocate appointed by the state, the church, or the medical profession—speak for them? It is clear that for the unborn but already conceived, for the newborn, for the young child, for the individual who is paralyzed and cannot communicate personal wishes, for those who are insane beyond the power of making judgments, for the senile, and for those whose hearts may still beat but whose brains are dead—for all these others must speak. The ethical question is who?

In a case where a mother who did not approve of blood transfusion but whose unborn child was judged by medical opinion to be jeopardized by her refusal, a Washington, DC court—in the name of the unborn child—ordered her to violate her own religious belief and her own body to accept a blood transfusion. The problem ranges from the right to decide on an abortion—for oneself, for the mother of one's child, for a citizen of a state where the officials judge a birth disadvantageous to the body politic—all the way to the right to turn off the respirator for a patient whose brain has already died. Who decides?

Who has the absolute power of life and death over any individual life, whether just conceived or just ending? On the basis of our oldest human forms of social organization, is it the family; is it the state, which has grown and taken over tremendous powers of life and death over its willing and unwilling citizens; is it the medical profession, which owes its very being to the preservation of life in all circumstances; or is it oneself, in the case of the right of an individual while of sound mind to determine how and when his or her own life shall end?

Is an unborn child a human being, with the full rights we accord a human being? If that child is such a human being, and if it cannot in the nature of the case defend its own rights, should it have an advocate appointed by the court, the protector of the civil rights of citizens, to plead its cause? When does an individual become a citizen over whom other citizens—including its father and mother—cannot exercise powers of life and death?

When Does Life Begin . . . and End?

Sixth, after all these issues are considered under the heading of rights to life, we are still faced with two questions: When does an individual come into being so that he or she can be said to have an individual life, and when does that life end, so that the individual can no longer be said to live? Here again both ends of the spectrum must be considered.

Does an individual exist from the moment of the first union of sperm and ova, from implantation, from the stage of the shaping of the fetus into recognizable human form, from the moment prenatal diagnosis declares the fetus without discernible defect, from the moment of birth when the child is fully enough developed to survive without extraordinary means (an incubator is just as extraordinary as a respirator), from the moment it is seen as having irremediable birth defects (does this include birth defects that demand fifty-five corrective operations so the child can participate in society?), from the moment the mother is able to feel the child is hers (which may take weeks if an anesthetic has been used at delivery), from the moment the infant has demonstrated it is strong enough to live, from the moment the father acknowledges it legally if he has not done so before?

Some societies do not consider a child a full human being—the inducing of whose death would be murder—until two weeks after birth, or six months, or even two years. . . . In other words, the right to life in such societies includes the demonstration that the individual infant has the capacity to live. All these considerations can be stated in reverse. When is an individual no longer a valuable member of society, crippled mentally or physically so as to be incapable of reproduction, self-support, or conscious participation?

A Simple Solution: Repeal the Laws

When all these considerations have been thought through—in relation to one another—then come the questions of the right of the state to impose these decisions and the right of some group of citizens who hold one view to impose their version of rights to life on other citizens who, in good conscience, hold other views. Here we come to the crucial question of the demand by both those who advocate abortion—and either active or passive euthanasia—and those who oppose them that the state should implement their particular views by imposing them on all citizens: either by imposing an absolute prohibition on abortion, or by the compulsory sterilization of those who may be expected to have defective children, or by passing a liberalized abortion law that in effect causes citizens who disagree to vote *for* abortion.

Both parties to this debate are attempting to impose their wills —those who demand a liberalized abortion law just as much as those who demand a law making abortion illegal. This is what the advocates of the right to an abortion fail to recognize. No one who believes that abortion is murder—at any stage from conception to birth—should be asked to vote for a law *legalizing* abortion. No one who believes that the pregnant woman, or the pregnant woman and the father of the child, should have a full right to determine whether this child should be born should be asked to vote for a law making abortion illegal.

The solution is simple. Both parties can in good conscience vote for the *repeal of laws* governing abortion and place abortion under the medical profession, and under the churches who may educate their own members and work to convert nonmembers to their point of view. When the issue is extended to the right to die with dignity, no one should be asked to vote for what they regard as suicide or murder, and again, the rights of the individual concerned should be respected. Quite clearly no Christian can vote for abortion or euthanasia as public policy for reducing the population or lessening the burden the support of the weak places on the strong. But the need for laws that permit individual interpretations of the beginning and end of life is manifestly very great.

Have the Unconceived Any Rights?

And once this set of temporal issues that relate to a single life span on this planet is resolved, we will be faced with a great many more issues, which again should be resolved by a law that protects the individual conscience in its attempt to obey the injunction "thou shalt not kill." For after the unborn come the unconceived. Have they rights? Those who oppose contraception implicitly act as if the unconceived already exist, and that properly wedded men and women should open the windows and "let the little souls fly in."

Does every individual who might be the result of a single sexual act between two persons, or two persons declared by church or state to be in a particular condition of potential parenthood, have a right to be actualized now, in this period of history, as a living person, regardless of whether this particular condition of birth will make the child defective, crippled, condemned to a life of poverty, born to parents who will reject and possibly harm her or him, born to a group that is starving or being subjected to genocide—hunted like animals in some jungle that an avaricious state or an amoral commercial interest wants to develop?

Or should we think instead of the other individuals (for each such possible conception is of course unique) who might—if the birth of some were postponed now, for this pregnancy, or this marriage, or this generation—be born to a better life, a life when prenatal defects could be corrected, when prenatal malnutrition had been abolished, when all human beings were treated as equally human regardless of race, color, religion, ideology, or technological level of their culture, a life in which men and women had been freed to become loving fathers and mothers?

Should we in fact have advocates for the unconceived who may claim that the children of the future have a right to live in another generation rather than in this, a right to be born to different parents, a right not to be born today or to particular parents whose inheritance or experience will doom them to lives of suffering and misery?

These are admittedly population rights, rights of a universe that contains millions, billions of children who may or may not be conceived. Can our imagination encompass them, and if so, how will we implement what we see—as Christians? How can we combine care for every child whom we pronounce to have a right to life—however defective this child may be—with public policies of the prevention of the birth of children into lives that are demonstrably and irremediably bad?

Here contraception as a public policy comes into play. Just as the state *should not* have power of life and death over its citizens of any age and in any condition, so *should* the state have the power to protect the population of a country from disease, from poverty, from conditions in which children are beaten and starved and abused. This seems to me a position that can be defended in the name of the Christian ethics of "thou shalt not kill" and "thou shalt love thy neighbor as thyself."

Those who advocate any portion of the whole argument should —in all conscience—scrutinize how they regard the rest. If they are willing to plead for the rights of the just-fertilized ovum, they should scrutinize their willingness to see a fellow adult, who is surely completely human in the capacity to sin, suffer and repent, be hung or electrocuted. Those who draw such appealing pictures of unborn infants should face their willingness to compel our young men to go to war and to pour napalm on the children of the people whom we have declared, by fiat, to be our enemies. And those who plead for the life of every unborn child, no matter how defective, should consider how they regard the care of the elderly and the helpless.

And there is another consideration that is coming to the fore in the increasing demand that only the strong and productive should be allowed to live. This is what happens to a society that does not care for its weak and its unfortunate, that does not respect individual consciences, that subjects those who regard war as murder to legal penalties, that punishes physicians who feel a woman should have a right to choose whether or not she will bear a child, or another child. What happens in a society in which a legal decision can cancel all rights of a father to his own child, and which permits conditions to continue in which a black child's right to survival may be one seventeenth as good as the right of a white child born on the other side of town?

The Ethic Changeth Not; Times Do . . . and People Can

Willingness to protect life as an individual understands it and to protect the individual's conscientious choice, and the willingness to find a place for the weak, the infant and the aged, the crippled, the defective, mutilated by accident or war are a measure of a good society. But this is only so if this willingness is joined by the most vigorous attempt to abolish the conditions that make these decisions so paradoxical, contradictory, and difficult.

Advocates for laws against all abortions, or even all contraception, and advocates of laws in favor of abortion, or of compulsory contraception, should sit down and think through all the ramifications of their fierce and unexamined advocacy. They might then agree on laws that require no citizen to violate what he or she understands as the will of God.

The debate might become, as it should be, a discussion of the way in which changing conditions of life, changing medical knowledge and skill, changing population size, and changing relationships between the environment and the stress placed on it by modern technological civilizations necessarily demand a rethinking of Christian ethics within the basic commandment "thou shalt love thy neighbor as thyself." The young lawyer who asked of Christ "Who is my neighbor?" could not have discussed prenatal diagnosis of fetal defects or the possible effects of the emission of gases from millions of automobiles into the atmosphere.

The basic ethic of "thou shalt not kill"—never realized yet except by a handful of prophetic forerunners of a better world—and of "thou shalt love thy neighbor as thyself" does not change. But times

13

do, and men and women can; and we may well ask whether the commotion made by the mass media and politicians over abortion is not a cover for unwillingness to face the mass murder of innocents in other parts of the world, murder that no longer can be rationalized by the argument of the defense of small, vulnerable homelands, necessary for the safety and well-being of our children's children.

3

The Woman's Right of Privacy

Sarah Ragle Weddington

My topic, "The Woman's Right of Privacy," has two facets: the constitutional protection of the privacy of our citizens, and the particular concern of women regarding pregnancy.

On January 22, 1973, the U.S. Supreme Court decided the case of *Roe v. Wade*. This decision specifically holds that a woman's right of privacy extends to the decision of whether to continue or terminate an unwanted pregnancy. The case is truly a landmark decision. Before discussing the basis for and the impact of the decision, I would like to make a few general remarks.

First, regarding the topic of abortion, it is important to divide what is said from the manner in which it is said. Those of us who favor availability of choice are at a disadvantage concerning semantics. Those who oppose availability of choice emphasize being pro-life. All of us would affirm the sanctity of life, the joy of life, the value of life. The points on which we divide include the definition of human life, the weighing of concerns for the pregnant woman and for the fertilized ovum, and the implications of constitutional law.

Second, those of us who favor the availability of alternatives are not "for" abortion. We are *for* such things as preventing unwanted pregnancies; I personally have sponsored legislation to make contra-

---

Reprinted from *The Perkins Journal*, Fall 1973, with the permission of the publisher.

SARAH RAGLE WEDDINGTON is a member of the Texas Bar, and served as an aide in the White House during the administration of President Carter.

ceptive measures more widely available. We *do not* advocate, for example, that every woman should seek an abortion; we *do* advocate that the alternative of abortion be an alternative available to pregnant women.

Discussion regarding abortion so often centers on the fertilized ovum and omits any focus on the woman involved. My comments will focus on the woman.

Pregnancy unquestionably has an impact on the woman involved. *Roe v. Wade* established that the impact of pregnancy is of such a nature and extent that the woman is entitled to constitutional protection in being able to choose among alternatives that include abortion.

The main plaintiff in the case, Jane Roe, at the time she filed suit was an unmarried adult. She filed on behalf of herself and "all other women who have sought, are seeking, or in the future will seek" a legal, medically safe abortion. She had not finished high school, had difficulty holding a job, and had no money for medical care associated with the pregnancy. Jane Roe had sought an abortion but had been refused since she was in good health and Texas law allowed abortion only for the purpose of saving the life of the woman.

Mary and John Doe, a childless married couple, were also plaintiffs. Mary Doe's health, but not life, would be seriously affected by pregnancy. Because of a neural-chemical disorder, she had been advised not to use oral contraceptives and not to get pregnant. The Does also filed a class action, pointing out that according to the 1965 National Fertility Study, among *married* couples in the United States, nearly 20 percent of all recent births were unwanted.[1]

The Constitution does not specifically enumerate a "right to seek abortion" or a "right of privacy." That such rights are not enumerated in the Constitution is no impediment to the existence of the rights. Other rights not specifically enumerated have been recognized as fundamental rights entitled to constitutional protection[2] including the right to marry,[3] the right to have offspring,[4] the right to use contraceptives to avoid having offspring,[5] the right to direct the upbringing and education of one's children,[6] as well as the right to travel.[7]

The plaintiff in *Roe v. Wade* sought to establish the right of individuals to seek and receive health care unhindered by arbitrary state restraint, the right of married couples and of women to privacy and autonomy in the control of reproduction, and the right of physicians to practice medicine according to the highest professional standards.

The federal district court agreed that a right of privacy was involved.

16

On the merits, plaintiffs argue as their principal contention that the Texas abortion laws must be declared unconstitutional because they deprive single women and married couples of their right, secured by the Ninth Amendment, to choose whether to have children. We agree.

The essence of the interest sought to be protected here is the right of choice over events that, by their character and consequences, bear in a fundamental manner on the privacy of individuals.

That view has been shared by a number of other courts which have considered the question and have affirmed the fundamental right involved. The progression of decisions by courts which have indicated their recognition of abortion as an aspect of protected privacy rights includes the following:

The fundamental right of the woman to choose whether to bear children follows from the Supreme Court's and this court's repeated acknowledgment of a "right of privacy" or "liberty" in matters related to marriage, family, and sex.[8]

For whatever reason, the concept of personal liberty embodies a right to privacy which apparently is also broad enough to include the decision to abort a pregnancy. Like the decision to use contraceptive devices, the decision to terminate an unwanted pregnancy is sheltered from state regulation which seeks broadly to limit the reasons for which an abortion may be legally obtained.[9]

It is as true after conception as before that "there is no topic more closely interwoven with the intimacy of the home and marriage than that which relates to the conception and bearing of progeny." We believe that Griswold and related cases establish that matters pertaining to procreation, as well as to marriage, the family, and sex are surrounded by a zone of privacy which protects activities concerning such matters from unjustified governmental intrusion.[10]

Without the ability to control their reproductive capacity, women and couples are largely unable to control determinative aspects of their lives and marriages. If the concept of fundamental rights means anything, it must surely include the right to determine when and under what circumstances to have children.

All too frequently it is presumed that people have access to and are able to use highly effective contraceptives, and are themselves at fault in cases of unwanted or unplanned pregnancy. This assumption could not be further from medical reality. First, there still is no such thing as a contraceptive device that is 100 percent safe and 100 percent effective. Second, there are still those in the United States who financially do not have access to medical care and contraceptives.

17

The California Supreme Court has recognized that "childbirth involves the risk of death."[11]

Nearly ten years ago a medical expert reported that "the risk to life from an abortion, performed by an experienced physician in a hospital on a healthy woman in the first trimester of pregnancy is far smaller than the risk ordinarily associated with pregnancy and childbirth."[12] A recent study of the death rate from childbirth in the United States revealed that twenty deaths per 100,000 pregnancies occur among American women.[13] The same study reported that the death rate due to legalized abortions performed in hospitals in Eastern Europe is three per 100,000 pregnancies. Thus, in the United States today, giving birth is nearly seven times more dangerous than a therapeutic abortion.

Further, women who have been unable to end an unwanted pregnancy by other means have sometimes resorted to illegal abortions performed by persons with little or no medical training. There is no need to detail the emotional and medical consequences.

From the moment a woman becomes pregnant her status in society changes as a result of both direct and indirect actions of the government and because of social mores.

Pregnancy, from the moment of conception, severely limits a woman's liberty. In many cases of both public and private employment, women are forced to temporarily or permanently leave their employment when they become pregnant. The employer has no duty to transfer a pregnant woman to a less arduous job during any stage of pregnancy (should the woman or her doctor consider this advisable); nor is there any statutory duty to rehire the woman after she gives birth.

Until 1972 a woman who became pregnant and was employed in Texas state government was forced to quit. She was not allowed to use accumulated sick leave or vacation time; she had no right to get her job back; and if she were rehired, she came back in the status of a new employee. This was true even if she wished to continue working and her doctor certified the advisability of such. Regardless of whether the woman wishes and/or needs to continue working, regardless of whether she is physically capable of working, she may nonetheless be required to stop working solely because of her pregnancy. In many if not most states, women who are public employees continue to be compelled to terminate their employment at some arbitrary date during pregnancy regardless of whether they are capable of continuing work.

In Connecticut a directive from the attorney general in 1938 stated that a pregnant woman could not be employed "during the four weeks previous to and following her confinement." This rule still exists. In fact, such employment is a criminal offense directed against the employer.[14]

This denial of liberty in one's work is accompanied by an unconstitutional taking of property, for Connecticut provides no maternity benefits. A woman is also denied unemployment compensation during her last two months of pregnancy, even when her unemployment is due to some reason other than pregnancy. If "total or partial unemployment is due to pregnancy," the woman is completely ineligible for benefits.

In Louisiana an amendment in 1968 of L.S.A.—R.S. 23:1601(6)(b) enables a woman who is forced to leave her employment either by contract or otherwise because of pregnancy to qualify for unemployment compensation. But as illustrated in the case of *Grape v. Brown,* 231 So. 2d 663 (Ct. App. La., 1970), the unemployment compensation in no way adequately compensates either for the actual wages lost or for the denial of liberty that forces a woman to receive unemployment compensation. Mary Grape was employed as a keypunch operator by Southwestern Electric Power Company. When she became pregnant she was advised that the company policy required expectant mothers to terminate employment no later than the end of the 150th day of pregnancy and that no leaves of absence would be granted. She was forced onto unemployment compensation and had lost her job.

Thus, the pregnant woman loses her job, her source of income, and is *forced* to become economically *dependent* on others. The law is harshest on pregnant women who are heads of households, and depended on as breadwinners. Statistics show that a high percentage of working women are in this position, i.e., they *must* work to support themselves and/or their children.

But restrictions on a woman's liberty and property only *begin* with pregnancy. A woman worker with children is considered "unavailable for work" (which means she cannot qualify for unemployment compensation) if she restricts her hours of availability to late afternoon and night shifts so she may care for her children during the day. Connecticut courts have often held that "domestic responsibilities" are "personal reasons unrelated to employment"[15] or "entirely disconnected from any attribute of employment."[16] In one decision the court said that a woman had just *five weeks* to rearrange her life and domestic responsibilities to try to make herself "available for work" according to Connecticut standards (i.e., ready for work at all hours of the day).

Once a woman has given birth, according to the Court of Appeals for the Fifth Circuit, she may still be barred from employment as long as she has preschool children.[17] If she needs or merely wishes to work while she has preschool children she cannot, unless she is fortunate enough to have a family who will care for the children or is wealthy enough to hire help. And although a housekeeper, nurse, or baby-sitter is a necessary expense, enabling her to work, she has not been able to deduct the salary of this person from her income tax [26 U.S.C. 214] and thus is normally left with little, if any, of her pay after these expenses are covered.

A further denial of liberty results from the fact that women are generally forced to arbitrarily end their education because of pregnancy. Until recently, girls who became pregnant were often forced to drop out of public school. Many women are also deprived of higher education because of college rules requiring that pregnant women leave school.

The importance of education in modern society has been stressed and restressed in recent years. It has been recognized that there are special problems for women in obtaining education, for although "men and women are equally in need of continuing education . . . at present women's opportunities are more limited than men's."[18] Nonetheless, women may be robbed of their education and opportunity for any development and self-fulfillment because of an unwanted pregnancy.

The incursions on the liberty of an unmarried woman who becomes pregnant are even more severe. She too may be fired from her job and is even more likely to be compelled to discontinue her education. Unable to terminate her pregnancy, she is often forced into marriage against her will and better judgment in an attempt to cope with the new economic and social realities of her life.

Of course, frequently, the man who is responsible for the pregnancy refuses to marry her. In Texas the illegitimate father has no common-law or statutory responsibility to provide support. The woman may be forced to become a welfare recipient, become part of this cycle of poverty, and expose herself to the personal humiliation, loss of personal liberty, and inadequate income this entails.

A woman who has a child is subject to a whole range of de jure and de facto punishments, disabilities, and limitations to her freedom from the earliest stages of pregnancy. In the most obvious sense she alone must bear the pains and hazards of pregnancy and childbirth. She may be suspended or expelled from school and thus robbed of her opportunity for education and self-development. She may be fired or suspended from her employment and thereby denied the right to earn a living and, if single and without independent income, forced into the degrading position of living on welfare.

Having been forced to give birth to a child she did not want, a woman may be subject to criminal sanctions for child neglect, e.g.,

D.C. Code §22-902, if she does not care for the child to the satisfaction of the state. In some states even here the disabilities for the woman are greater than for the man. The New York courts seem to have found as a matter of law that the mother has a greater responsibility for the child than the father. In the case of *People v. Edwards,* 42 Misc. 2d 930, 249 N.Y.S. 2d 325 (1964), although the father and mother were jointly indicted for failure to provide shelter and medical attention for their baby, the court held that only the mother could be punished for failing to bring the baby to a doctor when a condition that began with a diaper rash resulted in the child's death.

The impact of pregnancy is not restricted to economic and educational areas. Certainly there is a physical impact, as well as the emotional reaction to an unwanted pregnancy. These aspects are obvious, and I will not belabor the point.

The Supreme Court in its opinion in *Roe v. Wade* said:

> This right of privacy, whether it be founded in the Fourteenth Amendment's concept of personal liberty and restrictions upon state action, as we feel it is, or, as the District Court determined, in the Ninth Amendment's reservation of rights to the people, is broad enough to encompass a woman's decision whether or not to terminate her pregnancy. The detriment that the State would impose upon the pregnant woman by denying this choice altogether is apparent. Specific and direct harm medically diagnosable even in early pregnancy may be involved. Maternity, or additional offspring, may force upon the woman a distressful life and future. Psychological harm may be imminent. Mental and physical health may be taxed by child care. There is also the distress, for all concerned, associated with the unwanted child, and there is the problem of bringing a child into a family already unable, psychologically and otherwise, to care for it. In other cases, as in this one, the additional difficulties and continuing stigma of unwed motherhood may be involved. All these are factors the woman and her responsible physician necessarily will consider in consultation.

Thus, a woman's right of privacy extends to abortion. Can the state prove a compelling reason to regulate? No.

Briefly, Texas law has never treated prior-to-birth and after-birth the same. Murder, in Texas, is defined as the killing of one who has been born. Murder carries a penalty of up to life. Abortion was a completely separate offense punishable by a maximum of five years, unless the *woman's* consent to the procedure was not obtained, in which event the penalty was doubled. Texas courts had specifically held self-abortion was not a crime, and one case regarding abortion stated that the woman was the victim of the crime. Tort and property rights in Texas are contingent on being born alive.

The court responded to the state's argument as follows:

Texas urges that, apart from the Fourteenth Amendment, life begins at conception and is present throughout pregnancy, and that, therefore, the State has a compelling interest in protecting that life from and after conception. We need not resolve the difficult question of when life begins. When those trained in the respective disciplines of medicine, philosophy, and theology are unable to arrive at any consensus, the judiciary, at this point in the development of man's knowledge, is not in a position to speculate as to the answer.

It should be sufficient to note briefly the wide divergence of thinking on this most sensitive and difficult question. There has always been strong support for the view that life does not begin until live birth. This was the belief of the Stoics. It appears to be the predominant, though not the unanimous, attitude of the Jewish faith. It may be taken to represent also the position of a large segment of the Protestant community, insofar as that can be ascertained; organized groups that have taken a formal position on the abortion issue have generally regarded abortion as a matter for the conscience of the individual and her family. As we have noted, the common law found greater significance in quickening. Physicians and their scientific colleagues have regarded that event with less interest and have tended to focus either upon conception or upon live birth or upon the interim point at which the fetus becomes "viable," that is, potentially able to live outside the mother's womb, albeit with artificial aid. Viability is usually placed at above seven months (28 weeks) but may occur earlier, even at 24 weeks. The Aristotelian theory of "mediate animation," that held sway throughout the Middle Ages and the Renaissance in Europe, continued to be official Roman Catholic dogma until the 19th century, despite opposition to this "ensoulment" theory from those in the Church who would recognize the existence of life from the moment of conception. The latter is now, of course, the official belief of the Catholic Church. As one of the briefs *amicus* discloses, this is a view strongly held by many non-Catholics as well, and by many physicians. Substantial problems for precise definition of this view are posed, however, by new embryological data that purport to indicate that conception is a "process" over time, rather than an event, and by new medical techniques such as menstrual extraction, the "morning-after" pill, implantation of embryos, artificial insemination, and even artificial wombs.

In areas other than criminal abortion the law has been reluctant to endorse any theory that life, as we recognize it, begins before live birth or to accord legal rights to the unborn except in narrowly defined situations and except when the rights are contingent upon live birth. For example, the traditional rule of tort law had denied recovery for prenatal injuries even though the child was born alive. That rule has been changed in almost every jurisdiction. In most States recovery is said to be permitted only if the fetus was viable, or at least quick, when the injuries were sustained, though few courts have squarely so held. In a recent development, generally opposed by the commentators, some States permit the parents of a stillborn child to maintain an action for wrongful death because of prenatal injuries. Such an action, however, would appear to be one to vindicate the parents' interest and is thus consistent with the view that the fetus, at most, represents only the potentiality of life. Similarly, unborn children have been recognized as acquiring rights or interests by way of inheritance or other devolution of property, and have been represented by guardians *ad litem*. Perfection of the interests involved, again, has generally been contingent upon live birth. In short, the unborn have never been recognized in the law as persons in the whole sense.

In view of all this, we do not agree that, by adopting one theory of life, Texas may override the rights of the pregnant woman that are at stake.

The Court, however, did not recognize an absolute right of privacy. Rather, it stated, for example, that the state could constitutionally regulate to require that abortions be performed by licensed practitioners, that second trimester abortions be performed in hospitals, and that third-semester abortions be done only for the purpose of saving the life or health of the woman.

Pregnancy does affect a woman directly and profoundly. The Supreme Court therefore held that the constitutional right of privacy would extend to the choice of whether to continue or terminate a pregnancy. The state then failed to meet its burden of proving a compelling state interest; the great diversity of opinion that exists demonstrates the obvious difficulty of proof.

The year 1973 began with the establishment of a woman's right of privacy extending to the choice of whether to continue or terminate a pregnancy. However, as a practical matter, many women who seek medical services have great difficulty finding them. There are various moves in Congress to amend the Constitution to end the woman's right of privacy. Whether the right will become a reality soon remains to be seen.

Part II

Rules for Debate

Richard A. McCormick, S.J.
Gregory Baum
Commission on Faith and Order,
  NCCC in the U.S.A.

Rules for Abortion Debate

Richard A. McCormick, S.J.

THERE ARE A MILLION legal abortions performed annually in the United States. If this is what many people think it is (unjustified killing of human beings, in most cases), then it certainly constitutes the major moral tragedy of our country. In contrast, over many years fifty thousand Americans were lost in Vietnam. About the problem of abortion and its regulation, Americans are profoundly polarized, and there seems little hope of unlocking deeply protected positions to reach any kind of national consensus. Yet surely this is desirable on an issue so grave.

I have been professionally involved in this problem for well over twenty years, on podium, in print, and above all, in many hundreds of hours of conversation. Such experiences do not necessarily increase wisdom. But they do generate some rather clear impressions about the quality of discourse on the problem of abortion. I have to conclude, regrettably, that the level of conversation is deplorably low. On both sides, slogans are used as if they were arguments; the sound level rises as verbal bludgeoning and interruptions multiply; the dialogue of the deaf continues. Some of the most prestigious organi-

Reprinted from the July 22, 1978 issue of *America* with the permission of the author and America Press, Inc., 106 West 56th Street, New York, NY 10019. ©1978 All rights reserved.

RICHARD A. MCCORMICK, S.J., is Rose F. Kennedy Professor of Christian Ethics at the Joseph and Rose Kennedy Institute of Ethics, Georgetown University, Washington, DC.

zations of the news media (for example, *The New York Times*, *The Washington Post*) support policies that stem from moral positions whose premises and assumptions they have not sufficiently examined, let alone argued. The same can be said of some antiabortionists in the policies they propose. An executive assistant in the Senate told me recently that the two most obnoxious lobbies on the Hill are the antiabortionists and the proabortionists. Briefly, civil conversation on this subject has all but disappeared. Perhaps this is as it should be. Perhaps now is the time for camping in abortion clinics or beneath office windows of the secretary of Health and Human Services. But I think not, at least in the sense that such tactics should not replace disciplined argument.

Many of us have become bone weary of this discussion. But to yield to such fatigue would be to run from a problem, not wrestle with it. If stay we ought and must, then it may be of help to propose a set of rules for conversation, the observance of which could nudge us toward more communicative conversation. This is surely a modest achievement, but where the level of discourse is as chaotic and sclerotic as it is, modesty recommends itself, especially when so many begged questions and non sequiturs are traceable to violations of some of the fundamental points raised below. I do not believe these guidelines call for compromise or abandonment of anyone's moral conviction. At least they are not deliberately calculated to do this. Basic moral convictions have roots, after all, in some rather nonrational (which is not to say irrational) layers of our being. Rather, these suggestions are but attempts to vent and circumvent the frustrations that cling to bad arguments. In qualifying certain arguments as "bad," one unavoidably gives his or her position away at some point. But that is neither here nor there if the points made have independent validity. Perhaps the following can be helpful.

Attempt to identify areas of agreement. Where issues are urgent and disputants have enormous personal stakes and investments, there is a tendency to draw sharp lines very quickly and begin the shootout. Anything else strikes the frank, let-it-hang-out American mind as hypocrisy. We have, it is argued, seen too many instances where a spade is called a shovel. Serious moral issues only get postponed by such politesse. Well and good. But this misses an important point: There are broad areas of agreement in this matter, and explicitly speaking of them at times will at least soften the din of conversation and soundproof the atmosphere. Some of these areas are the following.

Both those who find abortion morally repugnant and those who do not would agree that abortion is, in most cases, tragic and undesirable. It is not a tooth extraction, although some heavy doses of wishful thinking and sanitized language ("the procedure") sometimes present it this way. Therefore, all discussants should be clearheadedly and wholeheartedly behind policies that attempt to frustrate the personal and social causes of abortion. One thinks immediately of better sex education (which is not equivalent to so-called plumbing instructions), better prenatal and perinatal care, reduced poverty, various forms of family support, more adequate institutional care of developmentally disabled children, etc. Furthermore, anyone who sees abortion as a sometimes tragic necessity should in consistency be practically supportive of alternatives to this procedure. While these two areas of agreement will not eliminate differences, they will—especially in combination with an overall concern for the quality of life at all stages—inspire the stirrings of mutual respect that improve the climate of discussion. This is no little achievement in this area.

Avoid the use of slogans. Slogans are the weapons of the crusader, one who sees his or her role as warfare, generally against those sharply defined as "the enemy." Fighting for good causes clearly has its place, as do slogans. The political rally or the protest demonstration are good examples. But slogans are not very enlightening conversational tools, simply because they bypass and effectively subvert the process of communication.

I have in mind two current examples. One is the use of the word murder to describe abortion. "Murder" is a composite value term that means (morally) unjustified killing of another person. There are also legal qualifiers to what is to count as murder. To use this word does not clarify an argument if the very issue at stake is justifiability. Rather, it brands a position and, incidentally, those who hold it. It is a conversation-stopper. Moreover, the word murder is absolutely unnecessary in the defense of the traditional Christian position on abortion.

The other example is "a woman has a right to her own body." This is not an argument; it is the conclusion of an often unexamined argument and therefore a slogan with some highly questionable assumptions. For instance: that the fetus is, for these purposes, a part of the woman's body; that rights over one's body are absolute; that abortion has nothing to do with a husband, etc. To rattle some of these assumptions, it is sufficient to point out that few would grant that a woman's rights over her own body include the right to take thalidomide during pregnancy. The U.S. Supreme Court has gone pretty far in endorsing some of these assumptions. But even justices not above the use of a little "raw judicial power" would choke, I think, on the above slogan as an apt way to summarize the issue.

Represent the opposing position accurately and fairly. Even to mention this seems something of an insult. It contains an implied accusation. Unfortunately, the accusation is too often on target. For instance, those opposed to abortion sometimes argue that the woman who has an abortion is antilife or has no concern for her fetus. This may be the case sometimes, but I believe it does not take sufficient account of the sense of desperate conflict experienced by many women who seek abortions. A sense of tragedy would not exist if women had no concern for their intrauterine offspring.

However, those who disagree with a highly restrictive moral position on abortion sometimes describe this position as "absolutist" and say that it involves "total preoccupation with the status of the unborn." This is the wording of the unfortunate "Call to Concern," which was aimed explicitly at the American Catholic hierarchy.[1] The track record of the hierarchy on social concerns over a broad range of issues is enough to reveal the calumnious character of such protests. As Notre Dame's James Burtchaell wrote apropos of this manifesto: "Ethicians are expected to restrain themselves from misrepresenting positions with which they disagree."[2]

Distinguish the pairs right-wrong, good-bad. Repeatedly I have heard discussants say of a woman who has had an abortion, "She thought at the time and afterward that it was not morally wrong." Or, "She is convinced she made the right decision." It is then immediately added that the moral character of an action depends above all on the perceptions of the person performing it.

Indeed it does. But the term "moral character" needs a further distinction. One who desires to do and intends to do what is supportive and promotive of others (beneficence) performs a *good* act. This person may actually and mistakenly do what is unfortunately harmful, and then the action is morally *wrong*, but it is morally *good*. On the contrary, one who acts from motives of selfishness, hatred, envy, performs an evil, or *bad* act. Thus a surgeon may act out of the most selfish and despicable motives as he performs brilliant lifesaving surgery. His action is morally *bad* but morally *right*. One's action can, therefore, be morally good but still be morally wrong. It can be morally right but morally bad.

The discussion about abortion concerns moral rightness and wrongness. This argument is not settled or even much enlightened by appealing to what a person thought of it at the time, or thinks of it afterward. Nor is it settled by the good and upright intentions of the woman or the physician. Those who destroyed villages in Vietnam to liberate them often undoubtedly acted from the best of intentions but were morally wrong.

Not only is this distinction important in itself; beyond its own importance, it allows one to disagree agreeably, that is, without implying, suggesting, or predicating moral evil of the person one believes to be morally wrong. This would be a precious gain in a discussion that often witnesses this particular and serious collapse of courtesy.

Try to identify the core issue at stake. Many issues cluster around the subject of abortion, issues such as health (fetal, maternal), family stability, justice (for example, rape), and illegitimacy. These are all genuine concerns and can represent sources of real hardship and suffering. Those who believe abortion is sometimes justifiable have made a judgment that the hardships of the woman or family take precedence over nascent life in moral calculation. Those who take an opposing view weight the scales differently.

The core issue is, therefore, the evaluation of nascent life. By this I do not refer to the question about the beginning of personhood; this is a legitimate and important discussion. But the definition of person is often elaborated with a purpose in mind—that is, one defines and then grants or does not grant personhood in terms of what one wants to do and thinks it appropriate to do with nonpersons. That this can be a dog-chasing-tail definition is quite clear. As Princeton's Paul Ramsey is fond of saying, "Does one really need a Ph.D. from Harvard to be a person, or is a functioning cerebral cortex quite sufficient?"

The core issue, then, concerns the moral claims the nascent human being (what Pope Paul VI, in a brilliant finesse, referred to as *personne en devenir* [a person in the process of becoming])[3] makes on us. Do these frequently or only very rarely yield to what appear to be extremely difficult alternatives? And above all, why or why not? This is, in my judgment, the heart of the abortion debate. It must be met head on. It is illumined neither by flat statements about the inviolable rights of fetuses nor by assertions about a woman's freedom of choice. These promulgate a conclusion. They do not share with us how one arrived at it.

Admit doubts, difficulties, and weaknesses in one's own position. When people are passionately concerned with a subject, as they should be in this case, they tend to overlook or even closet their own doubts and problems. Understandable as this is—who will cast the first stone?—it is not a service to the truth or to good moral argument.

For instance, those with permissive views on abortion (who often favor Medicaid funding for it) sometimes argue that denial of Medicaid funding means a return to the back-alley butchers for many thousands of poor. This is deceptively appealing to a sensitive social conscience. But it fails to deal with the fact that in some, perhaps many places, there is precious little price differential between the butchers and the clinics that now offer abortion services. So why go to the butchers? Furthermore, it conveniently overlooks the fact, noted by Daniel Callahan,[4] that the woman most commonly seeking an abortion is not the poor, overburdened mother of many children, but "an unmarried, very young woman of modest, or relatively affluent means whose main 'indication' for abortion will be her expressed wish not to have a [this] child [now]."

Or, again, it is occasionally argued that in a pluralistic society we should refrain from imposing our moral views on others. This was the solution of *The New York Times*[5] when it welcomed the *Wade* and *Bolton* decisions of the Supreme Court. The *Times* stated: "Nothing in the Court's approach ought to give affront to persons who oppose all abortion for reasons of religion or individual conviction. They can stand as firmly as ever for those principles, provided they do not seek to impede the freedom of those with an opposite view."

I agree with Union Theological's Roger Shinn when he says that this view is simplistic and disguises its own weaknesses. He wrote: "If a person or group honestly believes that abortion is the killing of persons, there is no moral comfort in being told, 'Nobody requires you to kill. We are only giving permission to others to do what you consider killing.'" The protester ought surely to reply that one key function of law is to protect minorities of all types: political, racial, religious, and, as here, unborn.[6]

The traditional Christian view on abortion (until recently, universally proposed by the Christian churches) was that the fetus was inviolable from the moment of conception. I believe that certain phenomena in the preimplantation period raise doubts and questions about evaluation, and that is all—namely, they do not yield certainties. I have in mind the twinning process, the estimated number of spontaneous abortions (thought to be huge), and above all, the rare process of recombination of two fertilized ova into one. To admit that such phenomena raise serious evaluative problems is quite in place, if as a matter of fact they do. Indeed, I would argue that it is a disservice to the overall health and viability of the traditional Christian evaluation to extend its clarity and certainty into areas where there are grounds for residual and nagging doubts.

Distinguish the formulation and the substance of a moral conviction. This may seem a refined, even supertechnical and sophisticated guideline better left in the footnotes of the ethical elite. Actually, I believe it is enormously important for bringing conversationalists out of their trenches. And it applies to both sides of the national debate.

For instance, not a few antiabortionists appeal to the formulations of recent official Catholic leaders in stating their moral convictions. Specifically, Pius XI and Pius XII both stated (and, with them, traditional Catholic ethical treatises on abortion) that direct abortion was never permissible, even to save the life of the mother. As this was understood, it meant simply and drastically, better two deaths than one murder. Concretely, if the only alternatives facing a woman and a physician were either abort or lose both mother and child, the conclusion was drawn that even then the direct disposing of the fetus was morally wrong.

This is a formulation—and almost no one, whether liberal or conservative, endorses the conclusion as an adequate and accurate way of communicating the basic value judgment (substance) of the matter. Some moral theologians would say, in contrast to the popes, that in this instance the abortion is indirect and permissible. Others would say, again in contrast to the popes, that it is direct but still permissible. For instance, the Catholic bishop of Augsburg, Josef Stimpfle, stated: "He who performs an abortion, except to save the life of the mother, sins gravely and burdens his conscience with the killing of human life."[7] A similar statement was made by the entire Belgian hierarchy in its 1973 declaration on abortion. Of those rare and desperate conflict instances, the Belgian bishops stated: "The moral principle which ought to govern the intervention can be formulated as follows: Since two lives are at stake, one will, while doing everything possible to save both, attempt to save one rather than to allow two to perish."[8] What is clear is that all would arrive at a conclusion different from the official one, even though the language might differ in each case.

The point here is, of course, that ethical formulations—being the product of human language, philosophy, and imperfection—are only more or less adequate to the substance of our moral convictions at a given time. Ethical formulations will always show the imprint of human handling. This was explicitly acknowledged by Pope John XXIII in his speech (October 11, 1962) opening the Vatican Council II. It was echoed by Vatican II in *Gaudium et spes:* "Furthermore, while adhering to the methods and requirements proper to theology, theologians are invited to seek continually for more suitable ways of communicating doctrine to the men of their times. For the deposit of faith or revealed truths are one thing; the manner in which they are formulated without violence to their meaning and significance is another."[9]

This statement must be properly understood. Otherwise theology could easily be reduced to word shuffling. If there is a distinction between substance and formulation, there is also an extremely close—indeed, inseparable—connection. One might say they are related as are body and soul. The connection is so intimate it is difficult to know just what the substance is amid variation of formulation. The formulation can easily betray the substance. Furthermore, because of this close connection, it is frequently difficult to know just what is changeable, what permanent. Where abortion is concerned, one could argue that the Roman Catholic Church's *substantial* conviction is that abortion is tolerable only when it is lifesaving, therefore also life-serving, intervention. Be that as it may, to conduct discussion as if substance and formulation were identical is to get enslaved to formulations. Such captivity forecloses conversations.

Something similar must be said of the 1973 abortion decisions of the U.S. Supreme Court. The court was evolutionary in interpreting the notion of liberty enacted in 1868 as the Fourteenth Amendment to the Constitution. No evidence exists that the Congress and the states understood this amendment to include the liberty to abort. Yet the court asserts that "liberty" there must be read in a way consistent with the demands of the present day. Therefore, it concluded that the right to terminate pregnancy is "implicit in the concept of ordered liberty."

This is but a formulation of the notion of constitutionally assured liberty, and to treat it as more than that, as an ironclad edict, is to preempt legal development. Indeed, the court itself gives this away when it treats the word person in the Constitution in a static and nondevelopmental way, as John Noonan has repeatedly pointed out. It looks at the meaning of the word at the time of the adoption of the Constitution and freezes it there—just the opposite of what it does with the word liberty. Such vagaries reveal that the court's decisions and dicta are hardly identical with the substance of the Constitution. To argue as if they were is to confuse legal substance and legal formulations, and to choke off conversation. In brief, we must know and treasure our traditions without being enslaved by them.

Distinguish morality and public policy. It is the temptation of the Anglo-American tradition to identify these two. We are a pragmatic and litigious people for whom law is the answer to all problems, the only answer and a fully adequate answer. Thus many people confuse morality and public policy. If something is removed from the penal code, it is viewed as morally right and permissible. And if an act is seen as morally wrong, many want it made illegal. Behold the there-ought-to-be-a-law syndrome.

This is not only conceptually wrong, it is also conversationally mischievous. It gets people with strong moral convictions locked into debates about public policy, as if only one public policy were possible given a certain moral position. This is simplistic. While morality and law are intimately related, they are obviously not identical. The closer we get to basic human rights, the closer the relationship ought to be in a well-ordered society. It is quite possible for those with permissive moral convictions on abortion to believe that more regulation is required than is presently provided in the *Wade* and *Bolton* decisions. Contrarily, it is possible for those with more stringent moral persuasions to argue that there are several ways in which these might be mirrored in public policy.

I am not arguing here for this or that public policy (although personally I am deeply dissatisfied with the present one on nearly all grounds). The point, rather, is that public discourse would be immeasurably purified if care were taken by disputants to relate morality and public policy in a more nuanced way than now prevails.

Distinguish morality and pastoral care or practice. A moral statement is one that attempts to summarize the moral right or wrong, and then invites to its realization in our conduct. As the well-known Redemptorist theologian Bernard Häring words it: Moral theology operates on a level "where questions are raised about general rules or considerations that would justify a particular moral judgment."[10] A moral statement is thus an abstract statement, not in the sense that it has nothing to do with real life or with particular decisions, but in the sense that it abstracts or prescinds from the ability of this or that person to understand it and live it.

Pastoral care (and pastoral statements), by contrast, looks to the art of the possible. It deals with an individual where this person is in terms of his or her strengths, perceptions, biography, circumstances (financial, medical, educational, familial, psychological). Although pastoral care attempts to expand perspectives and maximize strengths, it recognizes at times the limits of these attempts.

Concretely, one with strong convictions about the moral wrongfulness of abortion could and should be one who realizes that there are many who by education, familial and religious background, and economic circumstances are, or appear to be, simply incapable in those circumstances of assimilating such convictions and living them out, at least here and now. This means that compassion and understanding extended to the woman who is contemplating an abortion or has had one need by no means require abandonment of one's moral convictions. Similarly, it means that a strong and unswerving adherence to a moral position need not connote the absence of pastoral compassion, and deafness to the resonances of tragic circumstances. I believe that if more people understood this, the abortion discussion would occur in an atmosphere of greater tranquillity, sensitivity, and humaneness—and therefore contain more genuine communication.

Incorporate the woman's perspective, or women's perspectives. I include this because, well, frankly, I have been told to. And I am sure that there are many who will complain: "Yes, and you put it last." To which a single response is appropriate: "Yes, for emphasis." In the many discussions I have had on abortion where women have been involved in the discussion, one thing is clear: Women feel they have been left out of the discussion. This seems true of both so-called prochoice women and so-called prolife adherents.

But being told to is hardly a decisive reason for urging this point. And it is not my chief reason. Women rightly, if at times one-sidedly and abrasively, insist they are the ones who carry pregnancies and sometimes feel all but compelled to have abortions. Thus they argue two things: (1) They ought to have an influential voice in this discussion. (2) Up to and including the present, they feel they have not had such a voice.

All kinds of shouts will be heard when this suggestion is raised. We are familiar with most of them. For instance, some will argue paternal rights against the U.S. Supreme Court's 1976 *Planned Parenthood v. Danforth* decision. Others will ask: Which women are you talking about, prolife or prochoice? And then, of course, they will begin issuing passes to the discussion on the basis of predetermined positions. Still others will wonder why the fetus does not have a proxy with at least equal say. And so on. One can see and admit the point in all these ripostes. Nothing in femaleness as such makes women more or less vulnerable to error or bias in moral discourse than men, yet when all is shrieked and done, the basic point remains valid: The abortion discussion proceeds at its own peril if it ignores women's perspectives. As Martin I. Silvermann remarked in an issue of *Sh'ma,* "The arguments change when you must face the women."[11]

One need not make premature peace with radical feminists or knee-jerk proabortionists to say this. Quite the contrary. One need only be familiar with the growing body of literature on abortion by women (for example, Linda Bird Francke's *The Ambivalence of Abor-*

tion[12] or Sidney Callahan's essays on abortion) to believe that the woman's perspective is an important ingredient in this discussion. To those who feel this is tantamount to conferring infallibility on Gloria Steinem, it must be pointed out that in nearly every national poll, women test out more conservatively than men on the morality of abortion.

These are but a few guidelines for discussion. I am sure there are many more, perhaps some of even greater importance than the ones mentioned. Be that as it may, I am convinced that attention to these points cannot hurt the national debate. It may even help. Specifically, it may prevent good people from making bad arguments—chief of which, of course, is that it is only bad people who make bad ones.

5

Abortion: An Ecumenical Dilemma

Gregory Baum

Because of the delicate nature of the topic, I wish to begin with a personal remark. Emotionally I am strongly opposed to abortions. When I argue about the issue in my mind, I tend to conjure up selfish and insensitive opponents who are exclusively interested in their comfort and career. I tend to connect the trend toward abortions with the hostility to little children that characterizes our highly rational culture. In my mind, the demand for abortions becomes a symptom of an ultimate capitalism where people claim total control not only over their property, but over their bodies, a kind of *reductio ad absurdum* of the individualism our economic system has generated. What has been lost, I then feel, is a sense of wonder before life itself and the hidden forces operative within it.

I

It is only when I engage in more serious reflection that I remember that among the people who regard abortion under certain circumstances as a licit, moral, even if regrettable and extreme, form of birth control, are Christian thinkers and in fact several Christian churches. Many Protestant theologians whose work I admire and whose moral

Reprinted with permission from the November 30, 1973 issue of *Commonweal*.

Gregory Baum is professor of religious studies at Saint Michael's College, University of Toronto, Ontario.

judgment I respect look on abortion under certain circumstances as a moral choice. In some cases, according to them, it could even be a duty. I have read these theological essays and studied the ecclesiastical documents; while I always win the argument when I discuss the issue in my mind with the imaginary opponents, selfish and insensitive as they are, I must admit that I respect the reflections of Protestant thinkers and take the teaching of their churches seriously.

As an ecumenical theologian I must ask myself whether one should regard the moral teaching of these Christian churches, even though they differ from the traditional position, as a Christian witness. Of course, the possibility exists that churches betray the substance of the gospel. We recall the blindness of the so-called German Christians under the Hitler regime. Yet at that time, the new ecclesiastical trend was repudiated by other Christian churches outside the country and by courageous Christians in Germany. No one received the position of the German Christians as an authentic witness to gospel morality. Their nationalistic stand was a brief episode in the life of the church, which should never be forgotten, but there is no analogy here whatever to the position on abortion adopted by many Christian churches in the industrialized world. Here Christian thinkers, on grounds they regard as responsible, tested, and in keeping with the gospel, come to conclusions on abortion that differ from traditional teaching but are shared by great numbers of Christians in the highly developed countries, whose moral judgments on other issues, even if untraditional, deserve the greatest respect. This break with the moral tradition of the past, then, does not resemble the kind of betrayal mentioned above: it recalls, rather, the break with the tradition that has taken place on many moral issues in recent decades. Even when we disagree with the view on abortion, defended by many Protestant thinkers, we must respect it as part of the Christian conversation about the meaning of the gospel for modern life.

Vatican Council II has acknowledged this ecumenical dilemma. In the Decree on Ecumenism, in the section dealing with the attitude of Catholics to Protestant Christians, we read, "If in moral matters there are many (Protestant) Christians who do not always understand the gospel in the same way as Catholics, and do not admit the same solutions for the more difficult problems of modern society, nevertheless they share our desire to cling to Christ's words as the source of Christian virtue [No. 23]." When Catholics disagree with the teaching on abortion adopted by some Protestant churches and many Christian thinkers, they should respect this Protestant position as an attempt to deal in a Christian way with a difficult moral problem.

This respect, I propose, is all the more necessary because the Anglican and Protestant churches have exercised moral leadership in contemporary society on many issues, on which the Catholic Church still defended the moral stance of a previous age. We all remember the repeated papal condemnations of religious liberty that, as late as the fifties of this century, caused a good deal of trouble to the late John Courtney Murray. Similarly in regard to birth control, I hold that the Anglican and Protestant churches gave moral leadership in the conditions of modern life with all its ambiguities, at a time when the Catholic Church continued to teach moral norms from the cultural experience of the premodern age. From my own personal contact with Protestant moral thinkers, I have acquired great admiration for them and thus I do not find the words of Vatican Council II exaggerated when they recall that Protestant thinkers look to Christ as the source of moral wisdom.

I realize, of course, that Protestant thinkers are divided on the abortion issue. My point is that we must respect their various positions as part of the significant Christian conversation. It is my personal experience that the Protestant authors who repudiate abortion altogether and agree with the common Catholic position often entertain moral views on other issues, such as authority, obedience, war, private property, socialism, etc., that greatly differ from my own. I suppose it is inevitable that we test the strength of a moral argument offered by a thinker by turning to the moral conclusions to which her or his reflections have led on other issues. This may not be philosophically sound, but in the concrete conditions of life we do rely on the moral counsel of persons whose moral judgment we approve in many areas.

The first conclusion I draw from the above reflections is that one cannot approve of the language and the arguments adopted by Catholics in their defense of the traditional position, which imply that the defenders of abortion are immoral, selfish, insensitive, cruel, lacking in respect for life, or worse. Yet such language is found even in statements made by bishops and popes. While I am quite sure there are unprincipled people arguing in favor of abortion, people who have lost a sense of morality and look on life in a materialist, comfort-oriented way, it would be quite unjust, and therefore immoral, for Catholics to suppose that all people who favor abortion under certain circumstances, including Christian groups and thinkers, share this materialistic outlook on life. The dilemma is that there are Christians who think a liberal position on abortion is more moral, more in keeping with God's will, than the traditional one.

Since no one claims that the traditional position is revealed by God, Catholics should not adopt a tone of voice as if their position is beyond challenge. Catholics may hold that, from their point of view, a liberal position on abortion is immoral, possibly due to false consciousness induced by the social conditions of industrial society, but

40

they have no right whatever to suggest that the thinkers who differ from them are immoral, that their position reflects a lack of virtue, and that the theologians and the theologically oriented among them have refused to search the gospel to find God's will in regard to this contemporary problem.

The ecumenical ecclesiology, found in the Decree on Ecumenism, which has been commonly adopted by Catholic theologians in North America, demands that we regard the abortion issue as a complex one. While Catholics may repudiate certain extreme positions on abortion with vehemence and passion, I do not see how they can do this to the more nuanced and careful positions of Christian thinkers and their churches. The idea that Catholics can solve the moral and pastoral problems of the present age by themselves, without relying on ecumenical dialogue and cooperation and without hoping that wisdom and insight will be exchanged among various Christian communities, living as they do in such varied circumstances, seems, to me, contrary to the ecclesial foundation of the Christian faith. The first conclusion of this essay, then, is that Catholics should not employ language and arguments against abortion that do not recognize the ecumenical dimension of the problem.

II

How is it possible that Christians who take the gospel seriously come to such different conclusions? This, I think, demands an explanation. For it would not do to say that Catholics on the whole are wiser, and more moral, than Anglicans and Protestants. Nor has anyone suggested that we are dealing with a revealed truth that Catholics and some Protestants have preserved but which the major Protestant churches have abandoned. The reason why the position of the Catholic Church differs from that of many other churches is related to a difference in social and cultural background. While a theologian does not wish to reduce significant moral stands to diverse social conditions, he or she must recognize that the conditions of modern life have produced a changed outlook on such traditional issues as birth control, extramarital sex, divorce, etc. in the Anglican and Protestant churches, and that these same conditions are leading Catholic theologians in the highly industrialized parts of the world, encouraged by the present pluralism in the Catholic Church, to raise the same issues and come to similar conclusions. Abortion, however, is such a serious matter that every reflection on it is pushed to its very foundation.

To understand the difference between the traditional position, defended by the Catholic Church, and the position adopted by some Protestant churches, we must place the respective moral judgments into the wider vision of human life, to which they belong and from which they try to derive their validity. Individual moral norms never stand alone; they belong to a more total understanding of human life, to a more complete ideal of what human existence is about. Thanks to my conversations with Protestant theologian Herbert Richardson, my colleague at St. Michael's College in the University of Toronto, I have begun to understand more clearly the two diverse world views, traditional and new, in which the abortion question has been raised.

The traditional Catholic position, with roots in the ancient past, was dominated by the concept of nature. Here sexuality and procreation were understood as being part of nature, watched over by divine providence. I wish to call this position Model A. According to Model A, sexuality is a biological function directed toward the procreation of the human race. While there is pleasure attached to sexuality, it is oriented by its very nature to the begetting of children. Sexual intercourse outside of marriage is therefore sinful. The conception of children is part of the natural process, watched over by God's providence. It is not for parents to choose the number of children. To practice birth control or to provoke an abortion is an interference with the order of nature and hence gravely sinful. From this perspective, abortion is seen among the sins against nature, touching on the procreative process of human life.

Since in recent years the Catholic arguments against nonprocreative sexual expressions have become less convincing, especially since the traditional position on birth control is no longer accepted, it has been necessary to find new and stronger arguments against abortion. The arguments now given see it as a destruction of fetal life destined to become fully human or, according to some thinkers, even the destruction of human life simply speaking. What was condemned and abhorred in the past as a sin against the order of nature is today often described as the taking of innocent life or murder. Yet the Catholic tradition shows it is possible to oppose abortion and regard it as a grave moral evil, without solving the question of when fetal life in the mother's womb should properly be called a human person. No official teaching on this matter has been established; it is unlikely that this is a matter on which the Christian church is able to offer definitive teaching.

The more liberal position on abortion, adopted by some Protestant churches, fits into a world picture that is dominated by the concept of history. I shall call this position Model B. People do not enter into their destiny by conforming to a given order of nature, but by assuming responsibility for themselves and their environment and by creating their own future. God's providence is here not a guidance from above, but a gracious action within human life, freeing and enabling people ever to expand the area of their responsibility. Sexuality, conception, and procreation, while grounded in biology, belong properly to the sphere of history. Humans are called on by God to assume responsibility for them. Sexuality is here seen not just under its biological aspect: it is a wider human reality, with deep meaning and power, and men and women are summoned to integrate the sexual dimension into their lives in a healing, joyful, and reconciling manner. The biological orientation of sexuality toward procreation cannot be used as an argument against extramarital sexuality. Moralists here do not speak of the pleasure that accompanies sexuality, but of the multileveled meaning and power it has in bringing about responsible human growth and community. Here the number of children is the responsibility of the parents. God's providence is believed to be operative through the grace-sustained free choice of mother and father.

According to Model B, abortion is an extreme interference in the life process, prompted by people's responsibility for the future, which to many thinkers seems justified, at least under certain circumstances. They think the parents' responsibility includes the authority, in cases of emergency, to interrupt a pregnancy with a clinical intervention. We note, however, that the moral approval of abortion is by no means a necessary consequence of Model B. It is possible to adopt Model B for the understanding of sexual life and procreation, without acknowledging abortion as a moral option. Nonetheless, it is the world view of humankind's ever increasing responsibility for the future, for the number of children born and for the kinds of lives these children will have, that explains how theologians and Christian churches can come to acknowledge abortion as a moral choice in extreme cases.

The distinction between the two models enables me to make a significant point. I hold that the Catholic Church at Vatican Council II has shifted from Model A to Model B. This was done, not in a fully consistent manner in regard to all its consequences, but in regard to two significant issues. First, ecclesiastical teaching at Vatican Council II abandoned the view that children are the primary end of marriage: quite apart from its procreative role, sexuality is credited with an important function in the building up of the family in love. Second, Vatican Council II unambiguously adopted the ideal of responsible parenthood: divine providence can no longer be invoked as dispensing people from assuming responsibility for their procreative role. Since then, and despite the papal teaching reproving contraception, Catholic theologians have, on the whole, opted for Model B and developed its full implications for a new theological approach to sexuality.

This leads me to the second conclusion of this essay. The opposition of Catholics against abortion should place itself frankly on the side of humans' historical responsibility for their sexual lives. Catholics should argue against abortion out of the presuppositions of Model B. I am uneasy with a movement against abortion that does not advocate sexual education and birth control. The attempt of Catholics to use their opposition to abortion as a subtle way of returning to Model A, that is, of going back to a purely biological-procreative view of sexuality and to the traditional sexual morality corresponding to this, I regard as theologically indefensible. It is my view that since Catholics are against abortion and want to help to reduce the number of abortions, they should favor the spread of sexual information, the availability of birth control, and an enlightened attitude that increases people's sense of responsibility for their own sexual lives.

Catholic groups and ecclesiastical leaders fighting against abortion often adopt a language and a style of argument that promote the view that sexuality is primarily and essentially procreative. In addition to opposing abortions, they advocate the traditional view of sexuality. Their struggle against abortion thus pursues two ends. While they do not always admit it, they wish to achieve two distinct goals with their campaign. But by linking their opposition to abortion to a highly biological view of sexuality, they weaken their arguments. We occasionally meet people involved in a movement against abortion with a certain passion, adopting a certain style and tone of voice, that give the impression that their main concern is not really human life (they were not greatly upset about the deaths during the war), but sexual morality. They are greatly upset by a sexual morality that acknowledges the quest for sexual freedom within the bounds of reason and love. By linking a special view of sexuality to their struggle against abortions, their arguments actually lose credibility.

The argument of some groups that wherever more sexual information and ready access to contraception are available the result has always been more abortions rather than less, is not the point. What is involved, I think, is a matter of principle. Since I hold that the Catholic Church has moved over to Model B and since I am convinced that the older view of sexuality, however adequate it may have been for the culture that generated it, is harmful for the present day, it is for me a matter of principle to defend the right and duty of men and women to choose with responsibility the form and pattern of their sexual lives. In this sense we must hope that more adequate, more human, and more reliable methods of contraception will be invented. Society must overcome the violence of abortions by increasing the sense of power and responsibility people have over their sexual lives.

III

Moral theology usually puts the burden of freedom and guilt on the individual. From the study of sociology, however, it would appear that the social and cultural conditions in which people live create a certain mind-set that must also be taken in consideration when evaluating people's actions. These two aspects are dialectically related: there is an interaction between the consciousness induced by social institutions and the freedom to transcend their limitations. The Roman Catholic Church's preaching on the whole has paid attention mainly to the aspect of personal freedom, thus sparing the institutions from a critical analysis and exempting them from moral guilt. While moral theologians usually acknowledge that institutional pressures reduce personal freedom and limit culpability, they do not sufficiently appreciate the formative influence of institutions on human consciousness.

Moralists in church and society tend to lament people's selfishness, their lack of generosity, and their bad will without analyzing to what extent the crimes committed by them are related to the mind-set induced by the contradictions within society. Can we confine an analysis of why people steal to a consideration of their private lives? Or must we not also analyze the society that produces an impoverished proletariat, bombards these same people with advertisements for the easy life, and creates conditions of loneliness and personal alienation in which drug addiction thrives? If we only take a firm stand against robbery without submitting society to a critical analysis, we disguise the true causes of evil in society, defend the injustices implicit in the present social system, and perpetuate the individualistic illusion that is related to the problem. The moralistic preaching of church and society is here seen as a defense of the established order.

After the October 1970 crisis in French Canada—the kidnapping of two government officials and the accidental murder of one of them—the French Canadian bishops published a statement expressing their dismay at the outbreak of violence in their midst. Let us remember, they wrote, that violence is nourished by injustice.

If the root of evil is twofold, in personal consciousness and in the social institutions made by people, then we must learn to repudiate abortions in this dialectical manner. We cannot place all the blame on the trapped people who desperately seek a way out of their predicaments. If it is true that violence is nourished by injustice, then we must ask what are the social injustices that make people interfere with the life-giving process in a violent manner. The repudiation of abortion should then be accompanied by a critique of society that tries to define the contradictions operative within it that foster the violence of abortion. Few moralists have done this.

Even a cursory analysis reveals two kinds of oppression in society favoring abortion. First and foremost, it seems to me, is the alienation imposed on people, especially, although not exclusively, on the underprivileged, by the money- and profit-oriented, maximizing economic system. The present system, through its various institutions, tries to make people into customers. From childhood on, people are taught to dream of buying goods and symbolizing affluence through ostentatious consumption. As they become part of the world of consumers, be it only in their dreams, they become estranged from the deep things of life, from love, truth, and fidelity. Institutionally summoned to a false life, they fall into emotional and sexual chaos. The confusion, isolation, and terror created among the urban dispossessed, coupled with an authentic desire for ecstasy, traps vast numbers of women in unwanted pregnancies. And while they are quite incapable of looking after themselves, society expects them to look after their children.

A second contradiction, operative in another section of the population, is the oppression of women. In our generation, women have discovered that much of the emphasis that they are mothers and achieve their highest fulfillment as mothers looking after a family, is an ideology that prevents them from experiencing the self-realization that is open to men. They sense that what is involved in much of the opposition to abortion is the hidden trend of the male-dominated society, endorsed by many women, to keep the power relations between men and women as they are. Women struggling for their liberation regard any form of unwanted motherhood as an unjust imposition of society.

It is the task of the moral theologian—this is the third conclusion of this essay—to institute a detailed critique of society to see more precisely how violence is nourished by injustice. The secular liberal approach to abortion, represented by the recent decision of the U.S. Supreme Court, which regards the interruption of pregnancies as a purely private matter, refuses to recognize in the abortive practices a symptom of social ills and alienation. The secular liberal approach intends to persuade us that nothing is basically wrong with society. The moralist who puts the blame for abortion on the people who seek it or commit it, and who refuses to deal critically with the social system, also disguises the full cause of evil in society. What the moral theologian will have to find, through a more detailed analysis of society, is a set of arguments repudiating abortions, that do not strengthen the oppressions working in the social order but promote social change and the liberation of men and women. Only too often is the call for a return to virtue an attempt to make people look away from the discrepancies in the institutions and is thus a disguise for a reactionary political outlook. The opposition to abortion could thus go hand in hand with the continued oppression of women and with the approval of an individualistic, profit-oriented, money-centered, customer-producing society. Catholic theologians will want to make their rejection of violence as a licit means of birth control a statement that is politically and culturally responsible and that raises the consciousness of the community in regard to the contradictions operative in it.

6

A Call to Responsible Ecumenical Debate on Controversial Issues: Abortion and Homosexuality

Prefatory note: This document is issued by the Commission on Faith and Order of the National Council of Churches of Christ in the U.S.A. It is a study document, not a policy statement. It is not to be construed as an official statement of attitudes or policies of the National Council.

CONCERNED AS IT IS with all that disrupts or enhances the oneness of the church of Jesus Christ, the Commission on Faith and Order of the National Council of Churches has watched with dismay the growing division of Christians on the questions of homosexuality and abortion. It has not viewed the turmoil from a stance of undisturbed inner tranquillity. The same conflictive views on these two issues present in the broader Christian community exist within the commission's own membership. Hence it has seemed urgent that this commission, comprising as it does the most inclusive American ecumenical group doing theology for the sake of Christian unity, assist its own members and other Christians in discovering God's will in these thorny matters.

While we have formulated these guidelines out of an ecumenical sensitivity that aspires to a more reasonable, more edifying, and more faithful handling of opposing views on homosexuality and abortion, we offer them in the hope that they will apply equally in other issues on which the Christian community is divided, although, of course, we have not tested them in every instance.

The issues of abortion and homosexuality are dividing families, friends, congregations, and communities. Polarized positions on these issues of public policy and personal behavior reflect the absence of a moral consensus in the society and the presence of conflicting moral principles. The issues raise questions about the meaning and value of human life; individual people are affected in their private and public lives. At the same time, the issues raise questions about the common welfare, the proper use of law, and the political process in preserving the civil order in the midst of moral diversity. It is essential that such issues be discussed publicly and fully. Unfortunately, positions on these issues have become so hardened, emotions so inflamed, reason so confused that careful public debate is rare. Personal suffering, anger, and fear disrupt human relationships. Intensity of commitment has turned, in some cases, to violence. Some see every question of the public welfare through the lens of one issue, and the abundance and complexity of life in community is then reduced to a single burning question.

Denominations and individual Christians are part of this conflict. Here, too, there are sets of moral principles that are in tension or opposition. Some of this diversity is a reflection of Christian freedom in responding to God's call to us to live according to God's will. But there is also diversity that reflects a deep division among Christians in understanding God's will. The unity of the church, the Body of Christ, is a gift of God that we are called to live in fact. There is a mutual interdependence of Christians, all born into the same Body through baptism. We are called to "maintain the unity of the Spirit in the bond of peace [Eph. 4:3]." Denominations and individual Christians are held accountable when division over any issue fractures or tears this Body.

We are now divided on the issues of abortion and homosexuality, as well as on the larger questions of the nature and meaning of human sexuality and responsible relationships among women and men. Indeed, this division has already undone some of the ecumenical advances of recent decades and is disrupting life within denominations and congregations. The division reflects some deep differences in our understanding of how we are to be faithful to God's will in and for the world. These differences dare not be ignored. No part of the

49

Body possesses complete and faultless insight into God's will. Dialogue must be established and maintained. The discernment of God's will for human beings and all creation is not a private or parochial task; it is the task of all members of the church. The dialogue must be carried on across the lines of denominations and differing traditions, lines that all too often act as barriers or entrenchments. The following guidelines for ecumenical debate of controversial issues are offered in the hope that Christian unity may grow and be maintained.

Ecumenical Discussion of Theological and Ethical Differences

1. Christians, by virtue of their unity in baptism, are obliged individually and corporately to discuss and attempt to resolve conflicts of theology and ethics. The lack of widespread and intensive ecumenical discussion on divisive social issues is an offense and stumbling block to the unity of the church; it weakens the announcement and inhibits the acceptance of the gospel of Jesus Christ.

2. There are significant differences among Christians in their understanding of God, the whole creation, and the moral responsibility of human beings. Christians must hold one another accountable for the adequacy and appropriateness of their respective understandings to ensure that the debate is grounded in the faith of the community.

a. Such adequacy and appropriateness must always be tested over against these sources: the scriptures, Christian tradition, philosophic methods and principles, scientific information and principles, and the experience of human beings.

b. Choices are made in selecting the content from each of these sources. In ecumenical discussion the reasons for these choices must be openly acknowledged.

c. Much of the conflict within the church over issues of social ethics arises when different groups give different weight or interpretation to one of these sources. All too often the debate does not reveal this level; the assumptions remain hidden.

d. The ecumenical discussion must consider the validity and relevance of each of the sources and how each is weighted when conflicts arise.

3. This method of evaluating stances on issues of social ethics would serve to keep the debate open, and calls us beyond premature and partial answers to issues of social justice. Fundamental conflicts in our understanding of God's will challenge the illusion of security in firm stances on these issues.

4. Discussion must be carried on by laity and clergy, women and men, young and old, in seminaries and among church leadership. It must be ecumenical, with participants fully informed of the position of

their denominations and fully aware of their understanding of God, the creation, and the moral responsibility of human beings.

Public Policy

1. Political activity that seeks to bring the social order in line with ethical convictions based on religious commitment does not violate the separation of church and state. Christians individually and corporately have a right and a responsibility, as do all citizens, to influence public policy by participation in the political process.

2. Political activity and decision are not an appropriate substitute for necessary ecumenical debate on theological differences with social policy implications.

3. When extensive theological and moral differences preclude consensus on issues of public policy, it is unwise for individual Christians and denominations to advocate the closing of debate through restrictive laws.

4. When individual Christians and denominations seek to influence public policy, they have an obligation to examine and make explicit both the religious principles and the principles of reason on which they base the public policy they advocate. Freedom of religion demands that public policy be based on a consensus of reason, not a consensus of religious principles.

5. Individual Christians and denominations have a responsibility in public policy debates to use language that is a true witness to their own positions and to the positions of opposing parties in the debate. Stereotyped notions and caricatures of people and positions must be avoided.

6. In ecumenical debates over public policy, individual Christians and denominations have a responsibility to enable various perspectives on controversial issues to be heard fairly and fully.

7. The determination and protection of civil rights are of utmost importance. Individual Christians and denominations must call the state to account when the rights of citizens are denied or violated.

Some Critical Issues in the Debate over Abortion and Homosexuality

1. In our understanding of individual human beings, how much weight should be given to physical nature and how much to emotional, social, and other characteristics having to do with the personal quality of human relationships? In what way are the sanctity and quality of life related to both?

2. What is a responsible method of interpreting scripture within ecumenical debates? How does the Word of God challenge en-

trenched and competing uses of scripture in debates on social issues?
3. What sources are appropriate and adequate in determining that a given behavior or attitude is unnatural? Is it appropriate that scientific insights and human experience offer correctives to assumptions about scriptural or traditional understandings of natural law?
4. How do our differing views of nature and grace affect our stances on abortion and homosexuality? With respect to social ethics, in what way is human nature—including reason—affected by sin, and what effect does grace have?
5. How can the experiences of women be constitutive of a more inclusive understanding of the nature of human sexuality? How can we correct the long tradition that masculinity is normative for human nature?
6. Is our understanding of human nature too much a function of scientific definitions?
7. Can we reach agreement on the nature and role of reason in discerning justice in public policy questions? Does reason discern an objective moral order in the universe?
8. What considerations should be taken into account in deciding that an immoral action should also be illegal?

Part III

The State of the Question

J. Robert Nelson
Daniel Callahan
Paul Ramsey
Karl Barth

7

What Does Theology Say About Abortion?

J. Robert Nelson

IN TALKING ABOUT ABORTION, does theology matter? No—not for people who have no faith in God as Creator and Sustainer of human life. It does not seem to matter for a lot of Christians either. When these voice their reasons for recommending, condoning, or opposing abortion, they rely entirely on statistics and empirical data drawn from the fields of medicine, sociology, and politics; and they interpret these according to prevailing humanistic concepts.

The fact is that the Gallup poll has become more authoritative than the usual sources of Christian ethical understanding. What was said in Sweden in the 1950s now seems to apply in the United States: If a majority of the people hold an act to be moral, it is moral. Even if an airtight Christian policy on abortion were possible, with a theological plug in every hole and biblical verses caulking every seam, it is doubtful most Christians would rally to it.

But obviously such a uniform, univocal policy is not possible. Christians who do think theologically and act in the best of faith nevertheless disagree. One side seems wholly unsuccessful in convincing and converting the other, while those who seek a mediating position eventually realize that their words have little effect on the popular mind. The theological broom seems unable to sweep back the

---

J. ROBERT NELSON is professor of systematic theology in the School of Theology of Boston University, Boston, Massachusetts.

four waves of radical change—waves that David R. Mace (in his *Abortion: The Agonizing Decision* [Abingdon, 1972], pp. 60–62) identifies as the pressure groups for sexual freedom, population control, women's liberation, and medical practice. And when a certain position based on elaborate theological reasoning receives the strongest support from the *magisterium* of the Roman Catholic Church, many Catholic Christians disagree and disobey. How much more difficult it would be, then, for a Protestant denomination to impose on all its members an ostensibly authoritative teaching. As for attempting to devise a policy on abortion, the difficulties seem almost insurmountable.

Eight Beliefs

This rather melancholy introduction might seem to mark the end of the matter. But is theological reasoning indeed so impotent? I think not. In the discussion among disagreeing Christians there are enough hopeful signs to justify the pursuit of clearer theological understanding and consequent ethical conviction. When Christian writers on abortion think and write as Christians rather than in the manner of secular humanists, they appeal to one or more of *eight* fixed beliefs. It is in appropriating these beliefs, testing the grounds for them, and relating them to the specific question of abortion that Christians are able to deal with it as a theological matter. Quite clearly, too, they are able to find a common mind with religious Jews on several of these beliefs. Let me list them.

1. God is indeed the creator of life in general, of human life in particular, and of both the body and the soul of the human being. The unity of body and soul is fundamental to biblical anthropology (as distinct from various kinds of Greek and Indian dualism). It is also fundamental to the reality of incarnation, on which Christian faith is built. The eternal Word, *Logos*, could not have become flesh, *sarx*, if this unity were not the reality of mankind. But scholastic speculations about the time of "ensoulment" of the fetal life were inappropriate in their time and are misleading today.

2. God the Creator is omniscient and personal; God's name is Love. From the human perspective, the assertion that God knows and loves every human being is staggering, even incredible. But there is in this assertion a basic profundity that is discernible even though it may be expressed in the simplest Sunday school terms.

3. Men and women are procreators with God. In respect to genetics, they are certainly procreators of the physical body of the offspring. And though we know almost nothing of the generation of the soul or ego—this being beyond the analytical power of both the

56

geneticist and the psychologist—it is a credible idea that God gives this also through the parents.

4. This human creature, and every one of the billions of human creatures who have ever lived, can be said to have been made "in the image of God." Biblical scholars and theologians dispute the meaning of this phrase. But in one respect there is no room for dispute: It is the image that accounts for the *humanum,* the distinctively human character and quality of every one.

5. Each human being is unique and irreplaceable. In the realm of being, no one can take the place of another. This is self-evidently the case for every conscious person who knows herself or himself to be an ego. With respect to unborn human life, it has been assumed to be true; today it is *known* to be true. According to recent genetic studies, long before it is possible to imagine that a human being possesses individualized consciousness, the uniqueness of genetic structure has been determined by the union of male and female genes. Theodosius Dobzhansky, the Nobel laureate in genetics, says that the possible variations of human genotypes constitute so vast a number as to be equal theoretically to the number of atoms in the universe. Uniqueness does not wait on one's being born and becoming a conscious person; rather, each combination of ovum and spermatozoon initiates unique life.

6. True humanity is found not in individualization, but in human community. The Creator decreed that "it is not good" for the creature to live alone, and caused life to be relational and communal in its very essence. Within the womb and until the tomb, every human life is dependent on some other life. At whatever stage of development prior to birth, the unborn human entity has an indispensable relationship to the woman who can become the mother, and vice versa. And however remote and minimal their consciousness of it may be, other members of the woman's family and of society share in this human relationship, which can be reciprocated by conscious experience only after birth.

7. The definition and identity of human life must be given in terms of personhood, and not alone in terms of living tissue. Yet it is as difficult for theologians as for psychologists to determine the exact point in the continuum of tissue life when it can be said that personhood has been attained in even the least meaning of the concept; and it is equally difficult (which means impossible) to define categorically the point when a human being has crossed the threshold of real or authentic personhood. When is day truly day and night truly night, rather than the dusk or dawn that distinguished them? The belief in personhood is basic, but the definition remains in dispute.

57

8. For Christian faith, the definition of life in terms of personhood is determined by the acknowledgment of Jesus Christ as the true pattern of authentic human personhood and as the divine Lord of life. What can be known of life in a personal and moral rather than a physiological sense is learned from what we know of Jesus Christ. God's being in Christ to reconcile a wayward human race to himself means that God gave in Christ the one after whom and through whom humankind can be renewed. But what are the limits of humankind in the sense of the totality of the race created in God's image? Is membership in humankind conditional on a criterion of conscious personhood? And when in the continuum of human development does the relationship to Jesus Christ begin? When the individual makes a profession of faith? Or when this individual comes into existence?

Sanctity of Life

These are eight expressions of Christian faith that are widely held among Christians belonging to various denominations and having diverse ethical perspectives. I chose these eight because they pertain to the question of abortion, not because they are the only basic Christian affirmations. And they *are* affirmations, not speculative hypotheses or abstract principles. In some churches (notably the Roman Catholic Church) such theological affirmations are held to be revealed truth, and as such are regarded as premises from which certain deductions may be drawn. (The deduction generally drawn from the statements about the unbroken continuum of human life created by God for conformity to the pattern of Jesus Christ (i.e., for full humanity) is that abortion is willful destruction of human life; it is tantamount to murder.)

Reasoning that deduces so categorical a judgment from affirmations of faith, called revealed truth, fails to take into account the complexities of human experience. To employ a recently popular term, such a method of theological thought is not contextual. It focuses all attention on the unborn human life and decrees that this life, created by God and destined for salvation, must under no circumstances be destroyed. (Or only under the circumstance designated double effect, as when a fetus is killed during a surgical procedure to save a woman's life.) Contextual reasoning is concerned with all the persons involved in a case of possible abortion—most especially the woman, but also the family and widening circles of society. When unborn life that is not as yet viable threatens the health and well-being of the pregnant woman or others whenever it becomes viable, a simplistic, noncontextual theological rule will not

58

do. What is the alternative, if it is not to be just a callous disregard for the value of unborn life?

Sanctity of life—this is the primary criterion applied by many Christians who wish to think theologically in the whole context of an abortion problem. People who dispute over abortion appear to be invoking "sanctity of life" with increasing frequency. Since they seldom define either "sanctity" or "life," the phrase can be made to fit either side of the argument. One who holds a rigorously prohibitive view of abortion means to say that the living cells of the embryo or fetus, having been made and destined by the holy God, are literally holy. Thus the sanctity of life inheres in its being given by God and destined to be a human person who is to realize authentic personhood in communion with God. Whatever the context, the unborn human life is sacred and must not be killed.

However, the same phrase is cited by one who sees nothing morally wrong in the termination of a pregnancy if this will ostensibly contribute to the health, well-being and fulfillment of the woman concerned and in a small way will also mitigate certain ills of society. In this case, sanctity of life is really equated with another much-used phrase: quality of life.

Is it possible to rescue "sanctity of life" from ambiguity so that intelligent Christians, when discussing abortion, can use it with the same meaning? If not, the phrase should be abandoned. If so, there may be some progress toward a common Christian position on the issue. Let us try.

The word sanctity certainly conveys the meaning of holiness. It has a transcendent reference to God, who is holy. To be made holy, sanctified, means to be set apart by God in the order of things for God's own purpose. The way in which a human being rises toward, or falls away from, that divinely intended purpose is the complex story of human misery and human grandeur. It involves the immanent working of God's Spirit, the mystery of evil and sin, and the strangely terrible and wonderful uses of human freedom. For Christian faith, the story includes, above all, the redemptive work of Jesus Christ and the response of people to him. In short, sanctity, far from being a facile designation of humanness, summons up the whole range of belief and understanding about God's intention for human beings and their responsibility to God. If this is what we mean when we talk about the pregnant woman and the unborn fetus, then we can use "sanctity of life" in a legitimately Christian sense.

What now about the tacit identification of sanctity with quality of life? This latter—a jargon phrase if ever there was one, jargon being the substitute for thoughtful diction—seems to refer simply to a life worth living or, at the most hedonistic level, to a life of bourgeois comfort. There is no point in applying the word sanctity to the life of either the pregnant woman or the fetus if the fetus' coming to term will probably injure the quality of the life of both; that is, if giving birth to and/or caring for a child might interfere with the mother's aspirations and plans for happiness and fulfillment; and/or if the baby might have to develop in a situation entirely adverse to its chances for a life of quality. Either one identifies sanctity and quality, thus stripping the former of much theological content; or else one asks, What good is the sanctity of life if there is no real quality?

Discussion of abortion among Christians could be clarified considerably if they could agree on a full (not merely vitalistic) meaning of sanctity, and then recognize that quality is always to be subsumed under sanctity. Otherwise the archetypal experience of Job, the historical experience of Israel, and the *via crucis* of Jesus have taught us nothing about life.

Bios and *Zoe*

Life—what is life? We may dispute the meaning of sanctity and quality, but we assume that everyone knows what life is. This assumption requires some scrutiny.

The New Testament speaks a good deal about life, especially in the Fourth Gospel with reference to Jesus Christ. "In him was life, and the life was the light of men [1:4]"; "As the Father has life in himself, so he has granted the Son also to have life in himself . . . the Son gives life to whom he will [5:26, 21]"; and many more such.

As compared to the Greek, the English language is inadequate. Where our translations have the one word life, the Greek New Testament uses two: *bios* and *zoe*. As they did with many Greek words, the New Testament writers transmuted their meanings and virtually exchanged the meanings of the two terms; and modern English has done the same with the words derived from them.

Bios originally meant the way or conduct or quality of life. Accordingly, its English descendant, "biology," once meant the study of human life and character. But today biology as a life science is wholly concerned with what secular Greeks called *zoe:* the phenomena of living tissues and organisms.

The New Testament people, as I said, used *bios* to designate the mere sustenance for mortal existence and *zoe* to speak of the sanctity, reality, and qualitative dimension of human living. *Zoe* is the true and abundant life that God intends people to enjoy on earth and to have in eternity. "Where," T.S. Eliot asks the modern man or woman, "where is the life you have lost in living?" Where is the *zoe* you have lost in *bios*?

The point of this philological excursus is to show that our discussions of abortion are often confused by the failure of the English language to distinguish between these two concepts of life.

We observe, for instance, that pregnancy sometimes causes a conflict of life with life. True. But this has a double sense. Given a pathological condition on the part of the pregnant woman, there may be a conflict of *bios* with *bios,* and a choice must be made between one *bios* and the other. But in the case of an unwanted pregnancy, the conflict is between the *bios* of the fetus and the *zoe* of the woman —since the *zoe* of the fetus can become a reality only after it is brought to birth. Or again, those who argue for abortion on demographic grounds are saying in effect that the population crisis is such that preservation of *bios* in the case of millions of unborn children threatens the collective *zoe* of humankind. A secularized usage of the words—a usage that, as we say, seems sensible and useful to many Christians too—reduces *bios* to a matter of histology and physiology and considers *zoe* hedonistically or humanistically. In both cases the Christian meaning is debased.

For Christian faith, true sanctity can be found in *bios* and in *zoe,* but in differing degrees, so to speak. The Author and Finisher of creation is God, the Holy One, who sanctifies. As creator God sanctifies with grace the person who develops from the procreated human entity. Christian thinking about and debates on the issues of abortion —whether the general ethical issue or the case of a particular woman with child—would be greatly helped if this true meaning of sanctity were accepted by all as including both *bios* and *zoe,* with *zoe* always having the higher value. Then Christians would never think of the fetus, at whatever stage of development, as a disposable "thing"; nor would they have so strong a fixation on the preservation of the fetus at all costs that they would be callous to either the pregnant woman's *zoe* or to the well-being of society. Then they could respect fully the rights of women without being coerced into thinking that women are always right. Then they could have the perception needed to resist the notion that an unwanted child had better not have been born. And, very important, then they could see that a battle for the rights of the unborn is only half a war against inhumanity—since the other half, which has equal claim on them, is the hard social and legislative struggle to secure and realize the rights of both the bearer and the born for a good life.

8

The Roman Catholic Position

Daniel Callahan

Two POINTS NEED to be distinguished in talking about the Church's present position. The first concerns the matter of the *method* of the argument, and the second the *substance* of the argument. In general, as the position is argued in papal statements and manuals of moral theology, the method is deductive. Fundamental general principles are laid down; specific conclusions, applicable to abortion cases, are then drawn. The principles function as axioms, the conclusions, as consequences derived from the axioms. While this style of argumentation is most obvious in the manuals, where it is explicitly used, it is also present in the papal and conciliar statements. It is possible to look on this method in two ways. Viewed benignly, it represents simply a common method of moral argumentation: General principles are established and specific applications are made. Viewed more critically, it can fall under the kind of charge leveled by Protestant theologian James M. Gustafson and echoed by many contemporary Catholic moralists about the method of Catholic moral theology. Gustafson has pointed out, perceptively, that Catholic arguments about abortion are (1) "arguments made by an *external judge*"; (2) "are made on a basically *juridical model*"; (3) "largely confine the relevant data to *the physical*";

Reprinted with permission of Macmillan Publishing Co., Inc., from *Abortion: Law, Choice and Morality* by Daniel Callahan. Copyright © 1970 by Daniel Callahan.

DANIEL CALLAHAN is director of the Hastings Center Institute of Society, Ethics and the Life Sciences, Hastings-on-Hudson, New York.

(4) "are limited by concerning themselves almost *exclusively with the physician and the patient* at the time of a particular pregnancy, isolating these two from the multiple relationships and responsibilities each has to and for others over long periods of time"; (5) "are *rationalistic*"; and further that (6) "the traditional perspective seeks to develop arguments based on *natural law,* and thus ought to be persuasive and binding on all men."[1] Yet, while a general characterization of this kind is accurate, not all who argue the Catholic position necessarily argue in this fashion; instead, one can now find commonly employed a variety of styles (which will be indicated in the ensuing discussion).

The substance of the Catholic position can be summed up in the following principles, which are sometimes developed in a theological way, sometimes philosophically, and sometimes mixed together: (1) God alone is the Lord of life. (2) Human beings do not have the right to take the lives of other (innocent) human beings. (3) Human life begins at the moment of conception. (4) Abortion, at whatever the stage of development of the conceptus, is the taking of innocent human life. The conclusion follows: Abortion is wrong. The only exception to this conclusion is in the case of an abortion that is the indirect result of an otherwise moral and legitimate medical procedure (e.g., the treatment of an ectopic pregnancy and cancerous uterus).

God Alone Is the Lord of Life

When the Catholic position is argued theologically, this is a key proposition. "Only God is Lord of the Life of a man who is not guilty of a crime punishable with death," Pius XII said on one occasion, and, on another, "Every human being, even the child in its mother's womb, receives its right to life directly from God" (as quoted above). Norman St. John-Stevas argues in a similar way, as do other Catholic authors.[2] Variantly, this argument is often couched in terms of the right to life, especially when the inviolability of human life is approached from a philosophical–natural-law–perspective. Thus Fr. Thomas J. O'Donnell contends that the purposeful termination of a pregnancy "contains the moral malice of the violation of man's most fundamental human right—the right to life itself."[3] Other authors, although more rarely, have also seen in abortion the thwarting of the ends of nature, in this instance that of frustrating the good of the species in favor of the good of an individual (the mother).[4]

I am critical of the use of the principle of God's lordship as a premise in a consideration of the morality of abortion. To recapitulate, it presupposes that God intervenes directly in natural and human affairs as the primary causative agent of life and death. Not

63

only is this theologically dubious, it also has the effect of obscuring the necessity that human beings define terms, make decisions, and take responsibility for the direct care of human life. Moreover, to say that God is the ultimate source of the right to life, which is less objectionable theologically, still does not solve the problem of *how* human beings ought to respect that right or how they are to balance a conflict of rights. Normally speaking, the right to life takes primacy over other rights, since without life no other rights can be exercised. But abortion problems normally arise because other important rights appear to be in conflict with this right; unless a prior and fixed decision has been made to give always and in every circumstance the right to life a primacy over all other human rights, it is not clear how, without begging some important questions, the right to life can be invoked as the sole right in question in abortion decisions. But this is the procedure of many Catholic moralists when it comes to abortion.

Human Beings Do Not Have the Right to Take the Lives of Other (Innocent) Human Beings

This proposition is consistent both with Christian ethics, in the theological sense, and with Catholic natural-law morality. The word innocent, however, is crucial here. Traditional Catholic morality has defended the just war, i.e., defensive, limited war waged for the preservation of life or the protection of vital human rights. These wars have been justified even though they result, often enough, in the foreseen taking of innocent life, particularly the lives of noncombatants. The justification for thus taking innocent life is governed by the principle of double effect. Thus, innocent (noncombatant) lives cannot be taken unless, for the strict demands of self-defense, these lives are taken only indirectly, that is, by an action "designed and intended solely to achieve some other purpose(s) even though death is foreseen as a concomitant effect. Death therefore is not positively willed, but is reluctantly permitted as an unavoidable by-product."[5] Thus, while the proposition concerning the absence of the right of one human being to take the life of another is basic to Catholic morality, when argued both theologically and in terms of natural law, it admits of an important exception in two circumstances: when the life to be taken is *not* innocent human life (as in punishment for capital crimes and in the case of a just defensive war) and when it is innocent life but the taking of life is indirect.

Human Life Begins at the Moment of Conception

Whereas the first two propositions were general moral principles, this one is a specific proposition about the nature of the life in question in abortion decisions. While some Catholic moralists are attempting to revive the earlier distinction between the formed and the unformed fetus, the general trend in recent decades has been to eliminate the distinction and count as human the immediate product of conception.[6] Thus, Pius XII: "Even the child, even the unborn child, is a human being in the same degree and by the same title as its mother." These words were consistent with the words of Pope Pius XI, who had spoken of the conceptus as "an innocent child" and "an innocent human being." In line with phrases of this kind, the Catholic Hospital Association of the United States and Canada has specified as one of its principles: "Every unborn child must be regarded as a human person, with all the rights of a human person, from the moment of conception."[7] When speaking cautiously, many theologians would say that, in the absence of a philosophical or scientific demonstration that a conceptus is human, respect for life requires us to treat it as if it were.

It goes without saying that a decision to call a conceptus, whatever the stage of development, a human being or a human person presumes certain convictions about the proper way to read biological evidence. While the papal statements do not give the reasoning behind this decision, it is safe to assume that the ultimate motive behind so reading the evidence in this fashion is to extend protection to the earliest reaches of individual human life. It represents a moral policy, one which has chosen one possible way of reading the data and chosen this way, the safest way, as the most compatible with the moral aim: the protection of all innocent life. In addition, in a way consistent with the Catholic tradition, Catholic authors overwhelmingly tend to make the problem of the beginning of human life the major, indeed overriding, particular factual question to be answered in any approach to abortion. Once it is determined (as the tradition has determined) that the right to life is the fundamental human right, and that innocent life may not be taken, then the only remaining question of consequence is whether the conceptus ought to be considered human life. As Fr. Robert Drinan has put it, "Every discussion of abortion must, in the final analysis, begin and end with a definition of what one thinks of a human embryo or fetus."[8] For John T. Noonan Jr., "the most fundamental question involved in the long history of thought on abortion is: How do you determine the humanity of a being?"[9] David Granfield felt that the centrality of the question warranted beginning his book on abortion with it. For that matter, whether dealt with in terms of the question of the moment of animation or ensoulment or in some other more contemporary form, it is a question that has traditionally been given primacy.[10] This characteristic of Catholic argumentation is important because, by so ordering the priority of the questions to be asked, all other questions are thrown into a subsidiary position. Actually this makes it exceedingly difficult, within the Catholic problematic, to try and weigh other values—the mother's duty toward her children, her psychological state and freedom, her economic situation—or to raise or answer the other kinds of questions; the first question asked tends to preempt the others. An important aspect of the one-dimensionality of the Catholic position is thus its tendency to narrow the issues considered legitimate and important to very few; issues that, it turns out, bear almost exclusively (with the noted exceptions) on the status of the conceptus. No room is left for the integration of a full range of rights, personal and communal.

Abortion, at Whatever the Stage of Development of the Conceptus, Is the Taking of Innocent Human Life

Once the question of whether the conceptus from the moment of conception is human life has been answered in the affirmative, then it is only a short, indeed tautological step to state that abortion is the taking of innocent human life. While, as Noonan has shown, there have been theologians who have tried to develop the argument that, in some cases, the fetus can be counted as an aggressor, this line has had scant papal or theological support. The net result is that the act of abortion is, in the end, defined as an act that takes innocent human life, and thus by definition an act to be condemned and proscribed. If one stays within the framework of the Catholic argument, proceeding from premises 1 to 3, then this is a logical deduction and thus unexceptionable. With premise 2 taken as a principle of the natural law and the conceptus judged factually (biologically) to be human, no other conclusion is possible than a condemnation of abortion. As Josef Fuchs, S.J., has argued (exhibiting both the style and the substance of the argument):

> Any principle of the natural law remains efficacious in every situation that realizes the facts involved by this principle. For example, it can never happen that the prohibition of a direct destruction of unborn life—a principle of the natural law—could cease to be an absolute demand even in difficult concrete situations, or out of charitable consideration for a mother and her family.[11]

Put in terms of the four propositions above, the structure of the Catholic argument is comparatively simple and straightforward. It rests on no *obscure* arguments (even if they may strike many as fallacious), requires no elaborate steps to carry it off (as, for instance, Catholic natural-law arguments against contraception do) and draws on few idiosyncratic Catholic ways of arguing moral issues (conserva-

66

tive Protestant and Jewish arguments are not that dissimilar). But it seems to me that one cannot fully appreciate the Catholic position (or the vehemence with which it is supported) without observing a number of collateral arguments commonly brought to bear in support of it. Most commonly, it is contended that a justification of abortion has the force of a justification for treating all human beings as expendable and introducing a principle of expediency into human relations. As David Granfield has put it:

> Abortion is forbidden morally because it is an abuse of human power. It is a destruction of a human being by another human being, and as such it strikes at the heart of human dignity. The usurpation of authority which is abortion is not wrong simply because it kills unborn children, but because it results in the vilification of all men. To give moral justification to abortion is to condemn all men to the level of expendable things. Morally, the fight against abortion is not primarily to protect the human dignity of the unborn, but is above all to safeguard that dignity in all men.[12]

For Father Drinan, an acceptance of the American Law Institute's Model Penal Code on abortion would have the consequence of overthrowing a fundamental value of Anglo-Saxon law, the inviolability of human life: "At no time and under no circumstances has Anglo-American law ever sanctioned the destruction of one human being—however useless and unwanted such a person may be—for the purpose of securing or increasing the health or happiness of other individuals."[13] For Father O'Donnell, doctors who perform therapeutic abortions have adopted a philosophy of "medical expediency" that they are willing to place above any other moral standard.[14] Bernard Häring sees the possibility of a fundamental threat to motherhood: "If it were to become an accepted principle of moral teaching on motherhood to permit a mother whose life was endangered simply to 'sacrifice' the life of her child in order to save her own, motherhood would no longer mean absolute dedication to each and every child."[15] For Noonan, "abortion violates the rational humanist tenet of the equality of human lives."[16] Finally, it is not unfitting to mention that some older manuals of moral theology—still in use in some places—condemned abortion on the added (but theologically dubious) ground that "it deprives the soul of eternal life."[17]

Extrapolations of this kind, which often strike the non-Catholic as red herrings if not bizarre, make considerable logical sense once one realizes that the premises of the Catholic argument have *defined* abortion as the taking of innocent human life. At stake, in the Catholic view, is the principle of the right to life: if the principle is breached in one place, it could well be breached in another—a precedent has been established for violating the principle. One may

67

object (as I will) to the premises, but it is important to see that, once adopted, the conclusions Catholics draw from them are consistent. The practice of envisioning further erosions of respect for life if abortion is accepted is, in the Catholic view, a perfectly legitimate philosophical procedure, a way of trying to chart the consequences of a change in what are taken to be fundamental moral principles. It is a procedure, moreover, used commonly in all forms of moral argumentation and by no means restricted to Catholics; it is only to say, as others say when their own ox is gored, that the social consequences of a change in basic moral principles can be enormously harmful. Given the Catholic premises, it should at least be understandable (even if not acceptable) why many Catholics cannot but view with alarm the prospect of a moral acceptance of abortion. State the case as bluntly as John Marshall has done and it is easy to see social disaster as a consequence of an acceptance of abortion: "Direct abortion . . . is gravely wrong, because it constitutes the direct killing of an innocent human being."[18] It ought to be understandable why Catholics, given their premises, can envision the antiabortion cause as an attempt to hold on to very basic Western values, values by no means exclusively their own but rather the patrimony of the entire culture. A quotation from Fr. Richard A. McCormick will help to drive the point home: "The question 'What am I doing?' is the first question to be asked about induced abortion. It is all the more urgent because it is precisely the question our society nearly always neglects."[19] The Catholic answer is that the act being performed in abortion is the killing of an innocent human being; once reached, a conclusion of this kind dictates, at the cost of inconsistency and moral irresponsibility, vigorous opposition to abortion.

The Principle of Double Effect

Within the framework of traditional Catholic morality, it is exceedingly difficult for a Catholic—even if he or she would like to do so—to find a way of taking exception to the received teaching. This is, no doubt, one reason why few efforts have been mounted to change the teaching. With the exception of the premise that human life begins at conception (which can at any rate be challenged on biological grounds, where the evidence is open to varying interpretations), the other premises seem either securely fixed by the Christian tradition or represent straightforward deductions from natural-law premises already accepted. If, then, the traditional teaching is to be challenged within a Catholic framework (and, of course, it is simple to challenge it from an entirely different theological or philosophical framework), it must be done by a critical examination of (1) the premises themselves, (2) the validity of the conclusions drawn from the premises, and (3) the details and methods of argumentation. As for the premises, a number of objections have already been leveled at the theological belief that the lordship of God takes the matter of abortion decisions out of human hands, and at the philosophical belief that the right to life necessarily takes precedence over all other rights. Once this much has been seen and the premises thrown into question (but only that), then the way is open to dispute the conclusion drawn from these premises: that the direct taking of innocent fetal (or embryonic) life is always and necessarily immoral.

One detail in particular of the traditional Catholic argument opens the way for such a disputation: the principle of double effect. As noted, the only exceptions to the absolute prohibition of abortion are in the case of an ectopic pregnancy or a cancerous uterus. In both of these instances, the justification for the exception is that the indicated medical procedure to save the life of the mother (the removal of the tube or of the uterus) has as its direct intention the saving of the life of the mother; the death of the fetus is the foreseen but unintended and indirect result of the lifesaving surgery performed on the mother. By a use of this distinction, then, an abortion can be performed in the specified cases without directly violating the moral law that innocent life cannot be killed. The basis for the principle is the commonsense observation that an action can have a good and a bad effect or result. As a theological distinction, it was first employed by Thomas Aquinas, who built on it a justification for the taking of life in self-defense.[20] In essence, the point of the principle is this: An action that has both a good and a bad effect may be performed if the good effect accomplished is greater than the evil effect and if, in addition, at least four other conditions are met: (1) the act must itself be either good or indifferent, or at least not forbidden with a view to preventing just that effect; (2) the evil effect cannot be a means to the good, but must be equally immediate or at least must result from the good effect; (3) the foreseen evil effect must not be intended or approved, merely permitted—for even a good act is vitiated if accompanied by an evil intent; (4) there must be a proportionately serious reason for exercising the cause and allowing the evil effect.[21] The problem of an ectopic pregnancy illustrates what is considered a legitimate use of the principle:

> The removal of a pregnant fallopian tube containing a non-viable living fetus, even before the external rupture of the tube, can be done in such a way that the consequent death of the fetus will be produced only indirectly. Such an operation will be licitly performed if all the circumstances are such that the necessity for the operation is, in moral estimation, proportionate to the evil effect permitted.[22]

In this instance, the intent of the operation itself is good (as a standard operation to save life); although the fetus is killed, this effect, although foreseen, is not the intention of the operation (thus the death of the fetus is indirectly caused); the evil effect (the death of the fetus) is not the means to the good end (the saving of the life of the woman), but only the indirect result of the means (the tubal removal) necessary to save the life of the woman. Thus, the conditions for an application of the principle are met. By contrast, a fetal craniotomy to save the life of the woman would not be licit because, in this case, the life of the fetus is taken directly by the act of crushing its skull. The intention is good (saving the life of the woman), but the means employed are evil (directly taking the life of an innocent fetus); hence, fetal craniotomy is forbidden.[23]

Now, it has been contended that, far from being impersonal and legalistic, the principle of double effect represents "an attempt on the part of theologians to free us to do as much as possible, even though indirectly intended evil—in this case, the death of the unborn —results."[24] For Noonan, the making of exceptions on the basis of the principle represents an attempt to achieve a balance: "In Catholic moral theology, as it developed, life even of the innocent was not taken as an absolute. Judgments on acts affecting life issued from a process of weighing. In the weighing, the fetus was always given a greater value than zero, always a value separate and independent from its parents."[25] One feels compelled to comment, however, that the weighing in question is decisively one-sided, takes physical life alone as the only value at stake, leaving no real room for even investigating any other considerations that might come into play. It is evident, moreover, that a theology that would countenance the death of the fetus and the woman (rare in fact but pertinent in principle) rather than directly take the life of the fetus is one geared heavily to a preoccupation with preserving individuals from sin or crime. Its real interest in the extreme case of letting both woman and fetus die turns out, in effect, not to be the good of the mother (for, hypothetically, a fetal craniotomy would save her life), but the good conscience of those who might but do not act to save her. The basic moral principle of "Do good and avoid evil" is efficaciously rendered into the avoiding of evil alone.

The way in which a conflict of rights between a woman and a fetus is treated is illuminating of the consequences of this style of moral reckoning; for it is at this point that the style most clearly shows itself. Pope Pius XII in a statement has said that "neither the life of the mother nor that of the child can be subjected to an act of direct suppression. In the one case as in the other, there can be but one obligation: to make every effort to save the lives of both, of the mother and the child." But it is, of course, precisely the supposition of the hypothesis in these situations (however rare medically) that, unless the fetus is killed, the mother will die also: both lives cannot be saved. The assumption behind this form of reasoning is that there exists a fixed order of rights, before which humans must passively stand, whatever the physical consequences of their passivity. A passage from Josef Fuch's book brings this out:

> The difficulty of a conflict of rights can *easily* [my italics] be solved if one understands that there are no heterogeneous orders and demands of the natural law placed side by side without any relation to one another. There exists indeed *an order* of goods and values, of commands and demands through the very nature of things, so that there can be no true conflict of rights but at most an apparent conflict. The two obligations concerning a pathological birth, to preserve the life of the mother and not to kill the child, only seem to contradict one another. There is in fact no commandment to save the mother at all costs. There is only an obligation to save her in a morally permissible way and such a way is not envisaged in stating this given situation. Consequently only one obligation remains: to save the mother without attempting to kill the child.[26]

What seems apparent here is that, despite acknowledgment of an obligation to the mother, the *primary* obligation is fulfillment of the moral law, which exists independently of the obligations owed to particular human beings. Once the primary obligation has been discharged, fidelity to the moral law, no human obligations remain; the woman may be allowed to die. One consequence of a morality that centers obligation and responsibility in preservation of the law is to posit a sharp distinction between physical and moral evils. "Two natural deaths," David Granfield has written, "are a lesser evil than one murder. In the conflict of interests between mother and child, the rights of both to live must be preserved. The conflict cannot be resolved morally by the killing of the weaker party without thereby destroying all morality."[27] Even if one assumes the killing of the child in the instance of a moral conflict would be "murder," one has to ask why this "murder" would be a greater evil than the death of both. Would it not be a moral evil to let the woman die (when she could be saved), and an even greater moral evil if there were others (husband, other children) dependent on her? To imply that such an evil is physical is to posit a moral helplessness and lack of human responsibility in the face of natural disasters. On the contrary, it seems to me perfectly reasonable to say that what is initially a physical situation (an event in nature) becomes a moral situation when it enters the realm of potential human action. A choice not to act in the face of a physical evil for the sake of saving another becomes—assuming human responsibility—a moral choice.

In a rigid natural-law formulation the terms of the choice seem dictated by laws supposedly transcendent to the human beings affected by them. In Granfield's instance the preservation of the rights of both to life becomes nothing more than sheer formalism. For, when one or more human beings refuse to save the mother by the "murder" of the fetus, she is being refused by other human beings the de facto right to life; her rights are nullified. To say that "all morality" would be destroyed "by the killing of the weaker party" is only possible if one presumes that morality consists in observing a moral law regardless of the consequences for individual human beings. The range of human responsibility is thus narrowed to a point where the good conscience of those who could act and the abstract demands of the law take precedence over every other consideration. It becomes, at this point, virtually meaningless to speak, as Noonan has done, of the work of the moralists as one of "the weighing of fetal rights against other human rights."[28] For the terms allowable in the weighing are such as to ensure that, once the fetus has been defined as innocent human life, the weighing entirely favors the fetus. That two exceptions are admitted (and those medically uncommon) can hardly be said to constitute "balance." And it goes without saying, of course, that when the only aspects of the balance even worthy of consideration are those of physical life, then the whole network of other responsibilities the mother may have becomes morally irrelevant.

The Morality of Abortion

Paul Ramsey

Possible Meanings of Animation

ALMOST EVERYONE has a proposal to make concerning when in the course of its prenatal or postnatal development embryonic life becomes "human." At one extreme are the views of those who hold that life is not human until the individual is a personal subject or has reason in exercise. If to be human *means* to be a person, to be a self-conscious subject of experience, or if it means to be rational, this state of affairs does not come to pass until a long while after the birth of a baby. A human infant acquires its personhood and self-conscious subjective identity through "Thou–I" encounters with other selves; and a child acquires essential rationality even more laboriously. If life must be human in these senses before it has any sanctity and respect or rights due it, infanticide would seem to be justified under any number of conditions believed to warrant it as permissible behavior or as a social policy. In any case, those who identify being human with personhood or rationality adopt a modern form of an ancient theological position called creationism. According to this view, the

---

Reprinted from Daniel H. Labby, ed., *Life or Death: Ethics and Options* (Seattle: University of Washington Press, 1968) with the permission of the author and the University of Washington Press.

PAUL RAMSEY is Harrington Spear Paine Professor of Christian Ethics at Princeton University, Princeton, New Jersey.

73

unique, never-to-be-repeated individual human being (the "soul" is the religious word for him) comes into existence by a process of humanization or socialization in interaction with the persons around him. In the traditional religious language, he is "created" and "infused" into the already existing organism—sometime, gradually, after physical birth.

At the other extreme is the latest scientific view, that of modern genetics. Indeed, microgenetics seems to have demonstrated what religion never could; and biological science, to have resolved an ancient theological dispute. The human individual comes into existence first as a minute informational speck, drawn at random from many other minute informational specks his parents possessed out of the common human gene pool. This took place at the moment of impregnation. There were, of course, an unimaginable number of combinations of specks on his paternal and maternal chromosomes that did not come to be when they were refused and he began to be. Still—with the single exception of identical twins—no one else in the entire history of the human race has ever had or will ever have exactly the same genotype. Thus, it can be said that the individual is whoever he is going to become from the moment of impregnation. Subsequent development may be described as a process of becoming the one he already is. Genetics teaches that we were from the beginning what we essentially still are in every cell and in every human and individual attribute. This scientific account is a modern form of the ancient theological viewpoint called traducianism. According to this view the unique, never-to-be-repeated individual human being (the "soul") was drawn forth from his parents at the time of conception.[1]

What is this but to say that we are all fellow fetuses? That from womb to tomb ours is a nascent life? That we are, in essence, congeners from the beginning? What is this but a rather antiseptic way of saying that the Creator has beset us behind and before? While we know only the light of our particular span of conscious existence, this light and that darkness whence we came and toward which we go are both alike to the One who laid his hands upon us, covered us in the womb, and by whom we were fearfully and wonderfully made.

Between the extremes of traducianism at the conception and creationism gradually after birth, there are other accounts of when the human being originates and thus becomes a subject worthy of respect, rights, sanctity. None of the positions yet to be mentioned is quite as up to date and scientific as the genetic account of the origin of human individuality. Among these are religious and legal viewpoints that seem always to be based on prescientific notions and superstitions. Anglo-American law, for example, takes the moment of birth to

74

be the moment after which there is a "man alive" (for which the evidence is air in the lungs) and before which there was no human life, separable from the mother's, that could be murdered. When it is born a man alive, the child is, from this moment, already the one it thereafter becomes; not before, as genetics teaches. After it is born a man alive, a child is then and then only a possible victim of the crime of murder.

Where abortion is defined as a criminal offense in our legal systems, this creates another category of proscribed actions. It is not because the fetus is regarded as having sanctity or integrity or an independent right to life such as the law presupposes in the case of a man alive. The legal reason for prohibiting abortion is not because it is believed to be a species of murder; it is the religious tradition, we shall see, and not the law that inculcates the latter view. The law's presumption is only that society has a stake in the prehuman material out of which the unique individual is to be born. Or it may be that the law exhibits a belief that as a matter of public policy society has an interest in *men* and *women,* who have an interest in and by their actions take responsibility for the prehuman material out of which an individual human being is to be brought forth a man alive.

This brings us to the theories advanced by theologians and by church law—all doubtless to be classed, along with the law, as superstitious and prescientific in comparison with the genetic account of the arrival of the essential constitutive features of a human individual. Theologians propose an analysis of the prenatal development of the fetus. This means they assert that the fetus *before* birth may be the victim of the sin of murder. But this does not immediately entail that *all* destruction of fetal life should be classified as murder. Only modern genetics seems to lead to this conclusion, with its teaching about the unrepeatability or at least the never-to-be-repeated character of that first informational speck each of us once was and still is in every cell and attribute. Theology, however, is premicrobiology! Theologians debate the question, *when* between conception and birth the unique not-to-be-repeated individual human being has arrived on the scene. Wherever the line is drawn, the direct destruction of a fetus after this point will, by definition, be murder, while before this point its direct destruction would fall under some other species of sin or grave violation.

In the prenatal development of the fetus, animation is the point between conception and birth that is usually taken to be crucial, although animation may have more than one meaning. If animation and not impregnation or birth is the moment when an individual offspring first begins to be what he is to become and launches on a course of thereafter becoming what he already is, then direct abortion after animation would be to kill a man alive. It would be—morally, not legally—a species of murder. Then, on this view, to define a direct abortion before animation as an offense would require that such an action be understood to fall within a class of less serious violations. In no case would the destruction of a preanimate fetus raise questions regarding the respect due or the rights and sanctity of another distinct human life. The fetus is then not yet human; it is still only part of the mother's body, even though there may be a special responsibility for this prehuman material out of which is to come, at animation, a man alive.

The term animation may be understood in two different ways, and from this follows two different views concerning when in the course of the development of a fetus its direct abortion would be murder. Animation may most obviously be taken to indicate the moment fetal life becomes an independent source of movement in the womb, and modern thought would define animation in terms of physical motion. This should perhaps be called quickening, the better to distinguish it from the second, the classic and more philosophical interpretation.

It was once commonly believed that there were forty days for the male and eighty days for the female between impregnation and the time, long before quickening, when the fetus became animate in this other sense. The second and more fundamental meaning of animation is derived not from motion, but from *anima* (soul). The controlling philosophic doctrine was one that held that the soul is the *form of the body*. Thus *fetus animatus* = *fetus humanus* = *fetus formatus*. This did not entail another purely physical determination of when there was a formed fetus, or a fetus in human form or shape, on the scene. This would be earlier, of course, than when the fetus quickens. The meaning of the soul as the form of the body was too subtle a notion for that. It entailed a belief that there is a living human fetus, possibly much earlier than when there is either discernible motion or discernible human shape.

But the point to be noted here is that in theoretical speculation there has never been a certain or unanimous opinion among theologians to the effect that a *fetus humanus/fetus animatus* begins to be at the very moment of conception. In the controversies among theologians past and present, there has always been allowed a period of time between conception and animation. Scientifically or at the level of theory or doctrine, one cannot speak with certainty of a human fetus before the lapse, some say, of six days.[2] It is the modern science of genetics and not theology that theoretically closes this gap completely (unless segmentation in the case of identical twins is taken to be some sort of *rebutting* scientific evidence for identifying the moment of animation).

In any case, the older theologians distinguished between a formed fetus and a quickened fetus, and between nutritive, animal, and intellectual parts of the soul. They did not go so far as to say that all this was created and infused at impregnation. By the intellectual or human soul informing the fetus and by the doctrine that the soul is the form of the body, they meant an immanent constitutive element, not form in the sense of physical shape. Their reasoning entailed a distinction between *fetus formatus/fetus animatus* and a quickened fetus. This meant, of course, that the embryo became essentially human very early in its development—much earlier than could be concluded from form or animation in the gross physical senses of these terms.

In a remarkable way, modern genetics also teaches that there are "formal causes," immanent principles, or constitutive elements long before there is any shape or motion or discernible size. These minute formal elements are already determining the organic life to be the uniquely individual human being it is to be. According to this present-day scientific equivalent of the doctrine that the soul is the form or immanent *entelechy* of the body, it can now be asserted—not unreasonably—for the first time in the history of scientific speculation on this question that who one is and is to be is present from the moment the ovum is impregnated.[3]

One can, of course, allow this and still refuse to affirm that the embryo is as yet in any sense the bearer of human rights. In this case one would have to provide himself with some account (perhaps drawn from these ancient and contemporary accounts of the prenatal and postnatal development of human personhood) of how by stages or degrees a human offspring approaches sacredness, and he would have to say when a child probably attains life that has sanctity. One could, for example, take viability and not impregnation or animation or quickening or actual birth or one year of age as the point in time when nascent life becomes subject to the protections due to any human life. Glanville Williams has recently proposed another place to draw the line, this time between quickening and viability. "One might take," he writes, "the time at which the fetal brain begins to function," which can be determined by electrodes detecting the electric potentials or brain waves that are discernible in the seventh month or shortly before the time of viability, to be the beginning of justifiable protection for the fetus.[4]

Of all these demarcations, the time of birth would in many ways seem the least likely account of the beginning of life that has dignity and sanctity. A newborn baby is not noticeably more human than before. It can, of course, do its own breathing; but before it could, within limits, do its own moving, and it could definitely do its own dying. While its independence of its mother's body is relatively greater—even dramatically greater—a born baby is still a long, long way from being able to do its own praying, from being a "subject," an "I," or from being rational.

The Sanctity and Protection of Life

Having begun with all these distinctions and theories about when germinating life becomes human, it is now necessary for me to say that from an authentic religious point of view none of them matters very much.

Strictly speaking, it is far more crucial for contemporary thought than it is for any religious viewpoint to *say when* there is on the scene enough of the actuality of a man who is coming to be for there to be any sacredness in or any rights attached to his life. This is the case because in modern world views the sanctity of life can rest only on something inherent in man. It is, therefore, important to determine when proleptically he already essentially is all else that he will ever become in the course of a long life. Respect for life in the first of it, if this has any sacredness, must be an overflow backward from or in anticipation of something—some capability or power—that comes later to be a man's inherent possession.

One grasps the religious outlook on the sanctity of human life only if he sees that this life is asserted to be *surrounded* by sanctity that need not be in a man; that the most dignity a man ever possesses is a dignity that is alien to him. From this point of view it becomes *relatively* unimportant to say exactly when among the products of human generation we are dealing with an organism that is human and when we are dealing with organic life that is not yet human (despite all the theological speculations on this question). A man's dignity is an overflow from God's dealings with him, and not primarily an anticipation of anything he will ever be by himself alone.

This is why in our religious traditions fetal life was *so certainly* surrounded with protections and prohibitions. This is why fetal life was surrounded by protections for the time before anyone supposed that a man alive *assuredly* existed, and even when, in opinions then current, there was a great degree of probability that he did not. "When nature is in deliberation about the man,"[5] Christians through the ages knew that God was in deliberation about the man. This took some of the weight off of analyzing the stages in the course of nature's deliberations, and off of the proofs from nature and from reason that were nevertheless used.

The value of a human life is ultimately grounded in the value God is placing on it. Anyone who can stand imaginatively, even for a moment, within an outlook where everything is referred finally to God—who, from things that are not, brings into being the things that are—should be able to see that God's deliberations about the man need have only begun. If anything is incredible here, it is not the science, but the pitch of faith that no science proves, disproves, or confirms.

According to the religious outlooks and "on-looks" that have been traditioned to us, man is a sacredness *in* human biological processes no less than he is a sacredness in the human social or political order. This sacredness is not composed by observable degrees of relative worth. A life's sanctity consists not in its worth to anybody. What life is in and of itself is most clearly to be seen in situations of naked equality of one life with another, and in the situation of congeneric helplessness that is the human condition in the first of life. No one is ever much more than a fellow fetus; and in order not to become confused about life's primary value, it is best not to concentrate on degrees of relative worth we may later acquire.

The Lord did not set his love upon you, nor choose you, because you were already intrinsically more than a blob of tissue in the uterus or greater in size than the period at the end of this sentence. Even so, the writer of Deuteronomy, in 7:7-8, KJV, proclaimed to the children of Israel:

> The Lord did not set his love upon you, nor choose you, because ye were more in number than any people; for you were the fewest of all people.
> But because the Lord loved you, and because he would keep the oath which he had sworn unto your fathers, hath the Lord brought you out with a mighty hand.

Not only the prophet Jeremiah, but anyone who has a glimmer of what it means to be a religious man, should be able to repeat after him: "Before I formed thee in the belly I knew thee; and before thou camest forth out of the womb I sanctified thee; and I ordained thee . . . [1:5, KJV]." Or after the psalmist:

> O Lord, thou hast searched me, and known me.
>
> . . . .
>
> Thou has beset me behind and before, and laid thine hand upon me.
>
> . . . .
>
> Behold . . . the darkness and the light are both alike to thee.
> For thou hast possessed my reins:

Thou hast covered me in my mother's womb.
I will praise thee; for I am fearfully and wonderfully made:
marvelous are thy works: and that my soul knoweth right well.
—Psalm 139:1, 5, 12b, 13-14, KJV

Thus, every human being is a unique, unrepeatable opportunity to praise God. His life is entirely an ordination, a loan, and a stewardship. His essence is his existence before God and to God, as it is from Him. His dignity is "an *alien* dignity," an evaluation that is not of him but placed upon him by the divine decree.

In regard to the respect to be accorded these generic, nascent, and dying lives of ours, it does not matter much which of several religious formulations is chiefly invoked. This may be the doctrine concerning the origin of a human life, or man's creation in the image of God. It may be the biblical doctrine of God's covenant with his people and thence with all mankind, with the standard this provides for the mercy to be extended in every human relation. It may be the doctrine concerning man's ultimate destination. Nor does it matter much whether it is man's life from God, before God, or toward God that is most stressed in a religious philosophy of life, whether it is supernatural faith or divine charity or supernatural hope that bestows the value. In all these cases it is hardly possible to exclude what is nowadays narrowly called nascent life from our purview or from the blessing and sanctity and protection—a religious man is convinced —God places over all human lives. *Sub specie Dei* human procreation is pro-creation. This is the most fundamental "pro" word in our vocabulary. It means procreation in God's behalf. *Sub specie Dei,* it was not because it could be proved that after a certain point in our pre- or even our postnatal development we became discernibly "human" and thus a bearer of rights and deserving of respect, while before this we were not; it was rather because the Lord loved us even while we were yet microscopic and sent forth his call on us and brought forth from things that are not the things that are. *Sub specie Dei,* it is precisely the little ones who have hardly any human claims who are sought out and covered by his mercy. *Sub specie Dei,* it is precisely when all reasonable natural grounds for hope are gone that one needs hope and may hope in God, even as when all hope was gone Abraham hoped on in faith; and in this perspective it is hardly possible to exclude from the meaning of nascent life God's call sent forth among men that once again they have hope beyond and beneath the limits reason might set.

These biblical themes resound throughout Karl Barth's writings on respect for life and the protection of life. For the greatest Protestant theologian of this generation, the congeneric human situation is that ours is a fellow humanity held in trust. Respect for life means that a man should "treat as a loan both the life of all men with his own and his own with that of all men."[6] Respect is indeed too pale a term to use for the attitude and response of those who "handle life as a divine loan."[7] Or rather—since Barth uses the term—we must allow the word respect to be filled full of the meaning and awe derived from the fact that whenever a man's life is in question, the primary affirmation to be made about it is that from all eternity God resolved not even to be God without this particular human life.

> Respect is man's astonishment, humility and awe at a fact in which he meets something superior—majesty, dignity, holiness, a mystery which compels him to withdraw and keep his distance, to handle it modestly, circumspectly and carefully. . . . When man in faith in God's Word and promise realizes how God from eternity has maintained and loved him in his little life, and what He has done for him in time, in this knowledge of human life he is faced by a majestic, dignified and holy fact. In human life itself he meets something superior. . . . [The incarnation of Jesus Christ, the Word of God made *man*] unmistakably differentiates human life from everything that is and is done in heaven and earth. This gives it even in its most doubtful form the character of something singular, unique, unrepeatable and irreplaceable. This decides that it is an advantage and something worthwhile to be as man. This characterizes life as the incomparable and non-recurrent opportunity to praise God.[8]

Respect means to treat human life with "holy awe."[9]

Respect for life does not mean that a man must live and let live from some iron law of necessity, or even that there is a rational compulsion to do this, or a decisive rational ground for doing so. It is rather that because God has said "Yes" to life, man's "Yes" should echo His. First and foremost, this means that man can and may live; he can and may respect the lives of others with his own. Into the darkness of the void before creation, or of the suicide's despair, or of a woman's womb, went forth the divine utterance, "Thou mayest live." Because of God's decree and election, a man, in his own case, can and may live; he should ("must") accept his life as a trust superior to his own determination. Because the "can" and "may" that went forth also to summon every other life together with his own came from the same God and not from any human source, he can and may and must say the only human words that are appropriate or in accord with God's Yea-saying: "Thou, too, mayest live."

It is obviously because of this understanding of the meaning of life's sanctity that Barth can write, as it were, from above about nascent life, and not because of some pseudoscience or even a correct science describing prenatal life from the underside:

> The unborn child is from the very first a child. It is still developing and has no independent life. But it is a man and not a thing, nor a mere part of the mother's body. . . . He who destroys germinating life kills a man

and thus ventures the monstrous thing of decreeing concerning the life and death of a fellow-man whose life is given by God and therefore, like his own, belongs to Him.[10]

It is precisely because *it is only nascent* life, weak and helpless and with no intrinsic reason for claiming anything by inherent right, that Barth can say, "This child is a man for whose life the Son of God has died. . . . The true light of the world shines already in the darkness of the mother's womb."[11] Or again: "Those who live by mercy will always be disposed to practice mercy, especially to a human being which is so dependent on the mercy of others as the unborn child."[12]

Because it is the Lord who has beset him behind and before, the child is a bit of sacredness in the temporal and biological order —whether in the womb of the mother, in the arms of the father, playing hopscotch on the sidewalk, a professional football player, or a scientist at work in his laboratory (or whichever one you value most). Each has the same title to life immediately from God.

Specific Problems

Nothing in the foregoing solves any problems. In these meager times it is first necessary to create the problem; and this, I venture to believe, is more important than solutions to the problem—namely, the problems arising from the sanctity of life in the first of it.

Nevertheless, by endorsing a religious understanding of the sanctity of nascent life, I have made myself responsible for offering some minimal comment on the direction and the ingredients of actual moral decisions in the matter of abortion.

1. Roman Catholic theologians do *not* in principle teach that absolute preference is to be given to the child's life over that of the mother's in cases of fatal conflict between them. This may seem to be the case in practice only because of an extraordinary effort to do nothing that denies them *equal* rights and *equal* protection. Protestant Christians and everyone of whatever profound religious outlook must join our Roman Catholic brethren in experiencing extraordinary anguish in the face of situations that throw life against nascent life, each of whom has *equal* title to protection.

My first comment is that we must adopt the main "rule of practice," which Roman Catholicism unfolds for the charitable protection of human life in cases of irremediable conflict of equals. This is the distinction between *direct* and *indirect* abortion. To abort the fetus may be the foreknown, anticipated, and permitted result of surgical or other emergency action whose *primary thrust* is directed to the end of saving the mother's life. An action may in its *primary thrust* be to save the mother's life, while it is foreknown that the fetus will or will likely die or be killed in the course of thus giving medical attention to the mother. Alternatively, if the fetus is viable, the primary thrust of the medical action may be to save the nascent life, while it is foreknown that the mother will or will likely die or be killed as a secondary consequence of trying to save her child's life. My language distinguishing between the primary and the secondary *thrust* of an action may be a peculiar Americanism. If so, it has to be invented in these times and among Protestants and other Americans who have so far reduced the meaning of "the intention of an act" that it has come to mean only the motives of the agent. Today we seem able to analyze play-acting better than we can analyze moral action, in that we can distinguish the intention of a drama from the motives and meaning the author may have had in mind, but are scarcely able to grasp the fact that the intention of moral action is not exactly the same as the subjective motives of the man who is the agent. (These, too, should be righteous.)

It is in these terms that Catholics distinguish between direct and indirect, intended and unintended, abortion. The latter can be justified but the former cannot; and, of course, neither death should be subjectively *wanted*. This rule of moral practice seems to be both a logical and a charitable extension of ethical deliberation impelled by respect for the *equal* sanctity of both the lives that are in mortal conflict, and both of whom one wants to save.

Only a moment of reflection is required to see that a woman's psychological or mental life would be equally overriding—provided her unborn child is *as certain* a threat to this. If proof were offered that this is the case, the structure of the traditional Christian argument would surely yield the point. The fact is, however, that in the present age we have proceeded to abort for psychological reasons generally, without demonstrating the necessity. There are four possibilities in the case of the so-called psychological indexes for abortion: The woman on the brink of psychological destruction may (1) abort and then (a) go to pieces or (b) hold together, or (2) bring the child to term and either (a) go to pieces or (b) hold together. Presently there is considerable evidence that the psychologists not only do not know how to *predict* these eventualities but also that they cannot *retrospectively* diagnose why what took place! Their psychological diagnosis becomes secure only after adding in a socioeconomic factor. In any case, the point to be made is simply this: The life of the mother always prevails over the life of the unborn when both equals are in mortal conflict and she alone can be saved. There is no reason for not extending this to encompass mental or personal life as well as physical life, if the facts or our knowledge of the facts were sufficient to sustain an extension of this moral judgment to such cases.

2. My second comment addresses cases that cannot be covered by the justification of indirect abortion only. The conflict situation may be one in which the mother's life cannot be saved and both the mother and the fetus will die unless the main thrust of the medical action is to kill the fetus. I do not know how many *sorts* of birth-room emergencies fall under this classification. I suspect the incidence of this *kind* or of these *kinds* of cases is lower than ordinarily supposed by persons who do not know Roman Catholic medical ethics, and therefore do not know how far this has gone in resolving one type of case after another (including ectopic pregnancy) so as to permit the action to be taken that alone will save the one life that can be saved while allowing the fetus to die. Nor do I know how often unique, individual cases may arise, even under *kinds* of medical difficulties where ordinarily indirect abortion will save the mother's life, in which a conscientious physician must judge that, taking everything into account, more positive and direct action must be taken in *this* situation or else both will die. I suspect that the number of instances in which medical practice limited to indirect abortion would be a law that kills, or rather one that allows both to die, is greater than Roman Catholic moralists suppose.

It seems altogether likely, however, whether by reason of some critical *kind* or *kinds* of medical situations or by reason of unique situations falling under any of these kinds in all their individual features, that there is need for taking up the question of the possible justification of *direct* abortion in cases of mortal conflict between a mother's life and nascent life where only the mother can be saved. In cases in which both will die unless the mother's life is saved by an act of direct abortion, does the person who secures or performs this operation do something *wrong* that good may come of it?

I think not. This would be to do the *right* thing as means (where no other means are available) and not only to seek a good end. It is permissible—nay, it is even morally obligatory—to kill the fetus directly if, without this, mother and child will die together.

The usual arguments for this practice are quite inadequate. Christian, rational, moral reflection is needed to penetrate the act of justifiable direct abortion itself, and not only its justifying circumstances or good results. In particular, if we are serious about ethics, the Protestant Christian should wrestle with his Catholic brother over the verdict each delivers on this proposed action in the course of deliberations on the Christian moral life. It is not sufficient for the Protestant simply to *assert* arbitrarily that direct abortion is the right action to be performed, and then fix his attention on the results of such conduct, on the life that is saved by this means. The goodness of this result was never in question. No one doubts that the action in question respects the sanctity of the mother's life. The question that was raised, and the question every Christian must face, is whether direct abortion is not in every way incompatible with any remaining regard of the sanctity of the nascent life.

What can and may and must be said about direct abortion insofar as this is an action brought on the child? If Roman Catholicism is incorrect in prohibiting this as a choiceworthy means for saving the mother's life (which is only of *equal* value), then it must be possible for ethical reflection to penetrate the action proposed for situations of mortal conflict in a fashion that is, morally, significantly distinguishable from the Catholic moral penetration of it. It helps not at all to say that we should do what love requires in the consequences, since the question was whether every shred of respect for the sanctity of nascent life must not be abandoned ever to do such a thing *to the child* for the sake of these consequences. No one ever doubted that the proposed action in its effects would be charitable to the mother. It is therefore no argument to say that it is.

The first thing that should be said concerning a forced choice of justifiable direct abortion is that the *motives* of the agent toward the child should not be any different from his motives toward the mother's life. To want to save her, it is not necessary for him to *want* the death of the fetus. In fact, the death of the fetus can and should be radically *unwanted*. A person should perform or procure a direct abortion in the midst of a mortal conflict of life with life, while not *wanting* the death of either. To this degree and in the motivational realm, a person does not altogether deny the equality of these two lives to God, or direct his own human love on the one and not the other.

If it is objected that the fetus will be dead anyway, and moreover by an act of direct aggression on his life, the answer has to be that the motives of moral agents constitute a part, but only a part, of the meaning of righteousness, along with the intention and direction of action, the consequences, and so forth. It should also be said that the requirement that in the agent's *motives* the death of the fetus be never *wanted* (which I grant has no practical consequence in the case of direct abortion to save the mother's life) may be among the *deciding* factors in assessing proposals that abortion is justifiable under other circumstances. Just so, the distinction between direct and indirect abortion, between killing and allowing to die, has no practical consequences at all in cases in which medically it is possible to save the one life that can be saved only by direct action. Still, ethical deliberation must traverse this ground and clarify this distinction, if for no other reason than that it is likely to prove to be among the deciding factors or to be definitive of the action to be adopted in other cases or circumstances.

Having said this about the moral agent's not *wanting* motivationally the death of the child he encompasses, one has then to ask if anything more can be said about justifiable direct abortion. Can *the action itself* and *its intention* be further penetrated by Christian moral reflection, and not only the heart of the moral agent? Certainly, if there is more to be said, this should be traced out.

We must side with Karl Barth[13] against reducing ethics to motivation alone, and especially against reducing it to motivations that have in regard only the mother's life and have already put empty room in the place of nascent life.

As regards the intentionality and the direction of the act of direct abortion that we are discussing, the following analysis seems, to me, to be decisive ethically. The intention of the action, and in this sense its direction, is not on the *death* of the fetus, any more than are the motives of the agent. The intention of the action is directed toward the *incapacitation* of the fetus from doing what it is doing to the life of the mother, and is not directed toward the death of the fetus, as such, even in the killing of it. The child, of course, is only doing what comes naturally, i.e., growing and attempting to be born. But this, objectively and materially, is aggressing on the life of its mother. Her life, which alone can be saved, can be saved only if this is stopped; and to incapacitate the fetus from doing this can be done only, we are supposing, by a direct act of killing nascent life. Still, in this situation it is correct to say that the intention of this action is not the killing, not the death of the fetus, but the incapacitation of it from carrying out the material aggression that it is effecting on the life of the mother.

This is the way the Protestant Christian should wrestle with his fellow Catholic moralist for the verdict approving direct abortion as a means. Of course, the child is innocent; it is not "formally" or deliberately and culpably an aggressor. It is a most unchristian line of reasoning that makes so much of a distinction between guilt and innocence in measuring out sanctity and respect to life. If this is true, then finding a guilty one cannot be the basic justification for ever killing a man. Catholicism simply stakes too much on an autonomous natural justice in every one of its judgments about when a formally guilty aggressor forfeits his right to life (and the same applies to everything said about the fact that the fetus has done nothing to forfeit its right to life). The determination of right conduct should not stop at the distinction between the innocent and the aggressor, if our reflection on righteousness has in any significant measure been invaded by the righteousness of God, who makes rain to fall on the just and the unjust and has surrounded not only microscopic life but also ungodly lives with sanctity and protection.

We must argue, therefore, that precisely the fact and the effects of *material* aggression of life on life should be the main concern in our attempts to penetrate the meaning of the Christian life, not waiting to find a guilty aggressor before we are permitted ever to take one life in order to save another in a mortal conflict of lives and values. Just so, in warfare it is not guilty aggressors, but material aggression that ever warrants the taking of life to stop the action that is going on. Moreover, a proper analysis of the intentionality and direction of an act of war in killing an enemy soldier is exactly that proposed here in the case of justifiable abortion. It is the incapacitation of the soldier and not his death that is the intention of the action.[14] If a combatant surrenders and incapacitates himself the just and the actual objective in ever killing him has been secured; and nothing would then justify this death. The fact that he, as materially the bearer of the force that should be stopped, cannot otherwise be incapacitated than by death or surrender is the tragedy of war. The fact that the nascent life cannot incapacitate itself from materially bearing its force against the only life that can be saved, in the case we are supposing, is the tragedy of abortion. But in neither case is wickedness done. These actions are not *morally* evil, either in the motives of the agent or in the intention of the action, because the agent need not *want* the death of another human being nor by his action does he *intend* this. He wants and his action intends rather the incapacitation of a life that is exerting materially aggressive fatal force on the life of another. The stopping of materially aggressive action is the highest possible warrant for the killing of men by men (if life cannot otherwise be saved), not the aggressor-innocent distinction.

Quite possibly even a tradition-minded Catholic can agree with the foregoing analysis of acts of justifiable abortion in which the physical force of the action is directed on the unborn child. He would point to Thomas Aquinas' justification (cited above) of any killing of man by man if and only if this is indirect in the sense of stopping an assault and not for the purpose of killing *him*. He would quite properly call attention to the fact that traditional moralists spoke not of the physical target of the destructive action but of the "directly *voluntary*" and the "indirectly *voluntary*." This allows that the physical force of the action may be directed on the unborn child and yet his death is only indirectly *willed* as an aspect of the action whose objective is to stop the child's material aggression on the life of the mother.[15]

We are concerned, however, with the moral analysis and the reasoning to this sort of justifiable abortion, and not with who

(Catholic or Protestant) accepts it. Despite the niceties and validity of the distinction just mentioned, there may be some point in still calling this (in the meaning of the action's physical force or target) *direct* justifiable abortion. There are some conservative moralists who before agreeing that such an abortion is ever right would require that the *description* of the physical action be something like "emptying the uterus" (from which the death of the child unavoidably results) and not "killing the baby" to stop its destruction of the mother. At the same time there are a growing number of liberal moralists who, embattled against all such physical descriptions, have apparently forgotten that the heart and soul of the "rule of double effect" and its true origin is in a charitable attention to and respect for the two *personal* termini of a single action that to save one life must kill another.

3. My final comment concerns the principal value to be derived from steadfastly maintaining the verdicts that can be reached in ethical justification or prohibition from a religious understanding of the sanctity of life and also of nascent life. This is not always or primarily the praise or blame of individual actions or agents. These may, for a variety of reasons, be *excusable* even for wrongdoing, and the judgment of blameworthiness may fall elsewhere, e.g., on the moral ethos of an entire society or epoch. We need, therefore, to look to the fundamental moral premises of contemporary society in order to see clearly what is at stake in the survival or demise of a religious evaluation of nascent life.

This is an abortifacient society. Women readily learn to "loop before you leap," but they forget to ask whether the intrauterine device prevents conception or aborts germinating life. Such a device does both. A significant part of the efficiency of the loop arises from the fact that it is not only a contraceptive, but also an abortifacient. The pills that prevent ovulation are more totally effective than the combined capacities of the loop, and this fact alone, in an abortifacient civilization, will lead to preference for the pill in the practice of birth control.

American women who can afford to do so go to Sweden to avail themselves of more liberal legal regulations concerning abortion; but Swedish women go to Poland, which is at the moment the real paradise for legal abortions. Sweden's regulations are midway between American rigidity and Polish unlimited permissiveness. The stated reason why Sweden does not go further and adopt still more liberal practices in regard to legal abortion is because of the fear that, as one doctor put it, where abortion is altogether easy, people will not take care to practice birth control.[16] Abortion is therefore a contraceptive device in this age. Doubtless, it is not the most choiceworthy means or a means frequently chosen, but it is an alternative means. Loop before you leap, abort before you birth! The evidence seems to be that the latter may not be merely a last resort, but is actually an option for contraceptive purposes. If quite freely available, abortion may relieve the moral and psychological pressures that are exerted on their freedom to copulate by the remaining regard that men and women have for possible nascent life. Just as surely as this is a contraceptive society, it is also abortifacient.

We are not concerned here with what the criminal law should be in regard to abortion. Not everything that is legal is right, nor should every wrong be legally prohibited; and nothing that is right is right *because* it is legal. Perhaps the penal code regarding abortion should be reformed in directions that will lead to less evil being done than is done under our present more stringent laws.[17] In comprehending the meaning of describing this age as an abortifacient civilization (in contrast to societies based at all on a religious comprehension of the sanctity of life), it is illuminating to notice what happens when legal prohibitions of abortion are "liberalized." Glanville Williams has this to say about the Swedish experiment: "There is convincing evidence that it is to a large extent an entirely new clientele that is now granted legal abortion, that is to say women who would not have had an illegal abortion if they had been refused the legal one."[18] Thereupon Williams states and endorses the value judgment on these abortifacient trends that are characteristic of the contemporary period: "Although the social result is rather to add the total of legal abortions to the total of illegal abortions than to reduce the number of illegal abortions, a body of medical opinion refuses to regret the legal abortions on this account." This judgment is, of course, in no sense a medical opinion.

The foregoing analysis of our society as in its ethos abortifacient is pertinent to the question concerning the moral justification of (direct) abortion of a fetus that is likely to be gravely defective physically or mentally. The answer to this question seems obvious indeed to a simple and sincere humanitarianism. It is not at all obvious. A first step in throwing doubt on the proposal is to ask what was forgotten in the discussion of the blindness and deformities that will result from a woman's contracting rubella especially early in pregnancy. It is often hard to tell whether a woman has rubella; yet her child may be gravely damaged. Moreover, it is hard to tell whether an individual case of measles is rubella; this can be determined with a great degree of certainty only in the case of *epidemics* of rubella. It is proposed that women who have rubella while pregnant should be able to secure a legal abortion, and it is affirmed that under these circumstances fetal euthanasia is not only ethically permissible, but may even be morally obligatory for the sake of the child.

We are interested primarily in the ethical question. The proposal, as I understand it, is based on a kind of *interims ethik;* direct abortion is justified at least until medical science develops a *vaccine* aginst these measles and a reliable *test* of whether a woman has or has had German measles. In our abortifacient culture it is forgotten, or if mentioned it does not sink into the consciousness of men and women today, that there is an alternative to adopting the widespread medical practice and legal institution of fetal euthanasia. This optional social practice of medicine would be equally or more preventive of damage to nascent life from rubella. The *disease itself* gives complete immunization to contracting rubella again. The popular belief that a woman can have several cases of German measles is an old wives' tale, my pediatrician tells me, which arises from the fact that it is almost impossible to tell one sort of measles from another, except in epidemics. But there is one way to be certain of this, and to obtain immunization against the disease in the future. The virus itself, the disease itself, can be used, as it were, to vaccinate against itself.

Why is it not proposed that for the interim between now and the perfection of a more convenient, reliable vaccine, all girl children be given German measles?[19] Would this not be a more choiceworthy *interims ethik*? The answer to this question can only be found in the complete erosion of religious regard for nascent life in a technological and abortifacient era. Abortion when the mother contracts rubella is another example of the American way of death. In this instance, the darkness of the womb makes unnecessary resort to a mortician's art to cover the grim reality. As long as we do not see the deaths inflicted or witness the dying, the direct killing of nascent life has only to be compared with the greater or less inconvenience of other solutions in an antiseptic society where the prevention of disease at all cost is the chief light on our conscious paths. But that darkness and this light are both alike to the Lord of nascent and conscious life. On this basis it would not be possible to choose actions and practices that deliberately abort over an interim social practice of deliberate disease-giving. At least in the problem of rubella-induced fetal damage, it is not mercy or charity, but some other motivation in regard to sentient life that can look with favor on the practice of euthanasia for the child's sake.

The real situation in which our ethical deliberations should proceed cannot be adequately defined short of the location of moral agency and the action under consideration in the context of the lives of all mankind and the general social practices most apt to exhibit righteousness or to make for good. Moreover, our ethical delibera-

90

tions cannot disregard the fact that the *specific* contemporary context must include the erosion of the moral bond between moments in a single individual life without which there can be no enduring covenants of life with life—the erosion of the moral bonds between life and life, between soul and bodily life, and between conscious life and nascent life—which has brought about the divorcing, contraceptive, and abortifacient ethos of the present day.

A chief business of ethics is to distinguish between venereal freedom and the meaning of venereal responsibility in such a fashion that it is barely possible (or at least that this possibility is not methodologically excluded) that from the reflections of moralists there may come clear direction for the structural changes needed to address the structural defects of this age. If this is so, I suggest that a strong case can be made for every effort to revitalize a religious understanding of the integrity and sanctity of life, for unfolding from this at the outmost limits the distinction between direct killing and allowing to die and the distinction between intending to kill and intending to incapacitate the fetus to save the mother's life, and for retaining in the order of ethical justification the prohibition of the direct killing of nascent life. This would be to keep needed moral pressures on ourselves in many areas where a proper regard for life threatens to be dissolved, or has already been dissolved. This would be to endeavor to reverse the trends of a scientific and a secular age that have already gone far in emptying our culture of any substantive morality.

The first order of business would be to strengthen an ethics that contains some remaining sense of the sanctity of life against the corrosive influence of the view that what *should* be done is largely a function of what *technically can* be done, and against the view that morality is entirely a matter of engineering the consequences for the conscious span of our lives. Moreover, if we do not confuse ethical justification with moral excusability, compassion can still encompass the possibility and the reality of individual moral excusability for a wrong that had to be done or was done in a particular situation in this world where sin (especially the sin in social structures) begets sin.

10

The Protection of Life

Karl Barth

THE PROBLEM of the deliberate interruption of pregnancy, usually called abortion (*abortus,* the suppression of the fruit of the body), arises when conception has taken place but for varying reasons the birth and existence of the child are not desired and are perhaps even feared. The persons concerned are the mother, who either carries out the act, or desires or permits it; the more or less informed amateurs who assist her; perhaps the scientifically and technically trained physician; the father, relatives, or other third parties who allow, promote, assist, or favor the execution of the act and therefore share responsibility; and in a wider but no less strict sense the society whose conditions and mentality directly or indirectly call for such acts and whose laws may even permit them. The means employed vary from the most primitive to relatively sophisticated, but these need not concern us in the first instance. Our first contention must be that no pretext can alter the fact that the whole circle of those concerned is in the strict sense engaged in the killing of human life. For the unborn child is from the very first a child. It is still developing and has no independent life. But it is a person and not a thing, nor a mere part of the mother's body.

The embryo has its own autonomy, its own brain, its own nervous system, its own blood circulation. If its life is affected by that of the mother, it also affects hers. It can have its own illnesses in which the

Reprinted from *Church Dogmatics,* Part III, Vol. 4, pp. 415–22 by permission of the publisher, T.&T. Clark, Ltd., Edinburgh.

KARL BARTH (1886–1968) taught theology at Göttingen, Münster, and Bonn in Germany, and at Basel in Switzerland.

mother has no part. Conversely, it may be quite healthy even though the mother is seriously ill. It may die while the mother continues to live. It may also continue to live after its mother's death, and be eventually saved by a timely operation on her dead body. In short, it is a human being in its own right. I take this and other information from the book by Charlot Strasser, *Der Arzt und das keimende Leben*, 1948 (cf. also Alfred Labhardt, *Die Abtreibungsfrage*, 1926).

Before proceeding, we must underline the fact that one who destroys germinating life kills a person and thus ventures the monstrous thing of decreeing concerning the life and death of a fellow human being, whose life is given by God and therefore, like his or her own, belongs to God. This person desires to discharge a divine office or, even if not, accepts responsibility for such discharge by daring to have the last word on at least the temporal form of the life of a fellow human. Those directly or indirectly involved cannot escape this responsibility.

At this point we have first and supremely to hear the great summons to halt issued by the command. Can we accept this responsibility? May this thing be? Must it be? Whatever arguments may be brought against the birth and existence of the child, is it the child's fault that he or she is here? What has the child done to its mother or to any of the others that they wish to deprive it of its germinating life and punish it with death? Does not the child's utter defenselessness and helplessness, or the question whom they are destroying, to whom they are denying a future even before he or she has breathed and seen the light of the world, wrest the weapon from the hand of the mother first, and then from all the others, thwarting their will to use it? Moreover, this child is a person for whose life the Son of God has died, for whose unavoidable part in the guilt of all humanity and future individual guilt he has already paid the price. The true light of the world shines already in the darkness of the mother's womb. And yet they want to kill the child deliberately because certain reasons that have nothing to do with the child itself favor the view that it had better not be born! Is there any emergency that can justify this? It must surely be clear to us that until the question is put in all its gravity a serious discussion of the position cannot even begin, let alone lead to serious results.

The mediaeval period, which in this case extended right up to the end of the eighteenth century, was therefore quite right in its presuppositions when it regarded and punished abortion as murder. It is indeed an action that in innumerable cases obviously has the character of murder, of an irresponsible killing which is both callous and wicked, and in which one or more or perhaps all the participants play more or less consciously an objectively horrible game. If only the rigor with which the past judged and acted in this matter, as in child murder strictly speaking, had been itself more just and not directed against the relatively least guilty instead of the relatively most guilty! If only its draconian attitude had at least made an impression on the consciousness of the people and formed even in later recollection an effective dyke against this crime! But it obviously failed to do this. For no sooner had this attitude decayed externally than its inner strength also collapsed, and transgression swept in full flood over the land.

In the circumstances there is something almost horribly respectable in the attitude of the Roman Church. Never sparing in its extreme demands on women, it has to this day remained inveterate and never changed its course an inch in this matter. In the encyclical *Casti connubii* of 1930,[1] deliberate abortion is absolutely forbidden on any grounds, so that even Roman Catholic nuns raped when the Russians invaded Germany in 1945 were not allowed to free themselves from the consequences in this way.

This attitude of the Roman Church is undoubtedly impressive in contrast to the terrible deterioration, to what one might almost call the secret and open mass murder, which is the modern vogue and custom in this respect among so-called civilized peoples. This can be partly explained by the social and psychological conditions in which modern man finds himself, and by the estrangement from the Church and palpable paganism of the modern masses, the age of the *corpus Christianum* being now, as it seems, quite definitely a thing of the past. But there is more to it than this. It concerns both the rich and the poor, both those who suffer and are physically in danger and innumerable others who are in full or at least adequate possession of their spiritual balance. Nor is it restricted to the so-called world; it continues to penetrate deeply into the Christian community. It is a simple fact that the automatic restraint of the recognition that every deliberate interruption of pregnancy, whatever the circumstances, is a taking of human life, seems to have been strangely set aside in the widest circles in spite of our increasing biological appreciation of the facts. Even worse, the possibility of deliberate killing is sometimes treated as if it were just a ready expedient and remedy in a moment of embarrassment, nothing more being at issue than an unfortunate operation like so many others. In short, it can be and is done. Even official statistics tell us in a striking way how it can be and is done; and we may well suspect that these figures fall far short of the reality. It remains to be seen how legal regulation will finally work out where it is introduced, but the first result always seems to be a violent campaign for the widest possible interpretation.

Who is to say where the error and wickedness operative in this matter have their ultimate origin? Are they to be traced to the morality or immorality of the women and girls who are obviously for some reason troubled or distressed at their condition? Do they lie in the brutality or thoughtlessness of the men concerned? Are they to be sought in the offer of the sinister gentleman who makes use of both? Are we to look to the involved lack of conscientiousness in some medical circles? Do they originate in a general increase of self-pity in face of the injustices of life, which were surely just as great in the past as they are today? Or do they arise from a general decline in the individual and collective sense of responsibility?

We certainly cannot close our eyes to these happenings. Nor can we possibly concur in this development. Nevertheless, there can be no doubt that the abstract prohibition which was pronounced in the past, and which is still the only contribution of Roman Catholicism in this matter, is far too forbidding and sterile to promise any effective help.

The fact that a definite No must be the presupposition of all further discussion cannot be contested, least of all today. The question arises how this No is to be established and stated if it is to be a truly effective No. In face of the wicked violation of the sanctity of human life that is always seriously at issue in abortion, and that is always present when it is carried out thoughtlessly and callously, the only thing that can help is the power of the wholly new and radical feeling of awe at the mystery of all human life as this is commanded by God as its creator and giver. Legal prohibitions and restrictions of a civil, moral, and supposedly spiritual kind are obviously inadequate to instill this awe. Nor does mere churchmanship, whether Romanist or Protestant, provide the atmosphere in which this awe can thrive. The command of God is based on grace. God summons people to the freedom in which they may live instead of having to live. At root, persons who think they must live cannot and will not respect life, whether their own or that of others, far less the life of an unborn child. If it is for them a case of "must" rather than "may," they lack perspective and understanding in relation to what life is. They are already burdened and afflicted with their own lives. They will only too readily explore and exploit all the supposed possibilities by which to shield themselves from life that is basically hostile. They will also fall into the mistake of thinking that the life of the unborn child is not really human life at all, and thus draw the inference that they have been given a free hand to maintain or destroy it. Mothers, fathers, advisers, doctors, lawgivers, judges, and others whom it may concern to desire, permit, execute, or approve this action, will act and think in true understanding of the meaning of human life, and therefore with serious reluctance to take such a step, only if they themselves realize that human life is not something enforced but permitted, i.e., that it is freedom and grace. In these circumstances they will not be at odds with life, whether their own or that of others. They will not always desire to be as comfortable as possible in relation to it. They will not simply take the line of least resistance in what they think and do concerning it. Those who live by mercy will always be disposed to practice mercy, especially to a human being who is so dependent on the mercy of others as the unborn child.

This brings us back to the point at which we cannot evade the question where was and is the witness of the Protestant Church in face of this rising flood of disaster. This Church knows and has the Word of the free mercy of God which also ascribes and grants freedom to man. It could and can tell and show a humanity which is tormented by life because it thinks it must live it, that it may do so. It could and can give it this testimony of freedom, and thus appeal effectively for the protection of life, inscribing upon its heart and conscience a salutary and resolute No to all and therefore to this particular destruction of human life. Hence it neither could nor can range itself with the Roman Catholic Church and its hard preaching of the Law. It must proclaim its own message in this matter, namely, the gospel. In so doing, however, it must not underbid the severity of the Roman Catholic No. It must overbid its abstract and negative: "Thou shalt not," by the force of its positive: "Thou mayest," in which, of course, the corresponding: "Thou mayest not," is included, the No having the force not merely of the word of man but of the Word of God. The Protestant Church had and has this Word of God for man but against his depravity in so far as its task was and is to bear witness to it. For this reason it cannot have clean hands in face of the disastrous development. It need not enquire whether or not it has restrained this development, or may still do so. The truth is plain that it has not been faithful to its own commission in the past, but that its attitude has resembled far too closely that of the Roman Church, i.e., that it has been primarily a teacher of the Law. The truth is also plain that only now is it beginning to understand its commission, and that it has not yet grasped it with a firm hand. It is still almost with joy that we hear perspicacious doctors, perhaps of very different beliefs (cf. Lk. 16:8), express a view which the Protestant Church, if it had listened and borne witness to the Word of God, ought to have stated and championed long since, namely, the kindly and understanding No which will prevail as such.

At this point it may be interjected that when this No is established as a divine No, namely, when it is in virtue of the liberating grace of God that deliberate abortion is irrefutably seen to be sin, murder, and transgression, it cannot possibly be maintained that there is no forgiveness for this sin. However dangerous it might sound in relation to all that has been said thus far, it must also be said that in faith, and in a vicariously intercessory faith for others too, there is a forgiveness that can be appropriated even for this sin, even for the great modern sin of abortion. God the Creator, who by grace acquits and liberates humans that they may live and let live in the most serious sense, who in and by this liberation claims humans incontestably as the great protectors of life, who inexorably reveals the true character of human transgression as sin—this God is our Parent in Jesus Christ, in whom God has not rejected sinful persons but chosen them and reconciled them, in whom God has intervened for sinful persons who have violated God's command, in order that the latter may not be lost to them even in and by reason of this terrible transgression. God sees and understands and loves even modern humans in and in spite of all the dreadful confusions and entanglements of their collective and individual existence, including this one. Those who see themselves placed by the gospel in the light of the relevant command, and are thus forced to admit that they, too, are in some degree entangled in this particular transgression, and are willing, therefore, to accept solidarity with more blatant transgressors, cannot and will not let go the fact, nor withhold it from others, that the same gospel that reveals this with such dreadful clarity is the gospel that, proclaiming the kingdom of God to all, summons all to repentance and promises and offers forgiveness to all. Nor does it weaken the command and its unconditional requirement that the one free grace, which in its one dimension unmasks sin as such, implies in the other that God has loved this sinful world in such a way that God has given the Son, and in him God, on its behalf, that it should not perish. Without this second dimension we cannot really understand the first. Indeed, only those who really grasp the promise of divine forgiveness will necessarily realize that sin as such is inexorably opposed by the divine No, and will never be able to keep this either from themselves or others.

If the No is securely grounded as seen from this angle, it inevitably raises here, too, the problem of the exception. Human life, and therefore the life of the unborn child, is not an absolute, so that, while it can be protected by the commandment, it can be so only within the limits of God, who issues it. It cannot claim to be preserved in all circumstances, whether in relation to God or to other persons, i.e., in this case to the mother, father, doctor, and others involved. In grace God can will to preserve the life that has been given, and in grace God can will to take it again. Either way, it is not lost. Humans cannot exercise the same sovereignty in relation to it. It does not really lie in their power even to preserve it. And only by an abuse of their power, by a sinister act of overweening arrogance, can they willfully take it. But they do have the power, and are thus commissioned, to do in the service of God and for the preservation of life that which is humanly possible if not finally decisive. Trained in the freedom that derives from the grace of God, they can choose and will only the one thing. In the case of the unborn, the mother, father, doctor (whose very vocation is to serve the preservation and development of life), and all concerned can desire only its life and healthy birth. How can they possibly will the opposite? They can do so only on the presupposition of their own blindness toward life, in bondage to the opinion that they must live rather than that they may live, and therefore out of anxiety, i.e., out of gracelessness and therefore godlessness.

However, they cannot set their wills absolutely on the preservation of this life, or rather on the service of its preservation. They all stand in the service of God, who orders them to serve its preservation and therefore the future birth of the child. There is an almost infinite number of objections to the possibility of willing anything else in obedience to God. But it is not quite infinite. If an individual knows that she or he is in God's service and wills to be obedient to God, can this person really swear that she or he will never on any occasion will anything else as God may require? What grounds have we for the absolute thesis that in no circumstances can God will anything but the preservation of a germinating life, or make any other demand from the mother, father, doctor, or others involved? If God can will that this germinating life should die in some other way, might God not occasionally do so in such a way as to involve the active participation of others? How can we deny absolutely that God might have commissioned them to serve in this way, and that their actions have thus been performed, and had to be performed, in this service? How, then, can we indict them in these circumstances?

This is the exceptional case that calls for discussion. In squarely facing it, we are not opening a side door to the crime that is so rampant in this sphere. We refer to God's possibility and specific command. We cannot try to exclude this. Otherwise the No that has to be pronounced in every other case is robbed of its force. For, as we have seen, it is truly effective only as the divine No. Hence no human No can or should be given the last word. The human No must let itself be limited. God can limit this human No, and, if this happens, it is simply human obstinacy and obduracy and transgression to be absolutely logical and to try to execute the No unconditionally. Let us be quite frank and say that there are situations in which the killing of germinating life does not constitute murder but is in fact commanded.

I hasten to lay down some decisive qualifications. For these will be situations in which all the arguments for preservation have been carefully considered and properly weighed, and yet abortion remains as *ultima ratio*. If all the possibilities of avoiding this have not been taken into account in this decision, then murder is done. Genuine exceptions will thus be rare. If they occur too often, and thus become a kind of second rule, we have good reason to suspect that collective and individual transgression and guilt are entailed. Again, they will be situations in which all those concerned must answer before God in great loneliness and secrecy, and make their decisions accordingly. If the decisions have any other source, if they are only the results of their subjective reflection and agreement, this fact alone is enough to show that we are not dealing with the genuine exception in which this action is permitted and commanded. With these qualifications, there are undoubtedly situations of this kind.

And we can and must add that, even if only in general terms and in the sense of a guiding line, these situations may always be known by the concrete fact that in them a choice must be made for the protection of life, one life being balanced against another, i.e., the life of the unborn child against the life or health of the mother, the sacrifice of either the one or the other being unavoidable. It is hard to see why in such cases the life of the child should always be given absolute preference, as maintained in Roman Catholic ethics. To be sure, we cannot and must not maintain, on the basis of the commandment, that the life and health of the mother must always be saved at the expense of the life of the child. There may well be mothers who for their part are ready to take any risk for their unborn children, and how can we forbid them to do so? On the basis of the command, however, we can learn that when a choice has to be made between the life or health of the mother and that of the child, the destruction of the child in the mother's womb might be permitted and commanded, and with the qualifications already mentioned a human decision might thus be taken to this effect. It goes without saying that the greatest possible care must be exercised in its practical execution. That is to say, it cannot be left to the mother herself or to quacks but is a matter for the experienced and trained physician. More detailed consideration would take us rather beyond the sphere of ethics. The question obviously arises in what particular circumstances and from what standpoint the life of the mother might be regarded as in peril and therefore this alternative indicated. To try to answer this question, however, is to expose oneself to the risk of making assertions that inevitably prove to be either too broad or too narrow from the standpoint of ethics, especially theological ethics. We must be content, therefore, simply to make our general point.

Physicians and lawyers speak in terms of the "indication" of abortion, a distinction being made between medical (whether somatic or psychiatric) on the one side and social on the other. The Swiss Penal Code regards it as nonindictable in an emergency, generally defined as a danger to life, body, freedom, honor or capacity, which cannot be averted in any other way.[2] In practice, however, it allows it only where there exists an immediate danger which cannot otherwise be warded off, or the risk of severe and permanent injury to the health of the pregnant woman. It also insists that it be undertaken by a certified doctor who is under obligation to report it to the responsible cantonal authorities.[3] It will be seen that this is in line with what we have just said. It must be remembered, however, that by no means every action allowed and exempted from punishment even on a strict, less alone a laxer, interpretation of these rules is for this reason permitted and enjoined ethically, i.e., by the command of God, as if those involved did not have to keep to a much narrower restriction of "indication" than that of the law. On the other hand, while Swiss legislation finds valid reason for abortion in an emergency affecting the life or body of the pregnant woman, the same does not hold good of an emergency affecting her freedom, honor or capacity. This means that, whereas medical "indication" is fully accepted, sound reasons are seen for not including social, and therefore for its implicit rejection. It does not follow, however, that a doctor is generally and radically guilty of transgressing the command of God, though he may expose himself to legal penalty, if he thinks he should urge a socio-medical "indication," i.e., in terms of a threat presented to the physical or mental life of the mother, or of economic or environmental conditions. For occasionally the command of God may impose a judgment and action which go beyond what is sanctioned by the law, and this may sometimes serve as a summons to all of us to consider that a sound social policy might well be a most powerful weapon in the struggle against criminal abortion. The legal rules are obviously useful, and even have an indirect ethical value as general directions to those involved, particularly doctors and judges. On the other hand, they are not adapted to serve as ethical criteria, since obedience to the command of God must have the freedom to move within limits which may sometimes be narrower and sometimes broader than even the best civil law. The exceptional case in the ethical sense is in general something very different from an extension of the permissible and valid possibilities established by human law.

The required calculation and venture in the decision between life and death obviously cannot be subject to any human law, because no such law can grasp the fullness of healthy or sick, happy or unhappy, preserved or neglected human life, let alone the freedom of the divine command the obedience which we owe to it. Hence we shall have to be content with the following observations: (1) For all concerned what must be at stake must be life against life, nothing other nor less, if the decision is not to be a wrong decision and the resultant action murder either of the child or the mother. (2) There is always required the most scrupulous calculation and yet also a resolute venture with a conscience that is bound and therefore free. Where such thought as is given is only careless or clouded, and the decision weak and hesitant, sin crouches at the door. (3) The calculation and venture must take place before God and in responsibility to God. Otherwise, how can there possibly be obedience, and how can the content be good and right, even though apparently good human reasons and justification might be found in one direction or another? (4) Since the calculation and venture, the conviction that we are dealing with the exception, are always so dangerous, they surely cannot be executed with the necessary assurance and joy except in faith that God will forgive the elements of human sin involved.

Part IV

The Case for Change

James E. Kraus
Joseph T. Donceel, S.J.
Charles E. Curran
Helmut Thielicke

11

Is Abortion Absolutely Prohibited?

James E. Kraus

LIFE HAS BEEN one of the unexamined absolutes of moral teaching. As a result of the lack of examination, the concept of human life has often been reduced to a mere quantitative biological minimum. Even its absolute character or inviolability has suffered some practical exceptions: capital punishment, just war, etc. In spite of these, however, theology developed the legal concept of God's absolute dominion over life and death, and ascribed to this "law," with the exceptions noted, the absolute character the culture had attributed to its concept of life—however limited it may have been to the biological. This was probably done to stave off the obvious tendency to abuse that arises not only in the ordinary temptations to take a life as a solution to a problem, but especially so in the case of abortion or euthanasia.

But in our day we have witnessed a series of new sensitivities and attitudes. Some are insisting on looking at the quality as well as the quantitative presence of life. Others question the validity of the exceptions that were made for capital punishment or war. Others wish to consider exceptions in the cases of abortion or euthanasia. Let me state first of all that I do consider life to be an absolute value, a

Reprinted from the Fall 1968 issue of *Continuum*, Vol. VI, pp. 436–40, with permission of the editor. © 1968 Justus George Lawler and *Continuum* magazine.

JAMES E. KRAUS was sometime academic dean, The Pontifical College (Josephinum), Columbus, Ohio.

true absolute that does not yield to another value in any instance. But life, while absolute, is not simple, but complex, and it may be possible to justify abortion in some instances precisely for the sake of a greater reverence for life in a deeper and fuller sense.

It is a basic tenet of Christianity (and of the best of humanism) that life—all life—is an outpouring of the spirit of God. Even the most elemental form of life, plant or animal, is a victory of spirit over matter; it transcends it, it grows, it is counterentropic—without implying any Manichaean condemnation of matter. Where there is a greater outpouring of the spirit, there is a higher form of life, a greater degree of perfection, and a consequent holiness or sacredness about life, and also a corresponding inviolability or duty to protect it. Further, there is among these levels or forms of life a necessity of sacrificing lower forms of life that the higher may live. This is the pattern of nature, and we rightly consider those who, like Schweitzer, extend an absolute value even to animal life to be people who have gone to an extreme in their protection of a recognized value, especially if they attempt to impose it on others to the point of actually sacrificing higher forms of life to lower ones. When we come to human life we have an outpouring of the spirit that is literally substantially different, a form of life so far above the lesser forms that it lives beyond them; it is called the image of God, and as such it is never to be sacrificed.

Or is it? Maybe, if we see its complexity, the principle of sacrificing lower to higher may be applied, may even be called for as uniquely Christian. Certainly it seems to operate between the different levels of life that are open to an individual human being or a community already existing. One must constantly deny oneself or at least regulate certain lesser forms of life in order to give birth to higher forms. This in no way condemns the lesser appetite; it simply realizes that it must serve the higher. And Christianity, as well as all forms of religion and true philosophy of humanism, comes out on the side of the spirit, the higher form of life, as opposed to the unlimited and therefore crippling indulgence of the lower form of life. In this sense it is a peculiarly strange perversion of Christianity to emphasize only the quantitative aspect of life, the idea of peopling heaven with more and more souls, as contrasted with the manifestly Christian idea of developing to the highest degree the potential, the spiritual life of the limited number we are capable of caring for.

Perhaps it will be helpful to cite some instances of a qualitative and spiritual development taking precedence over a lesser more material form of human life. The form of life and love that exists between parent and child is eventually sacrificed to the higher form of life and love that exists between husband and wife. And significantly, the latter is higher because more spiritual, being based on choice rather than on biological heredity. This does not deny in any way the spiritual component of paternal and filial love or the physical component of marital love, but for this cause a person chooses to leave one to have the other. Recognition of the right or the wisdom, and even obligation, of families to limit their size is recognition that mere quantitative multiplication of life may be sacrificed to the seeking of quality for lives that exist. The same will-of-God argument now used to absolutely forbid abortion was used not long ago to forbid even rhythm. Certainly then, it seems legitimate to sacrifice one level of life to a higher one, and even to limit the further production of life for a truly higher quality (and not merely materially higher) of life for those in existence.

But can one sacrifice the life of a person already in existence for another or for the community? The principle of God's absolute dominion would seem to say No, thou shalt not kill. But we know of many exceptions: A man is allowed to lay down his own life for his friend. He may take another's to save his own. The community may, according to a common opinion, take the criminal's life, or it may even take innocent lives for just cause in a just war. Always the justifying argument seems to be or include the principle of sacrificing the lesser good or lesser instance of human life to the greater good—human life looked at more fully and deeply.

But it is difficult to accept this line of reasoning when it is applied to the cases of capital punishment and war. It seems to me that the security of the community is both too small a contribution to human life and can be achieved in other ways ever to justify taking even a guilty individual's life, especially when one considers, as we must, not only the actual, but the potential value of this life for self and for the community. Similarly, it is a rare war that can be justified when balancing the loss in human life with the possible enrichment the war might bring in standard of living or even human freedom, although one need not condemn those who, like Patrick Henry, insist on following their particular evaluation of liberty. Thus it is difficult to see why people who are so ready to accept this principle of sacrifice for war and capital punishment are so affronted when it is suggested in the case of abortion or euthanasia. One can see that in these instances the temptation of the individual to abuse is greater than in community actions, but the principle and responsibility remain the same. Perhaps for this reason the church may have been wise in placing an absolute ban on them in a primitive culture, when the need of the species for survival was all-important and individual moral judgment undeveloped. Perhaps this cultural argument of accommodation will explain the church's acceptance of the killing allowed in war—not being able to eliminate the killing, the church tried to limit it.

But in our day people are not, in many instances, so culturally undeveloped; the need to protect the quantity of life by reproduction is counterbalanced by a need to protect the quality of life by selective limitation; and the traditional absolute-dominion or will-of-God arguments, riddled by historic inconsistencies of interpretation, will not hold up. So we must ask the question anew: May we sacrifice the life of the unborn child for the life of the mother in the name of sacrificing the undeveloped lesser life to the greater more important life? As a general rule, one must answer No; as already indicated, what we must consider is not only the actual degree of perfection and development, but the potential that is here: the possible saint and benefactor to humankind whose life has begun and whose future is being decided. And no person can weigh that, nor can a society afford to let any person or group of persons make this decision.

But let us pose the classic case in which the principle of sacrificing lesser life for greater may possibly be applied with sufficient reason to justify it. A conception has taken place for which medical evidence gives every reason to believe there will be a high probability of a deformed child. There are other children who need this mother, who is herself a person with much to give them and others, with indeed much potential yet to be realized. May we weigh the one against the other and say that the probable lack of potential of this fetus, even the hindrance that the fostering of this biological life process (certainly human, but not even certainly a person) will most probably cause other lives, justify the termination of the lesser for the sake of the greater? Does not nature itself often—far more often than we feel comfortable about—by a natural process reject the conceived fetus rather than bring it deformed into existence? To ascribe this right to God and not to humans because it would be too cruel for humans is hardly flattering to God. After all, the abortionist—divine or human —is not killing souls (if they are present), and we are beyond the fundamentalist idea that unbaptized babies go to hell. True they are deprived of a fully developed human life, but in the case we are considering we are postulating that the probability is all against their having it, and the almost certain consequence is the deprivation for others already in existence. And we must act on the probabilities; we have no certainties.

It will be objected that it is precisely the retarded child who has been the cause of greatest blessing to many families. Occasion, yes, cause, no. And if such an occasion be needed—as it is not—to make people reverence and cultivate life where it exists, then there are plenty of unfortunate retarded children about to be brought to their slight potential without bringing more into existence. The further objections that this sorrow or burden of both parent and child may be redemptive for them and that this child may be dearer to God for his or her deformity, etc., is replete with assumptions about suffering and God's will that are insufficiently certain to impose them on people.

I have deliberately portrayed or overportrayed what I consider to be the strongest case in which an abortion may be justified. I am not fully convinced by my own argumentation. I maintain therefore that although many abortions should not be legally prohibited, the great majority of them are certainly immoral by Christian standards.

But this does not mean one must uphold the traditional absolute prohibition. At most it is a good defensible, legal, and pastoral position but not a divine absolute. It will be objected that the above views open the door to all kinds of abuse: in fact, the door is already open and abuses are thronging through. Rather, we are seeking to open the door to responsible handling of a difficult situation, not to the mere acceptance of tragedy. Furthermore, one may hope that as people become more conscious of the preciousness of life and more responsible and capable in controlling the initiation and development of it, abortion will become less and less a problem, that is, it will become less often necessary even to consider the drastic action of terminating a life process already begun but doomed to deformity and hurt for many.

Finally, if it is a terrible thing to play God by terminating physical life, it is also a terrible thing, in another sense, to play God by imposing as a divine absolute a prohibition that may cause immense suffering both to individuals and society. To put it emotionally, for every "little saint" snuffed out, one can see dead mothers and deprived children, part of the army of the living dead, that is, of those who are alive, indeed, but condemned to a level of life that is subhuman. If this be emotional, it is nevertheless a true picture seen all too frequently in our hospitals and utterly unlike the emotional horror stories that are related in the fictional autobiographies of aborted children who report their dreams for the future only to conclude, "Today my mother killed me."

All we can really do is develop our reverence for life at every level as much as we can and our scale of priorities as properly as we can, then help and trust one another to make decisions as best we can, and be ready to sacrifice life for life. There is Christian precedent.

12

Abortion: Mediate vs. Immediate Animation

Joseph F. Donceel, S.J.

T HE REASON WHY CATHOLICS are so strongly opposed to any liberali-
zation of the laws against abortion is their conviction that abortion,
performed at any stage of pregnancy, is the intentional killing of a
human being. In other words, they hold that from the very first
moment of conception the fertilized ovum is a human being. This
explains also the strong opposition of a number of Catholics to the use
of intrauterine devices (IUDs) as a method of birth control. For such
devices do not prevent fertilization but nidification; they somehow
make it impossible for the fertilized ovum, coming from the fallopian
tube, to nestle in the uterus where it may grow to maturity. However,
honesty and sincerity might invite the moralists to admit that these
opinions are not shared by all Catholic thinkers. True, they represent
the majority position, but there is also a slowly growing minority that
rejects some of these views. In the present climate of sometimes bitter
controversy this fact is not without importance.

Saint Thomas Aquinas did not hold that the ovum was a human
being from the first moment of fertilization. For him, there was no
human being before the seventh week of pregnancy. Hence an
abortion performed during the first six weeks was not, for him, the

---

Reprinted from the Spring 1967 issue of *Continuum*, Vol. 5, pp. 167–71,
with the permission of the editor. © 1967 by Justus George Lawler and
Continuum magazine.

JOSEPH F. DONCEEL, S.J., is professor of philosophy emeritus, Fordham
University, Bronx, New York.

murder of an innocent human being and, if he had condemned the use of IUDs for birth control, the reason for his condemnation would not have been that these devices resulted in murder.

Catholic philosophers and theologians generally agree with Thomas Aquinas that the human soul is created at the moment of its infusion into the body. Most of them, however, disagree with him concerning the time of this infusion. Whereas Aquinas held that it occurred sometime between conception and birth, more precisely between the sixth week and the third month of pregnancy, the great majority of Catholic thinkers hold that it happens at the moment of conception. Why did the Catholic scholars give up the opinion of their leading theologian on this important point?

Before trying to answer this question we must find out why St. Thomas was of the opinion that the human soul was infused and created not at the moment of conception, but several weeks later. He held that the human soul is the substantial human form, and that such a substantial form can exist only in and with a human body. Scanty as his knowledge of embryology undoubtedly was, he knew enough of it to be aware that during the first few weeks the fertilized ovum or the embryo could not be considered a real human body. Although he had not the slightest idea of genetics, of chromosomes and genes, he held that the embryo was, from the very beginning, a human body in potency, a virtual human body. Unlike many Catholic thinkers of today he did not admit that an *actual* human soul could be coupled with a virtual human body. This would have gone against the hylomorphic conception of humans that he firmly professed. This is why he taught what is known as the theory of mediate animation.

The hylomorphic doctrine of St. Thomas, according to which a human soul can exist only in a human body, was held by Catholic thinkers until the end of the eighteenth century. Throughout most of this time the law of the Roman Catholic Church forbade one to baptize any *foetus abortivus* that showed no human shape or outline.

Yet starting from the seventeenth century, a few authors began to propose the theory of immediate animation (the soul is infused at the moment of conception), not because they rejected hylomorphism, but as a result of erroneous biological knowledge. A few physicians of this time claimed that from the very beginning of pregnancy either the ovum or the sperm was a microscopic but real human body, a homunculus, with brain, heart, and liver. They professed what is known as the *preformation* theory. It teaches that organisms are present with all their basic parts and structures from the very beginnings of life and that their development consists simply of a gradual increase in size. The first proponents of immediate animation argued not without reason that if there was from the start a real human body, be it ever so tiny, there could also be a real human soul.

With the steady progress of scientific biology the preformation theory had to yield to the theory of *epigenesis,* according to which the organism, far from being preformed from the very beginning, autonomously develops all its organs and structures through a complex process of growth, cleavage, and differentiation. There is no human body in the fertilized ovum. True, this ovum contains the chromosomes, the genes, the recently discovered deoxyribonucleic acid (DNA) "code of life," which will infallibly guide its development, given a normal environment, into a human body, never into anything else. Yet this ovum is not a human body, and it seems that Catholic thinkers, who professed the hylomorphic interpretation of human nature (which the Council of Vienne, in 1312, had so strongly endorsed), should, together with the preformation theory, have given up the theory of immediate animation and reverted to the traditional doctrine of St. Thomas.

One of the main reasons why most of them did nothing of the kind was the decadence of scholastic philosophy and its contamination with Cartesian elements. It is well known that Cartesian philosophy was inhospitable to any kind of hylomorphism, and that it professed a dualistic conception of humanity. If, as Descartes taught, a human is composed of two distinct substances—a soul and a body—that are capable of interacting somehow as active and passive components, then there was no longer any reason for rejecting the presence of a real human soul in a virtual human body. If the soul is not the formal cause of the body, it might very well be present in the fertilized ovum. It might act as some kind of efficient cause of the body, which effects the ovum's development from its very start. The soul would be the architect of the body, and the code of life imprinted in the zygote's DNA would serve as some kind of blueprint for the future organism.

This way of interpreting the development of the human organism is by no means absurd and is quite compatible with the theory of immediate animation. But it is no longer the hylomorphic theory of humanity that it claims to be. It looks more like the Cartesian doctrine of humanity; it is dualistic. Because the present mood of philosophy is strongly antidualistic, this kind of explanation has lost much of its appeal. Moreover, as noted above, it goes against the doctrine of the Church, as proclaimed at the Council of Vienne.[1] If, by analogy, we are allowed to speak of the substantial form of a building, we would certainly not claim that the architect or the blueprint or both combined constituted the substantial form of the building. The formal cause can only exist in the finished building. The soul is not to the body as an architect or a blueprint is to a building, but rather as sphericity is to a ball. A deflated ball, although virtually spherical, does not possess the form of sphericity. Neither can a fertilized ovum or a morula or an early embryo be said to possess the substantial human form.

Of course, once we have given up the idea that the human soul is infused at the moment of conception—and this may well have been another reason for the long survival of the immediate animation theory—it becomes practically impossible to determine at what time the rational soul makes its appearance in the human being. St. Thomas spoke of six weeks for the male embryo and three months for the female embryo. The reasons which he advanced for this distinction have obviously lost all their value. In his spirited defense of mediate animation, Prof. Henri de Dorlodot, late of Louvain University, required that there be "present the first rudiments of the structures of the human brain. We might perhaps add that it is very probable that the organization necessary in order that the brain may be said to be human is completed only during the third month after conception, and in fact nearer the end of the month than the beginning."[2] The reason why the embryo should at least possess some kind of brain before being called human is that the brain is obviously required for spiritual activities. The question might well be raised whether the mere presence of a rudimentary brain allows us to affirm with certitude that a spiritual soul is present. Would it not be better to wait until the brain is able to function? And why not then wait until the brain is able to function? And why not then wait until the first spiritual activities are performed? It is at once evident that this kind of thinking leads directly to conclusions that are wholly unacceptable. The spiritual soul would be present only at the moment of birth—a proposition suggested by the moralist John Caramuel and condemned as "lax" by Innocent XI, in 1679. Or the soul would be present only when the child starts speaking or using the word true.

All this shows why those who wish to play it absolutely safe prefer to admit that the soul is present at the moment of conception. But the safest theory is not necessarily true. In my opinion the true opinion is that of St. Thomas. He did not propose the dates of six weeks or three months as certain, but he was quite certain (and with him Cardinal Mercier, Canon de Dorlodot, and many others) that there is no spiritual soul at the moment of conception and during the first few weeks of pregnancy.

Some people reject this view because science teaches that the embryo is alive from the very beginning. St. Thomas did not deny this. He claimed that during the first stages of its development the embryo possesses a vegetative or plant soul; next, it has a sentient or animal soul; finally, when it is sufficiently organized, God infuses into it a spiritual soul. Then and only then may we speak of a human being. In other words, centuries before the word itself was coined, St. Thomas professed some kind of evolution not for the race, but for the individual. It is quite safe to assert, although difficult to prove that Catholic opposition to the Thomistic doctrine of mediate animation was powerfully abetted by the long-lasting Catholic opposition to the theory of evolution. Catholic thinkers could hardly admit evolution in the womb and deny it in the history of the race. If ontogeny, why not phylogeny? Might it not be wise to drop our opposition to mediate animation, now that we have dropped it to evolution?

Hitherto I have explained the main argument against immediate animation: This theory is incompatible with the hylomorphic conception of humanity so solemnly endorsed by the Church at the Council of Vienne, so much in line with the present antidualistic, anti-Cartesian mood of philosophy. There is also a strong argument coming from biology, the existence of identical twins. Unlike fraternal twins, who derive from two different ova, fertilized by two different spermatozoa, identical twins derive from one ovum, fertilized by one spermatozoon. In this case there is one fertilized ovum, hence for the proponents of immediate animation, one human being, which splits up—very quickly it is true—into two or more parts that will develop independently. One human being splitting up into two or more human beings is, metaphysically speaking, hard to take.

Moreover, experimental embryologists have succeeded innumerable times in artificially splitting the fertilized ova of lower organisms and bringing the resulting parts to full-fledged maturity. Many of them do not see why eventually the same procedure might not be applied to the fertilized human ova. Is it not difficult to admit that such a divisible ovum or morula is a human being? It looks very much as if, during the first stages of development, each blastomere or cell of the growing morula possesses the virtuality of turning into a complete human organism. Does this not imply that the presence of such a virtuality does not, contrary to the theory of immediate animation, suppose the presence of a spiritual human soul?

At Columbia University, Landrum Shettles has for many years performed the experimental fertilization, in vitro, of human ova with human spermatozoa. Dr. Shettles has kept the resulting ovum and morula alive and growing for several days. It is hard to admit these microscopic organisms are human beings. I would rather call them vegetative organisms that—if supplied with their proper, unbelievably complex environment—might evolve into human beings.

13

Abortion: Its Moral Aspects

Charles E. Curran

A POSITION PAPER on the morality of abortion from the Roman Catholic perspective must of necessity be somewhat selective. The following pages will center on three specific facets: the correct statement of the official teaching of the hierarchical magisterium, the possibility of dissent, and the present state of debate within Roman Catholicism.

Proper Statement of the Teaching

The most succinct and correct statement of the official teaching of the hierarchical magisterium is: Direct abortion is always wrong. Pope Paul VI's encyclical *Humanae Vitae* condemns "directly willed and procured abortion, even if for therapeutic reasons."[1]

A very accurate summary of the reasoning and statement of the Catholic position was given by Pope Pius XII in a 1951 address to an Italian family group.

> Innocent human life, in whatsoever condition it is found, is withdrawn, from the very first moment of its existence, from any direct deliberate attack. This is a fundamental right of the human person, which is of

Reprinted from *The Jurist,* Vol. XXXIII (1973), pp. 168–83, with the permission of the author and publisher. The same essay was reprinted in *New Perspectives in Moral Theology* (Notre Dame, IN: Fides, 1974), pp. 170–93.

CHARLES E. CURRAN is professor of moral theology at the Catholic University of America, Washington, DC.

general value in the Christian conception of life; hence as valid for the life still hidden within the womb of the mother, as for the life already born and developing outside of her; as much opposed to direct abortion as to the direct killing of the child before, during or after its birth. Whatever foundation there may be for the distinction between these various phases of the development of life that is born or still unborn, in profane and ecclesiastical law, and as regards certain civil and penal consequences, all these cases involve a grave and unlawful attack upon the inviolability of human life.[2]

The ultimate basis of the teaching on abortion comes from the sanctity or dignity of human life. However, the precise teaching on abortion requires two more specific judgments before it can be accurately articulated and formulated. The first judgment concerns the question of when human life begins. The second judgment involves the solution of conflict situations.

On this question of the beginning of human life there has been and still is a difference of opinion among Catholic theologians. Catholic canon law in its history often acknowledged a theory of delayed animation and did not propose the same penalties for abortion before animation and abortion after animation although both abortions were considered wrong. Thomas Aquinas and a majority of medieval theologians held such a view of delayed animation.[3] Even in the twentieth century there were still many Catholic theologians maintaining the theory of delayed animation.[4] Pope Pius XII acknowledges this in a long citation from his address to "The Family Front." Although Catholic teaching allows diversity on the theoretical question of when human life begins, in practice the question was solved by saying that one must act as if life is present from the beginning. If there is doubt whether or not life is present, the benefit of the doubt must be given to the fact that there is human life present.[5]

Such an understanding should guide Catholic statements on abortion, especially when voices become raised and shrill with the attendant problems of oversimplification and sloganeering. Abortion from the viewpoint of Catholic teaching thus should not be called murder or infanticide, because even Church teaching acknowledges that human life might not be present there. One must strive to be as accurate as possible in these matters.

Likewise, one distorts the true Catholic teaching by claiming that Catholic teaching forbids all abortion. In reality Catholic teaching does acknowledge the existence of some conflict situations which are solved by the application of the principle of the double effect. Direct abortion is always wrong, but indirect abortion can be permitted when there is a proportionate reason. The two most famous examples of indirect abortion are the cancerous uterus and the ectopic pregnancy. Pope Pius XII emphasized that he purposely used the term direct abortion, or direct killing, because indirect abortion could be permitted.[6] He defined direct killing as a deliberate disposition concerning innocent human life which aims at its destruction either as an end in itself or as the means of attaining another end that is perhaps in no way illicit in itself.[7]

Unfortunately, statements in the past about the Catholic position have not always been as accurate and precise as they should have been.

Possibility of Dissent

Recently Roman Catholic theology has publicly recognized that a good Roman Catholic can dissent from the authoritative or authentic, noninfallible papal teaching on artificial contraception. The question also arises: Is dissent possible on the question of the condemnation of direct abortion?

The teaching on direct abortion does belong to the category of authentic or authoritative, noninfallible hierarchical teaching. This teaching has been proposed in various responses of different Roman congregations and especially in the encyclical *Casti Connubii* of Pope Pius XI. Pius XII frequently reiterated and explained in his allocutions the condemnation of direct abortion. The Pastoral Constitution on the Church in the Modern World of Vatican Council II spoke of abortion as an infamy and an unspeakable crime but unfortunately did not make explicit the necessary distinction between direct and indirect abortion.[8] However, this question was really not a central consideration in this document. Obviously, the comments made in this document are to be interpreted in light of the general Catholic teaching on the subject. *Humanae Vitae* carefully restated the condemnation of direct abortion even if done for therapeutic reasons.[9]

The historical tradition indicates there was a solid historical basis for the teaching that has been expressed with greater precision from the time of St. Alphonsus as the condemnation of directly willed and procured abortion.[10] Perhaps the greatest deviation in the historical tradition concerns the expulsion of an inanimate fetus to save the life of the mother and even the reputation of the mother. John of Naples, an obscure fourteenth-century theologian whose work is known to us only through citations from others, apparently allows the abortion of an inanimate fetus to save the life of the mother. The animated fetus cannot be aborted.[11] This opinion was also maintained by Antoninus of Florence. However, Antoninus expressly denied the liceity of abortion to save the life of the mother if the fetus is already animated. He also expressly condemned the abortion of an inanimate fetus if the purpose was merely to hide the sin of the mother.[12] Later, Sylvester da Prieras presented his opinion in the same manner.[13] The same opinion was maintained by the influential Martin Azpilcueta, better known as Doctor Navarrus.[14]

A theologian named Torreblanca exerted a great influence on some seventeenth-century theologians. Torreblanca taught that before animation a woman may procure an abortion if because of the birth she is in danger of death or even of losing her reputation. In this case the fetus is not yet animated and her action is not homicide. Torreblanca cites seven authors in favor of his opinion, but he mistakenly cites Antoninus, Sylvester, Navarrus, and Sanchez as favoring his position, which they did not do in the case of abortion to protect the reputation of the woman.[15]

Leo Zambellus, explicitly following Torreblanca, held that if it is licit to procure an abortion before animation to save the life of the mother, it is also licit to save her reputation.[16] John the Baptist de Lezana allowed abortion before animation in the case of a noble-woman or a nun who sinned with a man and feared death or loss of reputation or scandal if her sin were known, but he accepted the expulsion in these cases only if it is the last available means.[17] John Trullenchus cited Torreblanca and Pontius (wrongly in this case) as permitting the abortion of an inanimate fetus as the last remedy in preserving a pregnant girl's life or reputation. Trullenchus himself denied such an opinion, but he admitted that the affirmative opinion is not improbable.[18] Gabriel of St. Vincent also argued against the possibility of abortion of the inanimate fetus, but he did admit some extrinsic probability as did Trullenchus.[19] The majority of theologians did not accept such an opinion.[20] On March 2, 1679, among sixty-five errors condemned by the Holy Office was the following: "It is licit to procure an abortion before the fetus is animated lest the girl be killed or lose her reputation if the pregnancy is detected."[21]

This historical section is included because other writers do not mention Torreblanca and those depending on him. The recognition of this fact indicates that even in the historical development there was some vacillation among Roman Catholic theologians, but the opinion permitting abortion of the inanimate fetus to save the reputation of the mother did not really arise again after the condemnation of 1679. In the question of therapeutic abortion even of an animated fetus to save the life of the mother, John R. Connery claims there was no official condemnation by the Church until the nineteenth century.[22]

In comparing the teaching on abortion with the Church's teaching on contraception it should be noted that John T. Noonan Jr., who has extensively studied the historical tradition on both questions, argues strenuously in favor of the Catholic teaching on abortion, while he disagrees with the traditional condemnation of contraception.[23] There do exist some few vacillations in the historical development, but one could still find there the general basis for the present teaching of the Catholic Church. The crucial problem remains the fact that life itself changes and develops, so that one cannot give absolute value to a tradition which merely repeats the past and does not enter into dialogue with present experience and with the discontinuities which can exist in the present, even though one could also conclude there are no such discontinuities.[24]

Thus from the fact the condemnation of direct abortion belongs to the authoritative and authentic, noninfallible papal teaching, and from the fact there is a long historical tradition that despite some vacillations serves as a basis for such a teaching, one cannot legitimately conclude there cannot be dissent from, or possible change in, the Catholic Church's teaching on direct abortion. In fact, I argue there can be both dissent from and change in the accepted Catholic teaching denying direct abortion.

The possibility of dissent from authoritative, noninfallible Church teaching has been demonstrated on the basis of the Church's own self-understanding of the assent due to such teaching.[25] But it is necessary to understand the theological reason justifying the possibility of such dissent. The possibility of dissent rests on the fact that in specific moral judgments on complex matters one cannot hope to attain a degree of certitude that excludes the possibility of error. In more complex matters one must consider many different facets of the question and circumstances so that one cannot expect to exclude all fear of error.

The present teaching of the Church on abortion depends on two very important judgments: the judgment about when human life begins, and the judgment about the solution of conflict situations involving the fetus and other values, such as the life of the mother. Even our brief historical summary indicates that in the past there has been some dispute on both these issues. The following section will furnish additional proof of the possibility of dissent based on the fact that some Roman Catholic theologians are now dissenting from and disagreeing with the accepted teaching of the Church on the condemnation of direct abortion. One can rightly suppose that the dissent will become even more prevalent in the future. Thus even in the question of the morality of abortion it is impossible to speak about *the* Roman Catholic position as if there cannot exist within Catholicism a dissent from this teaching.

Present State of the Debate

Until a few years ago there was no debate within Catholicism on the question of abortion. Earlier there had been other discussions on the question of craniotomy and the possibility of killing the fetus to save the life of the mother, but there was no dissent from the authoritative teaching proposed in *Casti Connubii*. Today there is an incipient debate within Catholicism that deserves to be brought to public attention and discussed, but there is comparatively much less dissent on abortion than on artificial contraception.

Within the last few years most episcopal conferences have made statements defending the accepted Catholic teaching.[26] In the United States, Germain Grisez has published a detailed study on abortion that, with one small exception (the possibility of killing the fetus to save the mother), defends the traditional opinion. As mentioned, John Noonan and others have also defended the existing teaching. However, there are some theological voices both here and abroad that have begun to disagree with the official teaching.

The remainder of this essay will review the recent discussion within Roman Catholicism. The fact that this discussion is comparatively new in Roman Catholicism can be documented by comparing what is mentioned here with the discussion of Roman Catholic theologians as recorded by Daniel Callahan in his far-reaching study on abortion published in 1970.[27] Our present discussion will neither repeat the work done by others such as Callahan nor will it attempt to be totally exhaustive. Rather representative opinions will be outlined and criticized.

The first crucial question in the moral judgment on abortion concerns the beginning of human life. Here there have been some recent divergences from the Catholic teaching that insisted, at least in practice, on the fact that one had to act as if human life is present from the time of conception. Callahan, in his study, has described three generic theories about the beginning of human life—the genetic, the developmental, and the social consequences approach.[28] In the recent Catholic discussions I see two different approaches proposed. The first approach can be called the individualistic approach, with almost exclusive dependence on biological or physical criteria. The second type can be called a relational approach, which is unwilling to accept just physical criteria and argues for what it would call more personalistic criteria for the beginning of human life.

The first characteristic of the relational school is the unwillingness to accept a determination of when human life begins on the basis of biological criteria alone. The destination of the embryo to become a human being is not something that is inscribed in the flesh alone but depends not only on the finality inscribed in the biological aspects, but even more so on the relation of acceptance and recognition by the parents who engage themselves in the act of procreation. Thus it is fruitless to look for a biological moment in which human life begins even if it would be possible to determine such a moment.[29]

Bernard Quelquejeu likewise denies that fecundation alone marks the beginning of human life, for the fruit of conception becomes human only through a procreative will expressed by the mother, the parents, and in some way by society itself.[30] Jacques-Marie Pohier explicitly mentions the fact that in other societies the decision about accepting one into the life of the tribe or the society was made after birth. Although disagreeing with such an approach, he contends that the motivation behind it was an attempt to show respect for life and the obligation of the society to care for the life that is accepted into it. Such approaches do show the relational aspect of acceptance that is required for truly human life.[31]

If the biological criteria are not sufficient, then one must ask what are the criteria for determining the existence of human life. Based on the notion of procreation as a free act of the parents and on the importance of relationship, these authors indicate the need for an acceptance by the parents and to some extent by society itself. Louis Beirnaert rejects an objectivist view that sees the fruit of conception as a being in itself when contemporary epistemology shows the participation of culture and of a knowing or recognizing element in the very constitution of the object of discourse. A human interrelation implies the recognition of the other as similar—the human face of the other. But this similarity is not present in the fetus or embryo. But even before this face is present, the parents, by their acceptance of the fetus—especially through giving a name—make the fetus a subject who has a place in the world. It is not a child until the decision of the parents anticipates the human form to come and names it as a subject.[32]

One can raise the question about when the relational recognition and acceptance take place. At least in some explanations it appears that this can take place any time before birth. For example, Pohier argues that there are economic, psychological, cultural, and even faith aspects of human life in addition to the biological aspects. What is the human life God wants for a man or woman? In effect, all depends, even from the point of view of God, on the possibility that men and women have to sustain a human life for that which will be born from this embryo.[33] Bruno Ribes asserts that in all the cases in which the relationship between the infant and the parents does not exist now or will not exist at birth, one has the duty to ask about the legitimacy of allowing such a child to be born.[34]

These authors generally take very seriously the fact that many people in our contemporary society obviously do not have difficulty in terminating a pregnancy under certain somewhat broad criteria. Quelquejeu calls for an entirely new theological methodology in light of such experience. One can no longer begin with established moral principles and apply them to these different cases, but rather one must begin with the moral experience as manifested in these different decisions. The experience of women who decide to have an abortion definitely constitutes a true source of moral reflection—a *locus theologicus*.[35]

Although I admit to some uneasiness in making the judgment about the beginning of human life, I cannot accept the relational approach described above. In reality it seems that some of the authors themselves do still hold a biological and individualistic criterion, namely birth. Apparently, none of them is willing to apply the relational criterion once the child is born, but some would be willing to apply it before this time. If one accepts only a relational approach in terms of recognition by parents and somewhat by society itself, there seems to be no reason to draw the line at birth. After birth these relationships could so deteriorate that one could judge there was not enough of a relationship for truly human existence.

Likewise, it is necessary to realize the problems existing on the other end of life; namely, the time of death. All the standards acceptable today for determining death are based on individualistic understanding as determined primarily by physical or biological criteria. Death is understood by some as the breakdown of the three basic human systems of circulation, respiration, and brain function. Some might want to define death only in terms of brain death, but all these understandings of death and tests for the presence of death follow an individualistic model. There would seem to be great problems in allowing a relational criterion that could then claim death has occurred when human relationships are no longer present.

In addition, the relational criterion that is proposed does not itself accept a full mutuality of relationships. One could press on with this criterion to say that truly human relations must be mutual and thus the child needs to acknowledge and recognize the gift of the parents before there is a truly human relationship present.

I do not want to deny the importance of relationality in human life and existence, but at the very beginning of human life or at the end of human life we are obviously not dealing with human life in its fullest actuality. Here we are dealing with the bare minimum that is necessary for individual human existence. People do exist in relationships, but more fundamental and basic is the fact that human beings are individuals called to enter into relationships with others in the growth and development of their own human lives.

Some proponents of this approach are not the only ones who mention the theoretical importance of the fact that many women see no moral problems in their decision to have an abortion. I agree that, on the one hand, the experience of people is an important consideration in moral theology. Catholic moral theology itself must recognize this, for it has accepted a natural law on the basis of which all people can arrive at ethical wisdom and knowledge. Thus one cannot write off the experience of people who are not "good Catholics" or "good Christians." On the other hand, one must also recognize that the experience of people can be wrong. Human limitation and sinfulness affect all our judgments and decisions. In many aspects of life we realize that even conscientious people are not able to agree on what is right or wrong. We know from history that the human race has unfortunately accepted some human behavior, such as slavery and torture, which we are not willing to accept today. Yes, one cannot neglect the experience of people who have made their decision in a particular matter, but such experience must always be subject to critical reflection.

The second generic approach to the question of the beginning of human life sees the basis of human life in terms of the presence of a human individual and usually employs physical or biological criteria to establish this fact. Such an approach, like the previous one, could insist on a developmental or process understanding of the development of human life, but it will still be necessary to draw some lines about when individual human life is present.

One could, from this perspective, adopt the time of birth or even the time of viability. In my judgment, birth and viability tell us where the individual is or can be and not necessarily what the individual is. It is important to acknowledge that at this time, to my knowledge, no Catholic theologians explicitly propose birth as the beginning of human life.

Joseph Donceel has written often on the subject and espouses a theory of delayed animation that, in his judgment, is the teaching Thomas Aquinas proposed, not on the basis of his admittedly inaccurate biological knowledge, but on the basis of his philosophical theory of hylomorphism.[36] According to the Thomistic theory, the soul is the substantial form of the body, but a substantial form can be present only in matter capable of receiving it. Thus the fertilized ovum or early embryo cannot have a human soul. A human being's spiritual faculties have no organs of their own, but the activity of cogitative power presupposes that the brain be fully developed, that

123

the cortex be ready. Donceel admits he is not certain when the human soul is infused into the matter, and he draws what appears to be a somewhat strict criterion in light of his above understanding. The least we may ask before admitting the presence of a human soul is the availability of these organs: the senses, the nervous system, the brain, and especially the cortex. Since these organs are not ready early in pregnancy, he feels certain there is no human person until several weeks have elapsed.[37]

John Dedek, after reviewing some of the theological literature on the question of the beginning of human life, admits there is doubt. He resolves the problem in practice by balancing off the probability of life and the reasons justifying abortion. He allows abortion up to the beginning of the third week for such circumstances as rape or even grave socioeconomic reasons. He even states there is a prudent doubt until the twelfth week and perhaps even until the fetus is technically viable, although he has really given no proof for the latter part of this statement. Only very serious reasons, such as grave danger to the physical or mental health of the mother or some serious physical or mental deformity of the child, could justify an abortion during this time.[38]

Wilfried Ruff has proposed that the individual life begins with the cortical function of the brain. Spiritual animation takes place at this time. Contemporary medicine also tests for death by the irreversible loss of the functioning of the cortex. The same test seems to be logical for the beginning of human life.[39]

In a matter as complex as this I have to admit there is some basis for these proposals, but I cannot accept them. Actual human and personal relations do not really take place until after birth. Truly spiritual activity does not take place until after birth. In my judgment, the basis for these actions is not qualitatively that much more present because there is now a cortex in the brain. A great deal of potentiality and development is still required. I do not see the rudimentary emergence of these organs as a qualitatively different threshold that can determine the difference between human life and no human life.

The argument about the consistency of tests for the beginning of human life and the end of human life does have some attractiveness. Frankly, I see it as a good approach with those who do not believe human life is present until much later. In this whole question of life it is important to respond with some logical consistency to the questions raised about the beginning of human life and about the end of human life, but one must realize what the test is trying to measure. The irreversibility of the coma is the decisive factor in the test for death. The test tries to measure if there is present any immediate potentiality for spontaneous life functioning. At the beginning of life

124

this can already be present before there is measurable electrical brain activity.

My own particular opinion is that human life is not present until individuality is established. In this context we are talking about individual human life, but irreversible and differentiated individuality is not present from the time of fecundation. This single fertilized cell undergoes cell division, but in the process twinning may occur until the fourteenth day. This indicates that individual human life is not definitely established before this time. There is also some evidence for recombination—one human being is formed from the product of more than one fertilization.[40] Thus I would argue that individuated human life is not present before this time. Corroborating evidence is the fact that a great number of fecundated ova are expelled from the uterus before they could ever reach this stage of the fourteenth day.

Notice that my argument is based on the concept of individuality that employs biological data to determine when individuality is present. The appearance of rudimentary organs, in my judgment, does not constitute a qualitative threshold marking the beginning of individual human life, for much development is still necessary. I have purposely refrained from using the term person or personal life, because as argued above, the actual signs of such personal life do not seem to be present until well after birth. Obviously, many Roman Catholic theologians still argue that human life begins or probably begins at conception, and confirm this argument from genetics that reminds us there is present from the very beginning a unique genetic package. However, I do not believe the individuality that is required is yet present.

An important study that needs to be done in this whole area is the question of probabilism and what to do when there is some doubt. My own tendency is to draw the line earlier so as to give the benefit of the doubt to individual existing human life. The older official Catholic teaching, which is still maintained by many Catholics, explicitly employs probabilism in this question. In one way or another this must enter into all the judgments made on this question. It would be an important contribution to indicate how various authors deal with this concept.

The second crucial moral question concerns the solution of conflict situations in which the life of the fetus is in conflict with the life of the mother or with some other value. Catholic theology has traditionally solved such conflict situations in the question of abortion by the concept of direct and indirect abortion. Direct abortion is always wrong, but indirect abortion may be permitted for a sufficient reason. The basis of the distinction between direct and indirect, as noted

125

earlier, is found in the nature and direction of the physical act and its effects.

In the question of abortion according to traditional Roman Catholic teaching, the only possible conflict situation involves two innocent individuals and is solved by the application of the principle of direct and indirect effects. In cases outside the womb, Catholic theology admits the unjust aggressor situation in which the unjust aggressor, even if the aggressor is in no way subjectively guilty for what is being done, can be repulsed by killing if necessary to protect life or other values proportionate to life. Thus anyone familiar with Roman Catholic moral theology recognizes that more possible conflict situations have been admitted for life outside the womb than for life inside the womb.

There is comparatively widespread dissatisfaction among Roman Catholic theologians today about the resolution of conflict situations by the concept of direct and indirect effects. Even some who maintain most of the traditional Catholic teaching admit that in some cases the fetus may be killed to save the life of the mother even though the general and even official interpretation of the older teaching would not allow it.[41] Germain Grisez argues that the principle of double effect in its modern formulation is too restrictive insofar as it demands that even in the order of physical causality the evil aspect of the act not precede the good. Grisez then gives some illustrations in which he would admit abortion to save the life of the mother provided no other act must intervene to accomplish the good effect.[42]

Other Catholic theologians have given even more radical theoretical interpretations to the understanding of the principle of the double effect. Many Catholic theologians today would be willing to accept in principle my earlier stated solution to the problem of conflict situations in abortion.[43] "Conflict situations cannot be solved merely by the physical structure and causality of the act. The human values involved must be carefully considered and weighed. . . . As a Christian any taking of life must be seen as a reluctant necessity. However, in the case of abortion there can arise circumstances in which the abortion is justified for preserving the life of the mother or for some other important value commensurate with life even though the action itself aims at abortion 'as a means to an end.' "[44] Richard McCormick, after studying six different modifications of the concept of the direct effect, also concludes that one cannot decisively decide the morality of the conflict situation on the basis of the physical structure of the act but ultimately on the basis of proportionate reason.[45]

In this light the question arises about what constitutes a proportionate reason. In other conflict situations in the past, especially in the case of unjust aggression, Catholic theology has been willing to equate

126

other values with physical human life itself. Manuals of moral theology justified the killing of an unjust aggressor as a last resort in defense of one's life, bodily integrity, spiritual goods "of greater value than life or integrity," such as the use of reason or conservation of reputation in very important matters, and material goods of great value.[46] In my opinion such a balancing of values could also be present in conflict situations involving abortion. Thus abortion could be justified to save the life of the mother or to avert very grave psychological or physical harm to the mother, with the realization that this must truly be grave harm that will perdure over some time and not just a temporary depression.

From my theological perspective there is also another theoretical justification for abortion in some conflict situations based on a theological notion of compromise. The theory of compromise recognizes the existence of human sinfulness in our world because of which we occasionally might be in a position in which it seems necessary to do certain things that in normal circumstances we would not do. In the case of abortion, for example, the story as reported about women in Bangladesh who were raped and would no longer be accepted in their communities if they bore children out of wedlock illustrates a concrete application of the theory of compromise.

A fair assessment of contemporary Catholic moral theology indicates a growing dissatisfaction with the concept of direct killing, which in the case of abortion would call for a greater number of conflict situations, even though some might disagree with my understanding of proportionate values or with my other justification for abortion on the basis of compromise.

Although some Catholic theologians today are questioning and denying the traditional Catholic teaching in the area of abortion, it is necessary to realize precisely what they are saying. I have not read any Catholic theologian who holds that the fetus is just tissue in the womb of the mother, or that the woman may abort for any reason whatsoever. No Catholic theologian, to my knowledge, accepts abortion of the fetus as just another form of contraception needing no more justification than any other use of contraception. At times I feel that some Catholic theologians are so involved in intramural discussions about abortion they do not emphasize that their opinions also differ quite markedly from many others in our society who seem to see nothing at all wrong with abortion. My own position does differ somewhat from the accepted Catholic position both about the beginning of human life and the solution of conflict situations, but I am adamantly opposed to any position that does not recognize some independent life in the fetus and that justifies abortion as just another form of contraception.

In closing this summary of contemporary Catholic moral theology on the moral aspects of the question of abortion, it is important to recall that this essay has presented just the newer and different opinions that have recently appeared. These positions are not held by the majority of Catholic theologians, but there is sizeable and growing number of Catholic theologians who do disagree with some aspects of the officially proposed Catholic teaching that direct abortion from the time of conception is always wrong.

14

The Interruption of Pregnancy (Problem of Artificial Abortion)

Helmut Thielicke

CAN THERE BE A SITUATION in which I am allowed to destroy innocent life? Can I ever intervene as a judge when "nature" . . . allows two lives to be set in competition with each other? It is not only in the matter of abortion that this question becomes acute. It also arose in the concentration camps of national socialism and in the killing of the mentally ill, when the question was whether to sacrifice a few to save a thousand others.[1] The fact the possibility of a conflict of values exists is undisputed; and that it demands an interpretation which must employ the concept of a world that is no longer "whole" —that is recognized not only by Christian theologians on the basis of the story of the Fall but also by the tragic poets.[2] The only question is whether human beings are permitted to intervene in this conflict and solve it according to their judgment—no matter whether it is nature or history that confronts them with this conflict.

This pragmatic weighing of values seems the most obvious and natural thing to do right here where the conflict occurs, and the

Abridged from pp. 232–41 in *The Ethics of Sex* by Helmut Thielicke, translated by John W. Doberstein. Copyright © 1964 by John W. Doberstein. Reprinted by permission of Harper & Row, Publishers, Inc.

HELMUT THIELICKE is a leading Protestant biblical theologian and ethicist, who has taught at Tübingen and Hamburg, Germany.

question presents itself which life is the more valuable, that of the mother—on whom the care of the family and the rearing and education of the children so largely depend—or that of the fetus —which has still to face the test of life and which at first appears to be only a burden and not to have any productive value whatsoever. If we understand Catholic moral theology correctly, it would not simply dismiss the question of the relative rank of the two lives, but would only draw different conclusions from the answer to this question. That is to say, it would see the higher value of the mother, which presumably it would not dispute, precisely in the fact that the mother is capable, as an ethical personality, of making her own decision and thus making the sacrifice of her life, whereas the unconscious fetus may be merely the object of hostile manipulations directed against it. Does not the relative rank of humans consist precisely in their ability to sacrifice, in their quality of being able to make decisions? . . .

Before we proceed, let us say that we see no possibility of contradicting this idea of sacrifice—except of course, on the *one* condition that it be not put forward as a law whether of the state or of the church. It is only at this point that the gist of our opposition could lie; and here it must be expressed, since the Roman Church, by its strict prohibition of artificial abortion in *every* case, demands the sacrifice of the mother. Here the sacrifice to be made by the one of higher rank is simply drained of its meaning, because through this legalistic regulation the mother is made the object of a medical act of omission on the part, say, of strict Catholic physicians or nurses. Casuistical regimentation of the case cancels out the freedom that alone could provide the basis for the higher duty of the one who has the higher rank.[3] If this freedom is granted, then the freely made decision of the mother to offer the risk of her life and not allow the fruit of her body to be touched can only be respected by Christian ethics.

Naturally, there is also a subtle form of noninstitutionalized legalism that could threaten such a sacrifice. This is the case when a mother acts in the name of, and under the pressure of, a supposed dogma of the order of creation that possibly is not to be held in this form at all. This confronts us with the real question that concerns us here in this *special* connection, exactly as it did in connection with the problem of contraception, namely, the question of how far and in what way the demand of the order of creation is to be obeyed. Here again we must be prepared to meet the question whether, under the conditions of this fallen, no longer perfect world, the direct application of the order of creation might not be fanatical (*schwärmerisch*) and therefore destructive; whether, therefore, there is not theological significance in the fact that Jesus did not simply make the protological law of the original state and the eschatological law of the kingdom of

God the law of this aeon, but rather allowed both to be the *corrective* which calls in question this aeon.[4] There is no need to emphasize particularly the fact that when we face the question of killing, which is at issue here, the brokenness of the claim of the order of creation needs to be dealt with far more carefully than when we are facing the question whether possible life may be prevented from coming into being.[5]

On the question of the *claim* of the order of creation there is a profound difference between the Catholic and the Reformation teaching concerning the relationship of creation and sin.[6] The reduction of the Fall to a mere injury inflicted on nature (which remains otherwise intact), as Catholic theology teaches, makes possible a certain analogy and continuity between the norms of the original state and those of the (partially) fallen world. The doctrine of natural law formulates and systematizes these enduring normative axioms.[7] Its presupposition is that the Fall represents only an accidental break in the structure of the order of creation, that in establishing the ethical norms one can—to express it sharply—almost pass over it. Over against this, Reformation doctrine is impressed by the elemental change that sin has wrought within the structure of the world.

Therefore, Reformation doctrine arrives at a different doctrine of orders. It says that the orders—with the exception of the prototype (*Urbild*) of marriage and family—must be understood not as orders of creation, but rather as orders of necessity in the fallen world, as measures God provides to preserve the fallen world.[8]

With respect to the medical indication of abortion, this break between the original state and the conditions of this aeon becomes acute in that the conflict between life and life does not occur in the original order of creation and therefore the order of creation cannot provide a direct solution of the conflict. This is also evident in the example of the just war, which is justified only insofar as its purpose is to protect life that is committed to the care of the state, but which can do so only by destroying other life. This analogy of war is applicable only in a limited sense, not only according to Catholic but also our opinion, because in a just war it is presupposed that the life to be destroyed is that of an aggressor and thus of one who is guilty, whereas the unborn child is certainly not to be thought of as an aggressor in this sense at all, but rather as innocent life.[9] Here the point of comparison between war and abortion does not consist at all in the guilty-aggressive or innocent competition between two lives, but rather in the fact that both are opposed to the order of creation, that originally (*ap' arches*) life was not pitted against life, that it was incorporated in an order cosmos that had been wrested from the chaos (where everything was pitted against everything else). Because

131

all life was under God and related to God, all life was at peace with all other life. Because the vertical dimension was in order, the horizontal dimension, too, was in order. We have repeatedly emphasized and shown the biblical basis of this relation between peace with the Creator and the peace of the creatures one with another, between breaking away from the peace of the Creator *and* the loss of peace within creation itself.[10]

The consequence of this interrelationship is that what we see in the world as disorder can never be related directly to God's creatorhood and God's government of the world. Where there is war in the world, it may be that God is giving us a mandate in it; but this does not mean that God wills war, that war is part of the design of creation. Suffering and sickness cannot be interpreted as the result of God's proper will (*voluntas Dei propria*) but are actually the reverse of this real will of God—although the will of God is still carried out in the midst of that which opposes it and is able to make even the forms of this opposition to work for good (Romans 8:28). The eschatological emphases in the Bible make it clear that it is not God's *real* will that is at work in the perversity of the world: Jesus' healings of the sick are signs that point to the fact that in the kingdom of God there will be no more suffering, no crying, no tears; his resurrection points to the destruction of the "last enemy [1 Cor. 15:26]." It is not permissible (and, of course, we are not insinuating that Catholics do this!) to trace back directly and indiscriminately to the creative will of God both the birth of children and the crippling of children, both the blossom and the "frost that blights the springtime bloom"—and thereby transform God from the ruler of the order of creation into what is basically only the First Cause and a phantom of a *philosophoumenon*.[11]

This raises the following question: When illness would make the bearing of the child a mortal threat to the mother, dare we say that what happens here is simply to be attributed to the will of God in creation? Dare we interpret the conflict between life and life that occurs here simply as a statute of God's will to which we must submit? Is not all this rather the token of a creation that should accuse itself in the face of the *real* will of God? Or to turn the question around, would we not have to brand all medical action as rebellion against God, if we were to affirm that suffering, sickness, the hostility of the elements of the organism, and the hostility of the organisms to one another are dispensations of God? Would this not mean that medical and nursing care flies in the face of God's will, prevents God's will from being done?

To ask these questions is to answer them in the negative. The order of creation is not an outline plan for what occurs in this case of illness, this conflict of two lives. I cannot incorporate it directly into this plan.

132

But, you ask, can I not do this at least partially, in *certain* relations? For example, by learning from the order of creation that God desires to preserve what has been created and give it its *kairos*? True, but what does this mean when two forms of life created by God enter into mortal competition with each other? Our only point in asking these questions is to make clear that the appeal to the order of creation becomes problematical insofar as one seeks to obtain direct answers concerning its demand in this case of conflict. Outside of the conflict the demand may be clear and unambiguous, and there can be no question about the prohibition of abortion, and yet it appears to become ambiguous as soon as the conditions of this aeon and the order of creation are seen to be incommensurable.

We are faced with the alternatives. One is whether we should obey the demand of the order of creation by simply accepting the condition of this fallen world as a judgment and then interpreting a mother's dying because of her child as a kind of vicarious sharing in this sentence of judgment. If we do this, are we really refraining from intervening in the order of *creation?* When all this happens, is it really the order of creation that is involved at all? Are we not rather refraining from intervening in the order of *judgment* when we simply allow the decree of judgment to take its course? And when we do this, are we not, at most, merely paying respect to the order of creation by regarding it only as a judgmental law that applies the standard of the original state and condemns our fallen world?

Or—and this is the other alternative—do we not rather observe the claim of the order of creation if we grant to medical assistance the mission to set forth in a signlike (although admittedly imperfect) way God's *real* will for the world and allow it to be a reminder of the original perfect creation and a promise of the world to come? Is not the healing that is committed to the physician actually part of the signlike struggle against the brokenness and disturbance of the creation? And is not the physician's struggle actually a battle that is waged with means (medicines and techniques) drawn from the surviving store of created things? [In this reaction of the medico is there not a manifestation of that mystery of the world in which in this aeon the conflict is carried right into the order of creation itself and the fact that we always find it there whenever we ourselves begin to act; in other words, that the conflict of values manifests itself in the conflict of the elements of creation with each other, that the physician fights against the alien elements in creation in the *name* of creation and with its *means*, that, indeed, nature is marshaled and mobilized against nature?]

Here we catch ourselves arguing by means of questions. This may be due to the fact that here we are confronted with that utmost limit, where the exceptional case lands us, where even theological thought reaches its limit: where we get no farther by making subsumptions under given dogmatic axioms and even the concept of the order of creation loses its applicability. True, we may be able to say why it is that we face this limit of theological thought and to that extent we shall be arguing theologically. We can show how in the borderline situation there appears that distortion of perspective which demonstrates all too clearly the derangement of the order of creation and the conflict of values that has intruded into it. All this we can state at the level of theological argument. But we cannot proceed with the same style of argumentation and solve this conflict. For us to be able to proceed in this way the order of creation would have to be an immediately applicable standard. But this it is not.

The order of creation would be this kind of standard only if we did not view the incursion of sin as radically as did the Reformers, in other words, if we did not interpret it as a break in the continuity between the original state and the fallen world. If one accepts this almost unbroken continuity and introduces the doctrine of original sin accordingly,[12] then both members of the continuity remain commensurable and the order of creation can be taken as a critical rule and standard and can be applied directly to the realities of our world. This experiment took form in the Catholic doctrine of natural law![13] If, however, we are compelled to hold a doctrine of sin that almost completely breaks the commensurability of the original state and this aeon in certain borderline cases, then it is impossible to lay one's finger directly on the claim of the order of creation. To adhere to this commensurability under all circumstances leads, it is true, to a more practicable moral theology. For then one knows where one is with all the certainty of juridical deductions; one has fixed standards. And even though their application—as in the case of the absolute prohibition of abortion—can lead to extreme practical harshness and the reproach of doctrinaire disregard for life, it is nevertheless a triumph of practicability to achieve a situation in which the framework of standards remains unmoved and every case can be localized within it.

In saying this it should be understood that we are by no means saying that this whole Catholic conception was contrived for reasons of practicability, that it is therefore pragmatic in a remote sense. On the contrary, we are simply clarifying for our own benefit why it is we often admire the impressive clarity of this conception and its rigid consistency, why it is we too would like to have something like it, because, after all, if we had explicit directive norms at our disposal, this would reduce the hazardousness of making decisions—and why it is that we must nevertheless renounce all of this.

134

The desire for practicability, for some handy moral-theological application of the order of creation, must rather be subjected to the discipline of the question of truth. And the question of truth is this: Can we, dare we, interpret sin in such a way that this continuing analogy between the created world and the fallen world can be accepted and that therefore a commensurability exists between the two, and that thus the order of creation becomes a directly applicable standard? We cannot.[14] But then this means that we can no longer decide with precise theological exactitude—remembering clearly that this applies only within this limited radius of the borderline situation where life is in competition with life—what the basic alternative shall be: whether the mother should sacrifice herself or not; whether the fatality of this split world should be passively endured or resisted in the name of a signlike medical intervention; whether we should accept the order of creation as condemning law; or whether the life that creation desires should be saved at least partially and possibly at the cost of another life.

Here it becomes clear that nobody can relieve us of this decision and that the only help we can get from a theological ethics is that it may help us to see what the alternatives are and thus prepare the material for our decision.

Part V

Abortion as a Socioethico Issue

Joseph F. Fletcher
Charles E. Curran
Roger L. Shinn
Paul D. Simmons

15

Abortion and the True Believer

Joseph F. Fletcher

Most of us learn sooner or later how wise it is not to debate with True Believers. Debate with them ends as an exercise in futility. What follows is therefore not an argument for abortion, either therapeutic or personal; nor is it a retort to the arguments of the antiabortionists. It is simply a comment, as from the sidelines or the balcony, on the debate—which is essentially over the question whether a fetus is a person or not and, consequently, what rights if any ought to be assigned to uterine life.

I

Thoughtful people, not just dull old philosophers, are always bemused when they learn how a medieval notion called substance enters into the abortion debate, lurking behind and beneath the rhetoric of the right-to-life forces.

Spokespersons for the Roman Catholic hierarchy, backed by one Lutheran synod and most Orthodox Jews, say that a fetus is a person and that therefore abortion is murder, the killing of an innocent person. They claim that a human embryo or fetus is a person because it is potentially a person. By this they mean that the substance of a

Joseph F. Fletcher was a sometime faculty member of the School of Medicine at the University of Virginia, Charlottesville, Virginia.

person is already present in a fetus or unformed human. How sound or valid is this preformist idea? Well, it is like saying that the house is in the blueprint, the statue is in the marble, the book is in the writer's conception of it, the oak is in the acorn—and by the same token, and *a fortiori*, the person is in the fetus.

The substance doctrine is the one that holds up the sacramental theology of transubstantiation—the belief that even though the wafer in the Mass has the "accidents" of bread (its taste, color, consistency, cereal content), down underneath these accidents lies the real substance, the body of Christ, which cannot be seen or touched or tasted or smelled but is nonetheless *there*—not just prospectively or virtually, but actually.

In the same way, it is contended, the verifiable properties of a fetus are admittedly not personal; it has no cerebration or memory or ability to communicate or self-consciousness. But these things are, after all, only accidents. The person is actually there, unverifiably (mysteriously) yet knowable by faith. It follows, of course, that abortion is killing an innocent person, i.e., that abortion is murder.

The medieval theology of transubstantiation offers a kind of objective argument against abortion, if you can accept its ontology or supernaturalistic theory of material reality. Its basis lies solely in a faith assertion: in an unverifiable *belief* in something we might call a preformed person. However, if you accept the faith assertion of substance (a very big If, to be sure), the deductive argument from it may be said to be a logical one in the syllogistic sense. (All fetuses are persons; this is a fetus; therefore this is a person: everything hangs on the first premise.)

For those who believe in the metaphysics of substance and accidents, who are convinced that the medieval sacramental theology was a true account of real things, it makes sense to refuse to terminate fetal development. But one more assumption is required for the antiabortion argument. Even if you are willing to revive the medieval notion of the homunculus (a minuscule person down *in* the fetus, maybe even in the sperm or ovum), you still have to assume (judge) that life is the highest good *(summum bonum)*, thus taking priority over all other values—health, quality of life, resources for well-being, and so on. This is a vitalistic ethics, and it makes human life sacrosanct, taboo, untouchable.

On examination, all of this comes down to two highly challengeable jumps in reasoning. They are known, among those who do not indulge in them, as the error of potentiality (taking what could be as what already is) and the fallacy of the single cause (seeing the constant, ignoring the variable).

Thomas Aquinas rejected this line of argument. He distinguished

140

between life *in potentia* and *in situ* (in being), and held that the difference between potential humanness and actual humanness is an essential difference, not merely a superficial or accidental one. For St. Thomas, what changed the fetus from merely biological life into a person was the infusion of the soul or animation—which he, like Aristotle, thought takes place about the time of quickening. Some Catholics still hold to this opinion, but the Vatican's official teaching has discarded it.

Among antiabortionists there is, it should be noted, an alternative position. A few of them claim to have a revelation of some kind, written either in a book or in their hearts, that God's eternal will has sanctified the fetus. This group does *not* take its stand on the metaphysical ground. It is amusing to observe how Protestants who fiercely reject the substance theory at the altar accept it in the uterus; they repudiate transubstantiation sacramentally but swallow it whole fetally.

These two antiabortion arguments, the one metaphysical and the other revelational, are fused together in the debate, yet in fact they are quite independent of each other. Some nontheists (a few humanists also, as well as Mahayana Buddhists and the like) accept the metaphysical position but not the revelational, with a few theistic debaters (for example, evangelical Protestants, Orthodox Jews, and Jains in India) reverse things, holding to a revelation without recourse to any metaphysics.

II

Leaving metaphysical and supernatural grounds altogether, we find another group who opposes abortion on a different basis: on ethical rather than either metaphysical or revelational premises. They take their stand on what *ought* to be rather than on what is or at least is believed to be. Their starting point is a *value* commitment. Their contention is that because the potential of a fetus is personal value, we ought to preserve the fetus when we can for the sake of what is not yet actual but presumably will come to be.

Once you stake your antiabortion case on values rather than on alleged facts not in evidence, on what ought to be rather than on what is, you are landed in the whole ethical problem of values and preferences and choices, the problem of relative values and of proportionate good. This is a radically different order of argument against abortion.

It is one thing to say, "No matter what else has to be sacrificed (health, happiness, growth, resources), I will not murder a 'substantially' real person"; but it is a quite different thing to say, "No matter

141

what has to be lost in terms of present values, I will not weigh them against the future value of this embryo." The essential feature of this latter argument is not that it rests on moral rather than metaphysical or religious grounds, but that it *always* gives a first-order value to a fetus regardless of the situation or circumstances. When this posture is combined with substance metaphysics, we have a True Believer whose dogmatism rules out any kind of pragmatic or responsible judgment about down-to-earth cases.

The great majority of us—doctors, nurses, patients, people as people—look at the abortion issue in ethical rather than metaphysical or revealed terms. But even if we regard it ethically, we cannot deal with abortion dogmatically or absolutistically or by universalized generalizations. Whether present human values should be traded off for or subordinated to future fetal values would depend on a responsible assessment of proportionate good. Approached in this way, a good case can sometimes be made for abortion, whether it happens to be for medical reasons or personal reasons.

Surely no law should be tolerated that forces the substance theory on those who do not find it reasonable, either in the fetus or in the sacrament. At the political level—at any rate in a democracy—it is obvious that like the substance doctrine, the revealed and vitalist doctrines are very much matters of private opinion.

Opposition to abortion is certainly a part of the freedom of religious belief and practice we want to protect: people should be free to embrace it. But this freedom has to be protected for all, not just for some. It is difficult if not impossible to see how church metaphysics or divine revelations or individual value preferences can be imposed by law on those who do not believe them to be either true or wise.

This is, in a word, the recommendation of wise and thoughtful people on both sides of the opinion line—those who disapprove abortion as well as those who approve it.

16

Civil Law and Christian Morality: Abortion and the Churches

Charles E. Curran

THE RELATIONSHIP BETWEEN civil law and morality, especially Christian morality, continues to be a subject of great debate. The problem arises because, whereas most people admit a difference between civil law and Christian morality, nonetheless there is not a complete separation between the two. The overlapping between the two presents possible sources of tension. In the recent debates in England, Patrick Devlin underscores the complexity of the relationship as illustrated in how contemporary society adopts monogamous marriage as part of its social structure. The historically Christian roots of England explain how monogamous marriage came into the structure of society, but such marriage remains there now not because it is Christian, but because it is built into the house in which we live and could not be removed without bringing the whole house down.[1] Basil Mitchell accepts and develops this metaphor of an old and rambling

Reprinted from *Conversations*, Spring 1975, Graymoor Ecumenical Institute, Garrison, New York. The essay was reprinted in *Ongoing Revisions in Moral Theology*, edited by Charles E. Curran (Notre Dame, IN: Fides/Claretian, 1975), pp. 107–43.

CHARLES E. CURRAN is professor of moral theology in the School of Theology of the Catholic University of America, Washington, DC.

143

English house that has grown over the centuries and thus includes many things from the Christian ethos of the society.[2]

The question has been particularly acute for Roman Catholicism. There is a close relationship between this question and the related matter of religious liberty. In the past few centuries one can recall the long and tortuous development within Roman Catholicism before Vatican Council II could accept the teaching on religious liberty.[3] At the present time the Roman Catholic hierarchy in the United States is generally—and rightfully—identified in the popular mind as opposed to liberalized abortion laws and is seeking an amendment to the Constitution to overturn the recent ruling of the Supreme Court. In fairness it must be pointed out that Roman Catholics are by no means the only ones who are opposed to abortion, and at the same time one must also signal the incipient dissent within Roman Catholicism itself on the morality of this particular issue although this dissent currently is minimal.

This mode of action by the Catholic bishops of the United States is reminiscent to many of the Roman Catholic opposition to changing the laws of Connecticut that made the use of contraception a crime and also of the opposition to public policy promoting and distributing artificial contraception. In November of 1959 the American bishops condemned the use of foreign aid funds to promote artificial contraception in developing countries, since the logical answer was not to decrease the number of people, but to increase the food supply. This statement raised a political storm, especially in the light of the impending Presidential candidacy of John F. Kennedy. Bishop Pike, a well-known Protestant Episcopal bishop, asked if the statement was binding on Roman Catholic candidates for public office.[4] Although the Kennedy Presidency did much to alleviate the fears and questions about a Catholic President that had emerged in a somewhat divisive way in the context of the Smith candidacy of 1928, still the problem of the relationship of Christian morality, especially moral teachings held by Roman Catholics, to civil law remains.

Efforts by the Roman Catholic hierarchy in the United States to influence legislation in the light of Christian moral teaching have not always met with ecumenical rebuff and suspicion. In 1919 the administrative committee of the National Catholic War Council issued a document entitled "Social Reconstruction: A General Review of the Problems and Survey of Remedies." As a program for social reconstruction after World War I, the document advocated both specific short-term steps and long-term goals. The short-term strategies called for the state to pass laws on such things as child labor, a living wage, and to make comprehensive provision for insurance against illness, unemployment, and old age. The long-term goals called for

144

considerable modification of the existing system through cooperation and copartnership because of the existing defects of enormous inefficiency and waste in production, insufficient incomes for the majority of wage earners, and unnecessarily large incomes for a minority of privileged capitalists. It was more than a decade later that some of the short-term goals were enacted into legislation although the more radical long-range plans were never met. Many people in American society applauded the leadership exercised by the American bishops in this struggle for social justice.[5]

One could call to mind many other instances similar to these already mentioned, but the point is clear. There is a distinction but also an overlapping between civil law and Christian morality, and especially from the Roman Catholic perspective there has been a tendency to see a rather close identification of the two. What has been the approach of Roman Catholic theology to this question? What explains this teaching within Roman Catholicism? What should be the proper understanding of the relationship between Christian morality and civil law today?

Until recently there was one approach within Roman Catholic thought to the proper understanding of the relationship between civil law and morality. On the basis of some developments in Roman Catholic theology, especially as illustrated in the teaching on religious liberty proposed at Vatican Council II, a different approach to the question is required. This essay explains the basis for the older teaching and shows its application to particular questions before arguing for a different approach judged to be more consonant with accepted developments in Roman Catholic thought. In the light of this approach the legal aspects of the abortion question are discussed.

The Foundations of the Older Approach

To understand properly the older approach to the relationship of morality and civil law it will be most helpful to consider three questions developed in Roman Catholic theology that have contributed to this approach: the relationship of church and state, the origin and purpose of the state, and the role and function of positive law. These teachings developed in the context of historical circumstances that are quite different from the contemporary historical context. The society at the time of the Middle Ages was not generally democratic. The idea of a unified Christendom was still an ideal in the mind of many. Much less importance was given to political and civil liberties of individuals. These historical circumstances understandably influenced the development of the teaching in Roman Catholicism on the subjects under consideration, but also the basic tendencies in Roman Catholic thought also influenced such teachings. Roman Catholic moral theology in its historical development has insisted on the goodness of the human, the role of rationality, and the existence of a hierarchical ordering in all aspects of God's creation, with very little emphasis on the freedom of the individual. A brief consideration of the three topics will indicate how both historical circumstances and traditional Catholic emphases influenced the development of the teaching.

Church and state. Catholic theorizing in the Middle Ages about the relationship between church and state took place in the context of medieval theocracy. Without attempting an exhaustive treatment of this question in Thomas Aquinas, a consideration of chapter 14 of *De Regimine Principum* shows the general approach taken by him at least in this one place. Thomas here employs Aristotelian thought to explain the medieval theory developed earlier by the canonists and theologians. There is a twofold ordering of humans in this world and thus a twofold governing power the commentators often called the *Regnum* and the *Sacerdotium.* The temporal order and the spiritual order are two different orders with two different ends, but the end of the temporal order is subordinated to the more important end of the spiritual order. (This hierarchical ordering is typical of Thomist thinking.) The temporal or earthly realm is committed to earthly rulers. The object of human society is the virtuous life, but the person who tries to live virtuously is destined to a higher end—union with God. Such an end cannot be attained by human virtue alone, but only by divine grace. The government of this higher order belongs to Jesus Christ and is delegated not to rulers, but to priests—especially the Roman pontiff who is the vicar of Christ and successor of Peter.[6]

According to one modern commentator, in Aquinas' theory the temporal power is subject to the spiritual as the body is to the soul, as philosophy is to theology, as the natural is to the supernatural. However, in comparison with Pope Boniface VIII, Aquinas' understanding of the subordination of the temporal to the spiritual is somewhat moderate. By giving a solid independent base to the temporal order the Thomist teaching does provide for a clearer distinction between the temporal and the sacred orders, but in practice Aquinas emphasized the subordination between them. The theory of Thomas is the theory of the orthodox state.[7]

In light of such an understanding one can appreciate Aquinas' teaching on the proper attitude of the state toward those who do not profess the true faith. In general he is against conversion of infidels by force, but force can be employed against those who have left the true faith, such as heretics and schismatics.[8] The question then arises about the rights of infidels to publicly practice their religion and have their celebrations. The response is in terms of toleration. Human government should imitate God's way of governing, but at times even almighty God permits certain evils to occur that could be prohibited, lest greater goods would be prevented or greater evils would occur by taking away such evil. Thomas is willing to tolerate rites and celebrations of the Jews, which prefigure the truths of faith, and also at times the rites of infidels if it is necessary to avoid a greater evil. Heretics, since they have left the true faith, are not to be tolerated. By their own deeds they have merited not only to be separated from the church by excommunication, but also to be excluded from the world through death. The church can mercifully extend a period for conversion, but if the heretic remains obstinate, the twofold separation should occur.[9]

One can see how the Thomist teaching could serve as a basis for the position on the relationship between church and state and for the question of religious liberty as these were developed in Roman Catholic theology. Modifications were made especially in the nineteenth and twentieth centuries to recognize that external religious liberty could be accorded to non-Catholics, but this was still in terms of toleration to avoid greater evil. It was only at the time of Vatican Council II that a more satisfactory approach to these questions was officially promulgated by the hierarchical magisterium of the Church.

The origin of the state. The second question concerns the origin of the state and necessarily includes somewhat oblique references to the nature and purpose of the state. The Lutheran tradition and much of the Protestant tradition has seen the origin of the state in light of the sinfulness of human beings. The state is necessary to bring about order and prevent the chaos that sinful human beings will wreak on one another and on society. Coercion is the primary way in which the state functions to prevent chaos and bring about order. Such an approach with a heavy emphasis on sin also tends to see opposition and discontinuity between what is good for the individual and what is good for the society, and sees societal rules as constraints on the freedom and liberty of the individual person.[10]

Thomas Aquinas occupies a significant place in the historical development of the teaching on the origin of the state in Christian thought. In the eyes of most commentators, he signaled a break from the Augustinian tradition of the past to a more Aristotelian understanding, but he himself only gradually came to this understanding. Thomas' understanding of the origin of the state can be seen in his interesting discussion of the question whether there would have been authority *(praelatio seu dominium)* in the state of innocence. Is the state a natural society in the sense that the very nature of human beings calls on people to band together in a political society to work for the common good? Or is the existence of political society due to the sinfulness of human beings, which must be kept in check? Does authority or political rule that is characteristic of the state owe its origin to the nature of human beings or to the sinfulness of human beings? Many earlier thinkers made a distinction between authority parents exercise over children and the authority the state exercises over its people. This latter type of dominion and subjection, like the subjection of a slave to the master, would be a result of sin. The authority of the state is coercive authority that indicates its origin in human sinfulness and not in human nature as such.[11]

Thomas first discusses this question in his *Commentary on the Book of Sentences of Peter Lombard*—a context in which his contemporaries (e.g., Bonaventure and Albert the Great) also discuss the question. In responding to the question whether there would have been authority *(praelatio seu dominium)* in the state of innocence, Thomas distinguishes two modes of authority: one for the sake of government *(ad regimen ordinatus)* and the other for the sake of domination *(ad dominandum)*. Relying on a citation from Aristotle, Thomas compares the first way with the ruler's authority when the ruler governs for the good of the subjects; whereas the second mode is compared to the tyrant, who rules for his or her own good and not the good of the subjects. The second mode could not have existed in the state of innocence, because no human being would be subject to another for the other's good. Such a relationship of domination could exist only in the relationship of human beings to inferior beings whose finality is in the service of humans.[12]

After making this fundamental distinction, Thomas now considers further this dominion of the ruler over the subjects for their good, and distinguishes three aspects of this ruling authority, only one of which would have been present in the state of innocence. The dominion of the ruler over the subjects insofar as it directs subjects to what should be done would be present in the state of innocence; but insofar as it supplies for defects as illustrated in the defense of the people against enemies or insofar as it involves the correction of morals in that evil persons are punished and forced to do the good, such dominion would not be present in the state of innocence. Since the first function of ordering involves direction by one who has a greater gift of wisdom and a greater light of intelligence, it would be present even in paradise. Aquinas employs the above distinction to respond to some objections that all dominion comes from sin. Nature makes all people equal in liberty, but not equal in natural gifts. When individuals are being directed to their own good, there is no restriction of their freedom, and in fact the ruler in this case is not incongruously called the servant of the people.[13]

In the *Summa Theologica* Thomas again turns to the question of the origin of the state in the same context of whether human beings in the state of innocence would have had authority and dominion over other human beings. After mentioning some arguments in favor of denying the possibility of such dominion in the state of innocence, Aquinas points out that the condition of human beings in the state of innocence would not be higher than the state of the angels. Even among the angels some had dominion and authority over others, as is evident from the order existing among the angels. Thomas responds by recognizing that dominion or authority can be understood in two different senses: one sense in which it is connected with servitude and another sense in which it refers to any subject so that one who has the office of directing and governing children can be said to have dominion or authority. Obviously, the first was not present in the state of paradise, but the second could be present. The distinction proposed here by Aquinas, unlike the distinction found in the *Commentary on the Sentences,* proposes a general concept of dominion related to any subjection and a particular type that is based on sin.[14]

In the instance of slavery the slave loses freedom and is ordered to the utility and good of another. A subject is governed as a free person insofar as one is directed to one's own good or to the common good, and this dominion or authority would have existed in the state of innocence. Such dominion must have existed before the Fall for, according to Aristotle, a human being is by nature a social animal, and the social life of many would be impossible without someone directing all to the common good. As Aristotle says, when many are ordered to one, then there is found one who is the director. For a second reason it would not be fitting for a person who has received a greater gift of knowledge or justice not to use it for the good and utility of others. This argument presupposes what Thomas had developed in the previous question; namely, there would have been differences and disparities in the state of innocence even with regard to knowledge and justice. Thomas then goes on to invoke the authority of Augustine in a passage from the *City of God* that the just rule not through a desire for power, but through an obligation to give guidance; and this is what the order of nature prescribes, this is how God created humans. There is irony in such a citation, because Aquinas now uses Augustine for what Augustine himself did not admit: political authority is compared to the authority of the father of the family and not to the authority of the tyrant or the master over slaves.[15]

There is a significant change and development in Thomas' thought on the question that shows the growing influence of Aristotle on his intellectual development. When Thomas wrote the *Commentary on the Sentences,* he did not as yet fully know the *Politics* of Aristotle, although he was familiar with many other writings, including the *Ethics.* Thomas gradually came to accept the Aristotelian notion that humans are by nature political. Both Augustine and Aristotle could agree that humans are by nature social; but for Augustine the ideal society was the communion of the blessed in heaven, whereas for Aristotle the only society he knew was the *polis.* By insisting that the human being is *animal politicum et sociale* Aquinas came to accept the Aristotelian notion. Political life belongs to the very nature of human beings.[16]

The question Aquinas was really confronting in the passage cited above was how can political society be natural to human beings when it restricts their freedom and forces them to do things. Surely such restrictions and coercion that at times force people to act against their wills could come only from sin, according to the Christian perspective. But according to Aquinas, political authority merely directs human beings to do what, by nature, they should do and thus constitutes no violation of their freedom. Such an approach is possible for Thomas because he accepts the fact that there is no contradiction between the good for the individual and the common good. Also, individual persons have different gifts and qualities because of which they can work together doing different things to achieve the common good. The direction from political authority does not violate human nature, but rather acts in accord with it. Sometimes the shortcomings of the agent cause one to feel coercion, but in so feeling one acts against the true self.

The relationship of the individual to the political order does not involve any restriction of the freedom of the individual, for by nature the human being is called to achieve one's own end and the end of society. Such a view of human nature and freedom has important ramifications for problems raised about the relationship between law and individual freedom. Civil law in no way involves a violation of the individual's freedom, for its purpose is to direct the individual to do, by nature, what he or she is meant to do. There is no dichotomy between political authority and the freedom of the individual, but only a harmonious interplay.

Positive law. A third important teaching for our purposes concerns the very nature and function of positive or human law. Discussion is restricted to a brief overview of the teaching as proposed by Aquinas in the *Summa.* Although Aquinas does discuss law in other places, the manuals of moral theology were usually content just to refer to his

150

teaching as found in the *Summa*. Thomas acknowledges that human civil law is derived from natural law. Thomas defines human law as the ordering of reason for the common good made by the one who has charge of the community and promulgated to the subjects. Human law depends primarily on the reason of the lawgiver, for the lawgiver's function is to order the people to the common good.[17]

This ordering of reason which is human law according to Aquinas is derived in two ways from natural law, which is the rational creature's participation in the eternal law. The first is by way of a conclusion from more general principles such as the condemnation of murder. The second way in which human law is derived from natural law is by way of specifying or determining what itself is general and undetermined in the natural law; e.g., by determining what penalty should be attached to a particular crime. The second way relates more to art than to science as illustrated by specifying and determining in a particular way that which is general; e.g., the artist adapting the general concept of house to a particular type of house. The second type, which specifies for the common good what is left unspecified by nature, has the force only of human law, whereas the first type also has the force of natural law. This connection with eternal law and natural law explains the obligatory force of human law, but also furnishes a higher criterion by which human law can be judged. Thomas accepted the very basic axiom that an unjust law is no law and does not oblige. Human law always stands under the judgment of the eternal law and the natural law.[18]

However, Thomas also points out there is not an exact equation between natural law and the civil law or what others describe as the relationship between a sin and a crime. Law is ordered to the common good and therefore does not command all the acts of all the virtues, but only those that can be ordered to the common good either mediately or immediately. In this connection there is no virtue whose acts cannot be commanded by laws.[19] Likewise, it does not pertain to human law to prohibit all evils, because laws are imposed on people according to their condition. The majority of humans are not perfect; therefore, human law should not suppress all the vices, but only the more grievous vices from which the majority are able to abstain and especially those that are harmful to others, for such prohibitions are necessary for the preservation of society. Note the close connection between moral law and civil law and also the moral obligation of civil law, but also Thomas recognizes there should not be an identity between the two.[20] In another discussion Aquinas approves of Augustine's toleration and regulation of prostitution.[21]

The manuals of moral theology in a somewhat truncated way base their teachings on Aquinas. According to the typical teaching found

151

in the manuals, divine law is the objective norm and conscience is the subjective norm of morality. Over the entire universe there reigns the eternal law of God, which is the plan of divine wisdom directing all toward a final end. The eternal law is thus the source of all other laws. Corresponding to the twofold participation in revelation and in creation, eternal law or divine law is distinguished into divine positive law and natural law, the latter being the participation of the eternal law in the rational creation. Eternal law as found in the natural law cannot cover all the particular questions and changing circumstances of the individual and the community. The natural law gives the basic unchanging laws that are of universal obligation. The application of these laws to concrete sociological and historical conditions is the task of human law. In adding new prescriptions human law cannot contradict natural law. All human laws thus depend for their obliging force on the divine law and are bound up with this fundamental law by reason of their content.[22]

Formulation and Applications of the Older Approach

In light of these three considerations it is possible to understand better the formulation of the older approach to the relationship between civil law and morality. The civil law applies the natural law amidst the changing and particular cultural circumstances of a particular region either by directly promulgating the conclusions of natural law or by specifying and making determinate what has been left undetermined (e.g., which side of the street cars should use). Civil law is not exactly the same as natural law, for civil law legislates what is necessary for the common good and at times may even tolerate moral evil in order to avoid greater evil. Notice that no mention is made of the freedom and the rights of conscience of the individual, for a just law never constitutes an infringement on the true freedom of the individual. The basic thrust of this approach is to see civil law in its relationship with natural law even though there is not a perfect identity.

History, especially more contemporary history, shows that Roman Catholicism has often, although not always, urged the existence of civil laws in such questions as contraception, divorce, homosexuality, abortion, as well as social justice. Even though the theory acknowledged that civil law, since it looks to the common good, is not identical with the natural law, nevertheless, it was easy to argue that anything that is against the natural law as the plan of God will ultimately have bad consequences for society. Roman Catholics who urged the continuing validity of the Connecticut law making the use of contra-

152

ceptives a crime maintained that contraception is corrupting to the individual and furthermore undermines political morality.[23]

William J. Kenealy, in 1948, argued in favor of the Massachusetts law that forbade the sale, manufacture, exhibition, and advertising of contraceptives. He ended his remarks with the eloquent plea, "I urge all not to permit the majesty of our civil law to sanction a perversion of God's natural law."[24] In a later article, in 1963, Kenealy continues to see the civil law in relationship to the moral order and the natural law in relationship to the moral order and the natural law, but he distinguishes between private morality and public morality, with the latter coming under the power of the state. Kenealy does not support the Connecticut law that forbids the use of contraception but he approves of laws that prevent the public display of contraceptive devices in store windows. The use of public funds and public agencies to encourage and support artificial contraception is a matter of public morality, and hence he is opposed to it.[25]

The possibility of tolerating an evil to avoid a greater evil becomes an important consideration in this approach. A statement issued by the Roman Catholic Archbishop of Westminster (England), in response to the Wolfenden Report, which urged that there be no laws against homosexual actions between consenting adults in private, well illustrates how the older approach in Roman Catholic thought considers a question of morality and civil law. The Archbishop of Westminster argues that since homosexual acts are morally wrong, the state could, in view of the harm that would result to the common good from the practice of homosexuality, make such acts crimes and in no way exceed its legitimate functions. However, two questions of fact arise: Do worse evils follow if the law makes private acts of homosexuality a crime, and would a change in the present law harm the common good by seeming to condone homosexual conduct? These questions of fact are not clear, and Catholics are free to make up their own minds on these two particular questions of fact.[26] This position tolerates some moral evils because of possibly greater evils that a law against them would cause. Although the older approach in Roman Catholic thought sees the civil law primarily in light of the natural law, there is no perfect identity between them.

Toward a Revised Understanding of Civil Law

In my judgment, the older approach in Roman Catholicism to the relationship between civil law and morality is no longer acceptable. In attempting a better understanding of the relationship between law and morality it is necessary to revise some of the basic understandings

153

of law that have existed in the Roman Catholic theological understanding. Changes have already occurred in the teachings on church and state and on religious liberty, but there are still many who do not see the implications of such changes in the area of the relationship between law and morality. The change in the teaching on religious liberty and even more important the underlying changes in the basic understanding of the role and function of the state are most instructive for our purposes.

In any discussion of religious liberty it is important to recognize what precisely the term implies, for misunderstandings abound. Religious liberty means the immunity from external coercion in civil society in the worship of God, so that no one is forced to act contrary to religious beliefs and individuals are not restrained from acting in accord with their consciences in religious matters.[27] Two important developments in Roman Catholic theology lay behind the change in the teaching on religious liberty. The first involved a better understanding of the rights of conscience of the individual human person. The older denial of religious liberty in theory accepted the fact that truth was to prevail and error has no rights. However, in certain cases one could tolerate the public expression of such religious rites. "The duty of repressing moral and religious error cannot therefore be an ultimate norm of action. It must be subordinate to higher and more general norms which in some circumstances permit and even perhaps seem to indicate as the better policy toleration of error in order to promote a greater good."[28] This statement by Pope Pius XII, in 1953, was as far as the older approach could go in terms of practical toleration of what was wrong.

Some Catholic thinkers reasoned that the whole question had to be put in a different context. Such an approach did not give sufficient attention to the rights of the individual person and the freedom of conscience. An examination of the understanding of conscience, including its development within the context of Roman Catholicism, came to the conclusion that "a person has a right to follow his conscience, with freedom from state interference, in matters of religious choice, profession, and worship."[29] As the Declaration on Religious Freedom of Vatican Council II phrases it: "In all his activity a man is bound to follow his conscience faithfully. . . . It follows that he is not to be forced to act in a manner contrary to his conscience; nor, on the other hand, is he to be restrained from acting in accord with his conscience, especially in matters religious" (n.3). Thus a greater awareness of the dignity of the individual person and the rights of conscience provided a different context from which to view the question of religious liberty.

In the debates within Roman Catholicism in the 1950s and 1960s,

154

and even in the conciliar debates among those favoring religious liberty, John Courtney Murray pointed out that one school regards religious freedom as formally a theological and moral concept that has juridical consequences and begins from the single insight of the exigency of the free person for religious liberty. Among the problems with such an approach is the risk of setting afoot a futile argument about the rights of the erroneous conscience. Murray favors a second approach, which begins with a complex insight—the free human person under a government of limited powers—and thus recognizes religious freedom as formally a juridical or constitutional concept that has foundations in theology, ethics, political philosophy, and jurisprudence.[30]

According to Murray, there are four principles on which constitutional government is based. The first principle is the distinction between the sacred and the secular orders of human life. The second principle concerns the distinction between society and the state. The state is an agency that plays a limited role in society, for the purposes of the state are not coextensive with the purposes of society. The public authorities are entrusted with certain limited powers, using political means and the coercive force of law for the good of society, and these functions are defined by constitutional law in accord with the consent of the people. The third principle, following from the above consideration, is the distinction between the common good, which embraces all the social goods—spiritual and moral as well as material—that human beings pursue on earth, and the public order, which is a narrower concept whose care devolves on the limited state as such. The fourth principle is freedom under the law, which is the higher purpose of the juridical order itself. This principle can be formulated in the following way as the basic law of jurisprudence: "Let there be as much freedom, personal and social, as is possible; let there be only as much restraint and constraint, personal and social, as may be necessary for the public order."[31]

Two comments about Murray's position are in order. First, the Declaration on Religious Freedom of Vatican Council II affirms the teaching on religious liberty but wisely does not take a decisive stand on the underlying reasons for such teaching. The declaration just lists the various reasons that have been proposed by the different schools as the basis for the teaching and does not take an ultimate position on which one provides the best basis for the teaching (n. 3).

Second, it is important to recognize the changed understanding of the role and function of the state and consequently of the law Murray explicates. In his formulation there remains a danger that one does not give enough importance to the role of the state, especially in areas of social and economic justice. Some fathers at Vatican Council II expressed the same concern. The concept of public order reduces the role of the state to the role of the corner police officer after the fashion of nineteenth-century liberalism and thus denies the positive role of the state in terms of social and economic justice. The second introductory report of the fourth draft of the Declaration on Religious Freedom *(Textus reemendatus)* defended the concept of public order in matters involving religious freedom and pointed out that the text was not concerned with social questions. The right of the state to restrict personal freedom is qualitatively more limited than its right to redress social and economic injustices.[32] At the very minimum one should include here the concept of socialization that Pope John XXIII employed in his encyclical *Mater et Magistra* to balance off the principle of subsidiarity and justify the positive intervention of the state to bring about social and economic justice.[33]

These changes both in emphasizing the right to freedom of the individual conscience and in recognizing the different political structure of constitutional government, which came to the fore in the newer teaching on religious freedom, also affect our understanding of the role and function of civil law in society. The emphasis on a hierarchical ordering and a synthetic overall picture that see all the different pieces fitting together in perfect harmony under the direction of God and those who in some way are taking the place of God can no longer be the controlling concept in our understanding of the meaning of law. As a very first step the present understanding calls for the secular order to stand on its own two feet with its own finality, and it cannot be subordinated to the sacred order as in the past.

Greater importance must be given to the individual person living in society. At the same time there has been a greater recognition of the pluralistic society in which many contemporary human beings exist, for not all are in agreement about what is morally good. The function of the state and of civil law is not to direct the lives of all its citizens to the common good, and likewise the lawgiver is not the one who sovereignly directs all the individuals for the good of the whole. Our present constitutional understanding of government sees the role of the state as limited. Individuals must enjoy the freedom and creativity by which in their own way and in many other groupings they can work for the good of the whole. The law does serve the good of society, but today this means especially in areas of personal morality that the state and the law safeguard the personal freedom of the individual and restrict this freedom only when necessary.

Our present discussion is confined to questions generally associated with private morality as distinguished from social or public morality. It might be somewhat difficult at times to make an exact distinction between the two; but in general, private morality embraces those

156

actions of individuals that tend not to have much effect on others, whereas social morality involves actions which do have a much greater impact on others. In the area of social morality past Catholic approaches have rightly accentuated the need for state intervention for the common good and have denied the excesses of a laissez-faire capitalism with its distorted notion of freedom calling for no government interference in the economic life of society. However, in matters more closely associated with personal morality the action of the individual by definition does not have that much effect on others living in the society.

Formulation of a Newer Approach

The fundamental and primary criterion of the role and function of civil law in questions of personal morality is as follows: "For the rest, the usages of society are to be the usages of freedom in their full range. These require that the freedom of man be respected as far as possible, and curtailed only when and insofar as necessary." This is a direct quotation from the Declaration on Religious Freedom (n.7) and applies now in my understanding to the role of civil law in private morality just as the fathers of Vatican Council II applied it to the question of religious liberty. John Courtney Murray exultantly sees in this sentence the culmination of a developing tradition in the Roman Catholic Church. This is a statement of the basic principle of the free society that has important origins in the medieval traditions of kingship, law, and jurisprudence, but its statement by the Church has an air of blessed newness. Secular experts may well consider this to be the most important sentence in the document on religious freedom.[34]

This principle, in my judgment, is the fundamental governing criterion in the relationship of civil law and personal morality. Unfortunately, many Roman Catholics do not realize that the two fundamental changes concerning the dignity of conscience and the limited nature of constitutional government must affect and change the understanding of the nature and function of civil law. One can understand this failure, because the development has occurred so quickly and so recently that its ramifications have not been explicitly proposed in other areas. It is helpful to recall the slow and tortuous development that led to the newer understanding proposed in Vatican Council II.

In the nineteenth century the Roman Catholic Church opposed religious liberty and many of the new freedoms, as illustrated in the condemnations found in the *Syllabus of Errors*. Undoubtedly, there were excesses in the understanding of freedom proposed in the nineteenth century, as illustrated in the injustices found in laissez-faire

157

capitalism, which called for governments to respect the freedom of the economic order and not to intervene. In the twentieth century the Roman Catholic Church was faced with the growing threat of Nazism, fascism, and communism. Papal teaching in this context emphasized the freedom and rights of the individual against encroachments from the totalitarian state. This marked an important stage in the development of Roman Catholic teaching on the freedom of the individual, but one can note even as late as the pontificate of John XXIII the dawning realization of the importance of the role of freedom in human society.[35] In *Mater et Magistra,* issued in 1961, Pope John XXIII speaks of the reconstruction of social relationships in truth, justice, and love.[36] In 1963, in *Pacem in Terris,* the same pontiff adds a fourth to this triad: truth, justice, charity, and freedom.[37] Thus one can see even as late as the early 1960s that Roman Catholic teaching did not give the importance to freedom in the social life of human beings that it now attributes to it. It is only natural to realize that in the area of the role and function of civil law Catholic theology even today might not give the importance to freedom that is necessary in light of the contemporary understanding of the rights of conscience in civil society and the limited constitutional government in most contemporary societies.

What are the criteria to judge the intervention of civil law in matters of private morality? The first limit on any freedom is the responsibility of the individual person in the exercise of this freedom. We should all exercise our freedom in such a way as not to unnecessarily harm the rights and freedom of other people. However, in addition, it might be necessary for the state to intervene and place limits on the freedom of individuals. The function of the state in these matters is to safeguard the public order, and the criterion of public order guides the intervention of the law. This is in keeping with the function of the limited constitutional state. The public order includes an order of peace, an order of justice, and an order of morality.[38]

The Declaration on Religious Freedom proposes the same concept of public order with its threefold content as the criterion for legal limitations on the exercise of religious liberty.[39] Thus, for example, even in the matter of religious liberty, the state certainly has the right to intervene for the sake of domestic peace if one religion believes it is necessary for its followers to gather at 4:00 A.M. on Sunday morning and proceed with a hundred-piece band to march around the neighborhood. Since the state also exists to bring about justice, an order of justice including the rights of innocent individual persons will be a sufficient and necessary criterion for the intervention of the state. The third component of public order is an order of morality, but it is important to realize that the morality under discussion here

158

does not involve an agreement on all specifics of morality, but rather is the basic shared morality that is necessary for people to live together in society.[40]

There is another important consideration in determining the relationship between civil law and morality. This consideration involves the prudential, pragmatic, and feasible aspects of law in a pluralistic society. Within a pluralistic society one must recognize the rights of other people who might be in disagreement about the morality of a particular action. Respect for the rights of others, especially minorities, is an essential part of a proper functioning of the democratic process. If many other people in a society do not believe that something is wrong and harmful to others, this fact definitely must be taken into consideration in law-making.

In this same connection one realizes the way in which legislation is made allows for a great deal of political accommodation. For example, a legislator who believes human life is present from the moment of conception might think it more prudent to work for a law that would make abortion legitimate in the first twelve weeks of pregnancy but forbid it after this time, since in the judgment of such a legislator this particular law would be better than a law which would allow abortion on demand for a much longer period. In backing such a compromise piece of legislation, it might be possible to avoid the greater problem of no restrictions at all on abortion.

Other considerations of a feasible and more pragmatic understanding of the function of law involve the divisive effect of law on society. Even more important are the questions of enforceability and equitableness. If a law cannot be enforced, then it does not fulfill the characteristics of a truly just law. The fact that many people in a particular society at a given moment are not observing the law would be a good argument for doing away with such a law. Likewise, a law that discriminates against the poor or a particular segment of society is also a poor law. In both these cases law really is not properly exercising its function and is a cause of a general disregard for law in a particular society.

The above three criteria—as much freedom as possible for the individual, the criterion of public order to justify state intervention by law, and the recognition of pragmatic, prudential, and reasonable aspects in the law—constitute the framework for the proper understanding of the relationship between law and private morality. Note that in this understanding of law there is what some have called an idealistic function of law insofar as it must support peace, justice, and an order of morality, but there is also the recognition of the rights of freedom of individuals and at the same time the recognition of prudential and pragmatic judgments about the effectiveness and

159

function of law itself. In this way such an approach avoids the danger, on the one hand, of an idealistic approach that does not give enough importance to freedom and considerations of feasibility and, on the other hand, avoids the danger of a purely pragmatic approach that sees law as totally distinct from considerations of justice and peace and merely accepting the mores of a particular society at any given time.

Application to Abortion

The application of such criteria to particular questions will obviously allow for different possible interpretations, but it is important to recognize that these are the criteria by which civil law is to be judged. In the questions of the use of contraception or even of homosexual acts between consenting adults in private, I do not see how the criterion of public order, embracing as it does an order of peace, an order of justice, and an order of morality, justifies the intervention of civil law in these cases. However, one must admit that abortion is an entirely different case. For those who believe human life is present from the moment of conception or very early in pregnancy, then abortion involves the rights of an innocent human being, in addition to the rights of the mother. On the basis of the criterion of public order, one is totally justified in striving for a law that would prevent abortion, since this safeguards the rights of the innocent human being.

However, there are other considerations of feasibility that can be raised. What about the rights of very many people in our society (the exact number is impossible to determine) who do not believe human life is present in the fetus or at least do not believe human life is present immediately after conception? What about the fact that in most countries in which there have been very restrictive abortion laws that allow practically no abortions there has been the great problem of clandestine abortions? In other words, it seems that many people even now are flaunting laws prohibiting abortion. (In this connection it must be pointed out that many of the statistics that have been proposed as to the number of illegal abortions are often vulnerable to criticism.) There also arises the practical consideration that a law must be equitable. If a law prohibiting abortion prevents the poor from having abortions, while at the same time the rich are able to circumvent the law, then one can definitely question the equitableness of such a law. These are some of the considerations of feasibility that must enter into any discussion about a law on abortion in our contemporary society.

An understanding of the above criteria and their application to the

160

question of legislation in the matter of abortion indicates that one who believes human life is present from the moment of conception could adopt a number of different approaches to the question of the law concerning abortion. In practical terms this means that for Roman Catholics there is no such thing as *the* one Roman Catholic approach to abortion legislation. The existence of the prudential and the feasible aspect in law argues against the possibility of any immediate and necessary translation of a moral teaching into a matter of law. Roman Catholics and those in society who believe human life is present from the moment of conception can very well argue there should be a law against abortion. However, in light of some of the considerations of prudence and feasibility in a pluralistic society, one might argue there should be no law against abortion. If such a large number of people in our pluralistic society do not accept the fact that human life is present in the fetus, then one might argue there should be no law against abortion, for an abortion law would unnecessarily restrict their freedom.

My own approach to such questions is to attempt some type of accommodation. In the beginning I advocated a moderately restrictive law such as that proposed by the American Law Institute, which would allow abortion in certain particular situations. Such an approach was quite similar to the law existing in the state of Texas, which was overturned by recent Supreme Court decisions. In this same line of approach I could also support a law that would prohibit abortions after ten or twelve weeks in the development of the fetus but would also include ways of helping the mother who wants to bring the fetus to term. The important thing to recognize is that the difference between civil law and personal morality means one can truly be convinced abortion is morally wrong but still support legislation that allows for abortion. One must therefore conclude there can be no one Roman Catholic approach to the question of abortion legislation and that a good Roman Catholic legislator could vote for different types of abortion legislation.

The older Roman Catholic approach to the relationship between civil law and morality, in my judgment, is no longer viable in light of the developments pointed out above. However, despite these developments, official Roman Catholic statements unfortunately continue to adopt the older understanding of the relationship between civil law and morality. An illustration of such an approach is the Declaration on Procured Abortion, of the Sacred Congregation for the Doctrine of the Faith, issued on November 18, 1974.[41]

In its consideration on morality and the law, this declaration, in its very first paragraph, mentions many of the aspects that emerged in our discussion under the considerations of feasibility, but subsequent

161

paragraphs show the theological approach to this document to be of the older understanding of the relationship between law and morality. In paragraph 20 the document states: "It is true that civil law cannot expect to cover the whole field of morality or to punish all faults. No one expects it to do so. It must often tolerate what is in fact a lesser evil, in order to avoid a greater one." Such a consideration starts out with the understanding that the function of civil law is in terms of applying the natural law. That which is against the natural law ordinarily is also against the civil law, although it might be tolerated as a lesser evil to avoid a greater one.

The same line of reasoning appears in paragraph 21: "The law is not obliged to punish everything, but it cannot act contrary to a law which is deeper and more majestic than any human law; the natural law engraved in men's hearts by the Creator as a norm which reason clarifies and strives to formulate properly, and which one must always struggle to understand better, but which it is always wrong to contradict. Human law can abstain from punishment, but it cannot make right what would be opposed to the natural law, for this opposition suffices to give the assurance that a law is no longer a law." Insisting that civil law cannot act contrary to the natural law does not accept the understanding of civil law as ensuring as far as possible the freedom of the individual. The central framework of the discussion should not be that the civil law does not contradict the natural law; rather, it is the question of the civil law protecting and preserving as far as possible the freedom of the individual and interfering only when public order requires it. The civil law does not sanction actions contrary to natural law, but rather it safeguards the freedom of the individual in areas where public order is not involved.

Paragraph 22 of this declaration goes on to say that a Christian cannot take part in a propaganda campaign in favor of a law allowing abortion or vote for it. Again, on the basis of what has been said above, I would have to disagree with this particular conclusion. However, I definitely agree with the declaration when it asserts that doctors and nurses should not find themselves obliged to cooperate closely in abortions, but rather should have the right not to do so.

In contrast to the approach taken in the declaration issued by the Sacred Congregation for the Doctrine of the Faith, in 1974, a Declaration of the Permanent Council of the French Bishops on Abortion, issued in June 1973, adopts a somewhat more nuanced methodological approach to the question. The slightly more nuanced approach is indicated in the following statements. "In extending the legal possibilities of abortion, the legislator risks the appearance of encouraging and provoking a lesser estimate of human life."[42] "Even if a law is not destined by itself to pose moral rules, the legislator is not

162

able to deny to the measures which he takes an import or bearing on this order."[43]

Within the context of Roman Catholic thought not only significant theoretical reasons but also important practical concerns make it imperative to follow the second approach to the question of the relationship of law and morality in a pluralistic society. Such an approach indicates that Roman Catholics accept an understanding of the function of civil law that can also be maintained by many others in our society. Many disagreements will continue to exist about the law on abortion, but the tone of the public discussion will be better if both Roman Catholics and others accept the same general understanding of the function of civil law. Likewise, the approach advocated here dispels somewhat the charge that Roman Catholics are trying to force their morality on others. The adoption of the second approach to the question of law and morality by no means denies the fact that one can argue for a law condemning all abortion, but it does argue for a methodological approach that does not see the function of civil law primarily in terms of the application and reinforcement of natural law. This essay has been limited to discussing the basis, formulation, and application of two different approaches, and has opted for the second approach to understanding the relationship between civil law and private morality. Elsewhere I have discussed the contemporary literature on this subject.[44] There remains only one final question to be discussed.

Reaction to the Recent Supreme Court Decision

The Supreme Court decision in January 1973 decided that there could be no legislation against abortion in the first trimester, and in the second trimester, states could make laws only insofar as this is necessary to protect the health of the mother. Only in the third trimester did the rights of the fetus come into focus.[45] As noted above, I would have preferred a different approach to the law on abortion, even though I did not think a law absolutely prohibiting abortion would be a good one. In the midst of the conflicting opinions in our society, I would have hoped for a more compromise solution in which even greater emphasis might have been given to the rights of the fetus.

Recent literature has indicated many disagreements with the reasoning behind the decision of the Supreme Court.[46] I am not competent to comment on the legal and medical difficulties that have been raised against the reasoning of the court. For example, it is said without nuance that ancient religions did not ban abortion or that there has always been strong support for the view that life does not begin until birth.[47] It seems to me that both these statements are historically inadequate. Likewise, the court does not properly interpret the delayed animation theory.[48]

Justice Blackmun, in writing the opinion of the court, maintained: "We need not resolve the difficult question of when life begins."[49] In my judgment, for all practical purposes the court has solved the question of when human life begins, at least in terms of the legal protection of such life. The legal protection of life for all practical purposes is the only way in which society can recognize the existence of human life. In addition, Chief Justice Warren Burger, in his concurring opinion, concludes with the statement: "Plainly, the Court today rejects any claim that the Constitution requires abortion on demand."[50] This seems to try to twist the thrust of the decision that definitely does allow abortion on the woman's request for the first six months of pregnancy, even though in the second trimester some restrictions can be made but only in terms of the health of the mother.

Despite my strong disagreements with the reasoning proposed by the court, and despite the fact that my own approach to abortion law would be different, I can understand why the court has come to its final conclusion. In our American society the primary purpose of the law is to protect the freedom of individual people, and the benefit of the doubt must be given to this freedom. When one is confronted with an issue in which a very large number of Americans believe they should have freedom, then one can argue on the benefit of the doubt that their rights should prevail. It is difficult to determine what is the exact sentiment about the feelings of Americans on abortion. The two states that did hold a referendum on such subjects voted against liberalizing abortion laws. Public opinion polls seem to indicate a standoff on this particular issue, but if the court were assessing the general feeling of the population as being equally divided on this particular issue, then in light of the need to give the benefit of the doubt to the freedom of the individual their final conclusion makes sense. Here, too, I would rather have seen the period for abortions restricted to the first trimester, but the final conclusion of the court is understandable in terms of the legal tendency to give the benefit of the doubt to the freedom of the individual.

In the period following the decision of the Supreme Court a number of Americans have called for an amendment to the Constitution in the matter of abortion. Senator Jesse Helms, Republican of North Carolina, has submitted an amendment stating that every human being subject to the jurisdiction of the United States or of any state shall be deemed from the moment of fertilization to be a person and entitled to the right of life. Senator James Buckley, Conservative of New York, has proposed an amendment specifying that the word

164

person as it applies to due protection in the Constitution applies to all human beings, including their unborn offspring at every stage of their biological development, irrespective of age, health, function, or condition of dependency. But the Buckley amendment, unlike the Helms amendment, allows for abortion in the case of an emergency, when a reasonable medical certainty exists that continuation of pregnancy will cause the death of the mother.

It is important to recognize and underline once again that opposition to abortion is not identified only with the Roman Catholic Church in the United States. In fact, in the matter of the morality of abortion there are many Protestant ethicians who take a comparatively conservative stance; other Americans have also decried the Supreme Court decisions. However, many Roman Catholics, including the Catholic hierarchy of the United States, have advocated a constitutional amendment to change the decision of the Supreme Court. I personally am opposed to efforts aimed at obtaining a constitutional amendment. For one thing, it does not seem that a constitutional amendment stands any hope of success. Even though one might argue that a majority of Americans disagree with the Supreme Court decision, I am sure they will never be able to agree on what the law should be. Some will argue for a strict law from the moment of conception, whereas others will allow for some exceptions and perhaps not want to place the beginning of human life at the moment of conception. It seems to me impossible that a majority of Americans could ever agree on precisely what the abortion law should be. Again, I recognize the right of any American to work for a constitutional amendment in this area, but I personally am opposed to such an approach.

In light of the present situation, I believe it is imperative for the Roman Catholic Church to recognize as clearly as possible the relationship between civil law and morality. There is a prophetic or teaching aspect to civil law, but civil law cannot be seen primarily in terms of an application of natural law. Rather, civil law must ensure that the "freedom of man be respected as far as possible, and curtailed only when and insofar as necessary."[51] The proper role of civil law is more limited than in the older Catholic understanding. The Roman Catholic Church cannot and should not always depend on civil law to back up its own teachings, but rather, through education, service, and other means, should strive to develop an ethos in which its own moral teachings and values can be effectively mediated to its members. Even now I think the efforts of Roman Catholics could be better directed toward this work of education and service rather than absorbed by attempts to amend the Constitution.

Personal Decisions and Social Policies in a Pluralist Society

Roger L. Shinn

I

YOU HAVE ASSIGNED ME a topic that presents an insoluble issue. I am constantly amazed that people think they know the solution. The issue is riddled with authentic dilemmas. Yet we cannot give up on it. Some nonsolutions can destroy a society or civilization; others make life and some social progress possible.

Every society demonstrates some interplay between personal decisions and social policies. Ideally, of course, there is a harmony between personal and social good. In Marx's utopian hope "the free development of each is the condition for the free development of all." Actually, there is some tension between personal freedom and social demands. Societies work out various balances between the two. And the balances change from time to time.

Our society, for example, allows more freedom than most in some areas. It is fairly easy (despite the FBI and the CIA) to ridicule the President (although not to influence him); people can propagate heresies that once might have brought death; they can get rich on

---

Reprinted with permission from *The Perkins Journal,* Vol. 27, No. 1 (Fall 1973), pp. 58–63.

ROGER L. SHINN is professor of social ethics, Union Theological Seminary, New York, New York.

sexual exhibitionism that has often been forbidden. However, this same society restricts freedoms that have often been familiar. It requires children to go to schools that may or may not do them good; it tells people by red and green lights when they must stop and go; it forbids them to own dogs without buying a license. I mention such examples simply to show that the balance between social and personal decisions is not fixed once for all; it moves about, depending on social organizations and situations.

Even so, in our society the problem has new dimensions. One is that we are an avowedly pluralistic society. In this we are not entirely new; post-enlightenment societies generally are more or less pluralistic. But with our variety of creeds, subcultures, and interest groups we have pushed pluralism pretty far. Some exult in it and want persons and groups to do their own thing. Others may say, like historian William L. O'Neill, "This country has all the diversity it can stand."[1] In either case, despite the dominating effect of mass media and mass production, we are pluralistic.

Another new dimension is the speed of change. The fixed points by which people have often guided their lives are no longer sure. Walter Lippmann has described the "feeling" of modern people "that almost nothing they think today about social, political and worldly morals is sure to be valid in thirty years."[2]

When ethical traditions, centuries old, are overthrown in a decade or two, people must wonder: Is this an exhilarating act of liberation? Or is it the swift disintegration of a decadent civilization? Or is it a mixture of many things? And how do we judge which it is?

In such a setting we are thinking about abortion as it enters into personal decision and social policy. I should like to be both fair and candid in discussing so controversial an issue. I should like to describe opposing positions with enough fairness that their advocates will feel they have been genuinely represented—even though, I'm sure, without all the eloquence the advocates might wish. I should also like to be candid in stating my own judgments. I don't know whether I can be both fair and candid, but I think I have a better chance to be fair if I am candid than if I am not.

II

Let us get at the subject by looking at a popular slogan. "You can't legislate morality." We hear this often. Actually, I doubt anybody believes it *entirely*. One might answer, "If you can't legislate morality, what can you legislate?" Apart from purely administrative legislation (income taxes are due on April 15 rather than April 10 or 20) the reason for legislation is to achieve justice. And justice is a moral issue. There are moral reasons for laws against murder, robbery, fraud, denial of civil rights, race discrimination, etc. While no law is ever 100 percent effective, law has some effect in controlling harmful behavior and securing human rights. To some extent there is a possibility and desirability of enforcing morality. In recent American history the role of law has been *extended* into some areas of racial and economic justice that were once left to personal decisions of the powerful.

But probably nobody would want all his or her personal moral beliefs legislated. Some kinds of morality (forgive your enemies seventy times seven times) are unenforceable by nature. On other moral issues people should have freedom to disagree about morality and to live by their own beliefs. In recent American history the moral role of law has been *withdrawn* from some areas; for example, there is an increasing belief that the private sexual behavior of consenting adults should not be the business of police and courts.

How do we decide what morality to legislate and what to leave to personal decision? There is some help in dividing the question. First, what morality is it *right* to legislate? Second, what morality is it *possible* to legislate?

III

On the issue of rightness both the advocates and opponents of legalized abortion pitch their cases on moral grounds. My assignment, of course, is not to argue a conviction about abortion, but to ask what a society does when its members disagree in their convictions. But to do this, I must look at the moral logic of opposing cases.

The case for freedom of abortion centers on the moral right of a woman to make a decision on an issue that concerns her intimately. She has the overwhelming stake in her own pregnancy. To be forced to give birth to a child, against her will, is an overwhelming violation of her freedom. Granted that everyone's freedom is limited by some moral, legal, and physical restraints, this is a peculiarly personal and immensely important infringement of freedom. Morality and government may tax away incomes, regulate conduct in countless ways, even draft people into armies and send them to death; but none of these cases infringes on inner personal life quite so intensely as the requirements to bear a child. This should be voluntary. Coercion at this point is a violation of dignity and of selfhood.

It is sometimes argued that—except in cases of rape—nobody forces women to become pregnant, that they should exercise their freedom of choice prior to pregnancy, and that after pregnancy they should carry the baby to birth. To the woman, trapped in an unwanted pregnancy, this course of action seems to victimize her. Whether pregnant because of ignorance, accident, error, or sin, she is not the sole cause of her pregnancy; but she is solely pregnant.

168

Furthermore, thousands have done what she did and have escaped pregnancy. To insist that she must see her act through to its consequences is to single her out when others are escaping. Again, her freedom and dignity are violated.

Those who take this position vary in some of the reasoning by which they support it. Most argue that the embryo or fetus is not a person and does not have the moral rights of a person. The most militant case holds that the woman has the sole right over her own body—that she has the same rights over a fetus that she has over her tonsils, teeth, or toenails. Probably this case is not usually intended literally. Biologically, every cell in the fetus is distinguishable by its genetic constitution from every cell in the mother's body. And, as Leon Kass has pointed out, nobody argues that a pregnant woman has a right over her own body to take thalidomide.[3] However, it may still be persuasive to argue that a pregnant woman has a moral obligation, if she bears a child, to do what she can for the health of the child —without arguing that she has a moral obligation to bear the child.

A more moderate case maintains that the fetus is a potential person, but not fully a person—certainly not a person who, like the mother, can think and feel emotions, envision futures with hope or despair, agonize over various possibilities, make decisions and take responsibility for them. Hence the rights of the woman are more important than whatever rights the fetus may have.

Let us now turn to an opposing case. The ethical opposition to abortion, as expressed in many times and places, affirms that the fetus is a person with a moral claim to life or a potential person entitled to some share in human dignity and sanctity. Often in human history the protest against abortion has expressed a moral sensitivity to the value of human life, actual or potential.

Thus Christians, in the ancient Mediterranean world, set themselves against the prevalent infanticide and abortion. Their faith and ethic, with its biblical concern for the poor and the weak, extended to infants and the unborn. Eventually, this ethic became widely accepted in Western societies, although it was never entirely heeded. There were, in fact, debates within the church about the exact time when a fetus became a person; so there was no consistent judgment that an abortion of an early fetus was the equivalent of infanticide.

Today, it is sometimes argued, modern biological and genetic knowledge has resolved these traditional debates. At conception a new genotype appears, radically different from the genotype of the mother. Landrum Shettles, M.D., of Columbia University, famous for his bold approach to genetic experimentation and uninhibited by "any known religious influence," nevertheless argues that "a new composite individual is started at the moment of fertilization." He continues: "From the moment of union of the germ cells, there is under normal development a living, definite, going concern. To interrupt a pregnancy at any stage is like cutting the link of a chain; the chain is broken no matter where the link is cut." Dr. Shettles does not himself use this reasoning as a basis for a moral judgment, but he does object to basing arguments for abortion on denial of "a truth."[4]

Persons and groups morally opposed to abortion do not necessarily believe that their conviction should be enacted into law. But sometimes they do, on the ground that one function of law is to protect human rights. If the fetus is a person, he or she is entitled to the rights of persons.

Opponents of legalized abortion often maintain that sensitivity to human rights has meant a continuous expansion of these rights to include persons not formerly protected by law. Rights once reserved in some societies to adult white male land-owners have been extended to include women, children, the poor, and black people. The question of whether a person is wanted or not is irrelevant to human rights. In some times and places the unwanted have included many groups: barbarians, Jews, heretics, female children, racial enemies, the sick, prisoners, and others. A humane society recognizes the right of all people. To deny human rights to the fetus is a backward step, a regression to the attitude that only those have rights who have the power to demand and enforce them.

Both these cases—the case for freedom of abortion and the case against abortion—involve a metaphysical judgment about what it means to be a person. We might prefer not to build law on perennially debatable metaphysical judgments. Yet it is hard to detach morality from metaphysics. The reasons why we think it morally different to eat steers than to eat human beings are metaphysical reasons.

There can be attempts to whittle away at the problem without resolving the metaphysical issue. The National Council of Churches is trying. On its books is a resolution of 1961: "Protestant Christians are agreed in condemning abortion or any method which destroys human life except when the health or life of the mother is at stake." Now the National Council of Churches is embarrassed because many of its members are not "agreed" on this stand. But agreement on a substitute is hard to find. One current attempt is to state that pluralism means no religious community should try to enact its beliefs "unless there is within the community a moral consensus on the issue or it can be empirically proven that society itself is harmed by the act proscribed." But there are gaping holes in this proposal. First, the National Council of Churches has often acted against popular moral consensus. Second, is the moral issue whether society is harmed or whether persons are harmed? And what is empirical proof on such an issue?

Suppose we agree that pluralistic society is possible only if groups refrain from trying to impose their peculiar (sometimes called sectarian) standards on other groups whose consciences differ from their own. On this basis the Rev. Robert Drinan, S. J., has felt that he could consistently uphold the traditional Roman Catholic objection to abortion, yet urge that abortion be removed from legislative control. If everyone could agree on such a proposal, the issue would be nicely simplified. This was the solution of *The New York Times,* commenting on the Supreme Court decision of 1973: "Nothing in the Court's approach ought to give affront to persons who oppose all abortion for reasons of religion or individual conviction. They can stand as firmly as ever for those principles, provided they do not seek to impede the freedom of those with an opposite view."[5]

But this reasoning is surely simplistic. If a person or group honestly believes abortion is the killing of persons, there is no moral comfort in being told, "Nobody requires you to kill. We are only giving permission to others to do what you consider killing." The protestor will reply that one function of law is to protect rights of minorities—of religious minorities, racial minorities, political minorities, persecuted and disregarded minorities, powerless minorities, and—in this case —of unborn persons.

Hence I see why those who believe abortion is the killing of a person cannot be satisfied with the glib answer that the present ruling does nothing to interfere with their moral convictions. For this reason, I think the present arguments, not only about the morality but also about the legality of abortion, represent a real conflict of values and convictions that will not easily be reconciled. The most we can expect, in the present situation, is a way of living with conflicts.

IV

This brings me to the second question: what is it possible to legislate? I have already said that no legislation is 100 percent enforceable. But some failures of legislation throw the legislation into question.

The total prevention of abortion is apparently not a social possibility. In most modern industrialized societies abortion is a fact, a conspicuous widespread fact. When such societies discourage abortion, either through legal restrictions or through moral inhibitions that affect the practice of medicine, they do not eliminate abortion, but they limit access to it.

Thus abortion is frequently available for the wealthy, the sophisticated, and all who know how to maneuver through the institutions of society. It is less available to others. Illegal abortions, although common enough in human experience, are likely to be dangerous. They may take place in a criminal subculture that is not concerned for the health or the personal well-being of the women involved. Abortion can be made available with safety, compassion, human concern, and something approaching equality of access to all.

Those who want freedom of abortion, out of concern for the freedom of women to make their own decisions, will certainly want abortion accessible to all. Some, who have severe moral reservations about abortion, may still argue that, in a world where abortion is frequent, it should be equally available to all under optimal conditions.

One requirement of law is usually that it rise out of a wide moral consensus in society. Law need not represent unanimity; in fact, when there is unanimity, law is scarcely necessary. But law must rest on a fairly broad basis, not on particular beliefs that are not widely shared. There may be exceptions: civil rights legislation has required some communities to act contrary to their dominant beliefs including their professed moral beliefs. But even in such cases the law usually has appealed to a very fundamental moral principle, often also a constitutional principle, that people were reluctant to deny, even though in their prejudices they temporarily opposed it. I think it is a fact that there is no such consensus in this society about the immorality of abortion or about its fundamental presupposition that a fetus is a person possessed of human rights. In such a case I think laws based on presuppositions not widely shared are futile.

Thus I find the Supreme Court decision a reasonably adequate framework for this society at this point in history. I am not arguing that it was well researched and well written. Nor am I sure that it was good judicial practice; it may be argued that the court was not so much interpreting the Constitution as it was legislating in a sticky controversy. What I am saying is that the decision offers a better way of living with a profound conflict of moral convictions than most alternatives.

The court gives the clear primary to the freedom of the woman until the point of viability of the fetus. After that, it permits—but does not require—states to recognize rights of the fetus when they do not interfere with "the life or health of the mother." My own moral belief is that the fetus has *some* rights, especially in the later stages of development, but that the woman also has rights to freedom. My own preference would be for weighting the law on the side of the woman's rights, even when the fetus is viable, not because I think the rights of the fetus are insignificant but because I think the problems of

172

defining the health of the mother are extremely difficult. There is something morally problematic in rounding up panels of doctors to judge such subtle issues as whether a woman's mental health will or will not be harmed by continuing a pregnancy. Most physicians find late abortions abhorrent and are inclined to refuse to do them; so total freedom for the woman is not easy to achieve. All this means that laws and legal procedures are never perfect; they are more often ways for living with problems than ways for solving them.

Whatever the details of the legal systems, which vary from state to state, my conviction is that they should make allowance for conscientious objectors among doctors and nurses. People should not be required to participate in abortions against their own consciences. The question of hospitals is more difficult. In a city with several hospitals I see no reason why a hospital should not be permitted on moral grounds to refuse to do abortions, free from legal or financial sanctions governmentally imposed. In small communities that have only one hospital, more painful compromises may be necessary, and I am not sure what the best answers are.

V

A final comment concerns the social context of human decisions. The social context has much to do with the options available to people, the pressures they feel, and their moral imaginations. No matter how much people may talk about freedom of decision, the culture is operative in their decisions. As Margaret Mead has put it, culture has everything to do with decisions on a question like abortion.

Consider two examples. The first is the effect of social injustice. I have touched on this question already. Some representatives of minority groups feel that the movement to liberalize abortion is aimed against them. Others say that limitations on abortion victimize them. Both could be right. Our society works things out so that *any* policy on abortion is likely to work against the people who suffer injustice. Hence I conclude that abortion *per se* is not a racial or class issue; but in a society marked by racial and class differences, it becomes such an issue. The arguments on both sides of the issue may be veiled expressions of class interest. As a test of whether they are that, I would use two questions. To the opponents of abortion, I ask: what are you doing to improve the quality of life for the children that you insist should be born? To the advocates of freedom of abortion, I ask: what are you doing to enhance the freedom of those who want to bear children but feel the pinch of poverty when they try to take care of their children? I do not claim that these questions have simple answers, but I do claim that they are important. The case *for* or *against* liberal abortion policies, although sometimes insincere, can be an expression of human concern.

Second, there are the moral and social pressures on people. A society may so impose pressures as to virtually dictate conclusions. It may idealize large families or small families. It may make abortion shameful and childbirth a mark of honor; or it may make motherhood for an unmarried woman a sign of shame while abortion (especially if done in secret) is no dishonor. When people make decisions about abortion, they make them in a cultural context that does much to shape the decision. Recently so ardent a champion of freedom of abortion as Howard Moody has said that by now it is perhaps more important to give some women the freedom to bear children than to give them the freedom for abortion.

VI

I began by saying that you had assigned me a topic embodying an insoluble issue: "personal decisions and social policies in a pluralist society." So I make no apology for failing to solve it.

But I also said that some nonsolutions can destroy a society, while others keep social life possible. One part of any morality, in situations of moral conflict, is the grace to recognize that people who oppose us may be acting out of a moral concern as authentic as ours. Such grace I commend to all parties in the continuing controversies over public policy on abortion.

18

A Theological Response to Fundamentalism on the Abortion Issue

Paul D. Simmons

A NEW AND FRIGHTENING FACTOR has been added to the politics of abortion: the powerful movement of fundamentalists into the antiabortion cause. What is frightening about this development is the way religious fervor has been combined with reactionary political movements. The result is a type of neofascism that threatens the very foundations of American life.

What Is Fundamentalism?

Fundamentalism must be described not only on the basis of doctrine, but in terms of its spirit or style. Its five doctrinal bases were set forth in *The Fundamentals*, published between 1910 and 1915.

This essay has been adapted by the editor from an address delivered at the Symposium on the Theology of Pro-Choice in the Abortion Decision, sponsored by Religious Leaders for a Free Choice, and the Religious Coalition on Abortion Rights, which took place at Stephen Wise Free Synagogue, in New York on October 9, 1980. Reprinted with permission from *Church and Society* (March–April 1981), pp. 22–35. Portions of this essay are to be published in *The Bible and Bioethics* by Paul D. Simmons (Philadelphia: Westminster Press, 1982).

PAUL D. SIMMONS is associate professor of Christian ethics, Southern Baptist Theological Seminary, Louisville, Kentucky.

175

Central among them is the notion of biblical inerrancy and infallibility, which is the current test for orthodox belief and for Christian fellowship in this group. However, the spirit of Fundamentalism is even more determinative of the nature of the movement. It is a mind-set or temperament—a certain style of religious mentality or perspective characterized by an arrogance that considers itself normative in all matters of theology and morals. It is a type of Gnosticism. It is ideological, intransigent, and inflexible, expecting and priding itself on doctrinal and moral conformity among its churches and their affiliated institutions.

Fundamentalism is a religious zeal that sees itself as God's movement or agent for the salvation of the world. Thus Protestant Fundamentalism finds kindred spirits in every religion of the world, from Torquemada to the Ayatollah Khomeini and various sectarian and cultic leaders of fringe movements in mainline religions.

Historically, Fundamentalism is a product of Puritanism, frontier revivalism, and the scientific revolution. Puritanism and revivalism shaped its moralizing and reformation-minded temper. Modern science provided Fundamentalism's reason for being by negation. Fundamentalism is profoundly biased against science and any world view that might be informed by scientific perspectives, such as evolution. Thus its defining virtue is that of resisting modernism and humanism in all their forms. Those persons or movements that do not conform to its standards of orthodoxy and orthopraxy are labeled modernists or liberals, and become the subjects of intensive opposition and resistance, even to the point of exclusion or banning —whether from church, denomination, or politics.

The flip side of this mentality is the martyr syndrome. As with the followers of the ayatollah, fundamentalists are willing to die for their cause. Even in defeat, they consider they have won because they are the saints of God being persecuted for their faith. They are never open to correction, because they have their own accrediting agencies. They may be victorious or defeated, but they are right in either case.

Fundamentalism and the Abortion Issue

These characteristics are discernible in the current involvement of fundamentalists in the abortion debate; not since the Prohibition era have they been so involved politically. Fundamentalist preachers find common cause in opposing abortion, the Equal Rights Amendment, gay rights, sex education in public schools, drugs, pornography, SALT II, the department of education, and cuts in defense spending.[1]

Thus New Right religion aims to forge a coalition of nearly 30 million conservative Christians with right-wing politics. Their platform is pro-God, pro-family, and pro-America. They are aggressive, affluent, highly organized, and ambitious, aiming to take control of legislative centers of power by 1985.[2] It amounts to a coalition of ultraconservative religion, laissez-faire capitalism, and American nationalism. The result is a fervent religious movement that could equally pass for a reactionary political movement—a type of neofascism.

This summary of the fundamentalist antiabortion movement is sufficient to show the nature of its spirit or mentality, the sources of its power and influence, and the alliances it has formed. It also helps to focus a theological ethical response to three major areas that form the foundation of Fundamentalism's efforts at political and moral reform: (1) civil religion, (2) doctrine of providence, and (3) the fetus as person.

Fundamentalism and Civil Religion

Civil religion is the emotional, if not ideological, commitment to American nationalism as the most concrete expression of God's will for governmental life. It is a simple identification of Christianity with nationalism—a "God with us, for us, all the way" mentality. This is a peculiar brand of Puritanism mixing religious zeal with political leverage to reform society. At stake is what fundamentalists regard as the central moral issues of the time—abortion being a primary concern. This gives them common ground for a coalition with the antiabortion stance of traditional Roman Catholics and creates a powerful voting bloc. Never before have these two groups been allies in American politics.

Harold O.J. Brown stated the position this way: "Law and public policy in our country should be in harmony with the fundamental Biblical principles of Judaeo-Christian civilization."[3] Wrapped up in this statement are several assumptions basic to civil religion: (1) that public policy should be based on religious perspectives, (2) that the policies advocated are those taught in the Bible, and (3) that America is and should be a Judaeo-Christian civilization.

The problem is this betrays a theocratic underpinning that does not build on the ideal of religious freedom. Church and state may remain separate institutionally, as the fundamentalists claim, while religious pluralism is being denied. The uniqueness of the American experiment lies not in religious toleration, but in religious freedom. This means freedom *of* religion from political interference, freedom *from* religious tyranny or the imposition of religious dogma, and freedom *for* religion to exercise its prophetic and missionary tasks in society. Fundamentalists have strongly asserted freedom of religion. Their political activism was launched by their reaction to efforts by the Internal Revenue Service to tax Christian schools that did not set racial quotas for their student bodies. They rightly saw this as undue governmental interference in religious matters.

It is the second tenet that is violated by fundamentalistic fervor. Their advocacy of prayers in public school classrooms and of placing the ten commandments in every classroom are the most serious points at which their church-state ideas may be challenged. James Wall[4] and Ellen Goodman[5] among others have wondered aloud whether an uneasy "toleration" may not be replacing a hard-earned, dearly treasured right of religious liberty.

The threat of persecution and of oppression in the United States seems not to be so much from government toward religious groups as religious intolerance using the arm of government power to persecute others. As Roland Hegstad put it strongly: "History tells me that persecution comes, generally, not from bad people trying to make other people bad, but from good people trying to make other people good."[6]

This is an ancient and sordid story in Christian history—a mentality based on what Roland Bainton called the crusade ethic. Whether the "war" is fought against foreign enemies of state or against domestic enemies of morality, it has four characteristics: (1) it is a holy cause, (2) it is fought with God as leader, (3) the crusaders are holy and the enemies are unholy, and (4) the war is to be prosecuted unsparingly.[7]

This tunnel-visioned approach to morality is willing to compromise the many small truths for the sake of the one truth being pursued. Anything goes as long as it serves the end being sought.

We cannot fault the fundamentalists on efforts to be politically involved. They are right in saying that separation of church and state does not mean separation of God and government. A great deal of criticism leveled at them is either misguided or motivated by jealousy of power and influence. Fundamentalists have heard the liberal message that Christians should be involved in politics, and they are doing so with a vengeance.

The problem is fundamentalist civil religion allies itself with the most fervent forms of nationalistic pride. For fundamentalists, America is God's chosen nation of all those on the face of the earth. Its special place is one of election and grace, but its task is to be the leader in world commerce and strength. A positivistic reading of history has traced God's movement among the nations from Israel, the Roman Empire, Germany, Great Britain, and now the United States. The decline of nations in the past is related to moral disintegration and loss of the sense of manifest destiny in God's plan for the world. That

America might be bypassed as the bearer of the torch of God among the nations of the earth is a genuine fear of Fundamentalism.

This helps to explain the commitment to a strong military and a hawkish foreign policy. America's enemies are God's enemies, and they are to be resisted with all the ferocity of Old Testament holy war. These enemies may be internal or external. Secularists, humanists, modernists, and liberals, as well as atheists, agnostics, and others who support immoral policies, are a danger to America and are the enemies of God.

Serious objections need to be raised concerning fundamentalist civil religion.

1. *America is not a Christian country, but a country in which many Christians happen to live.* America, or every country on earth, is called of God to seek justice and serve the common good of humanity. This is not a place of special privilege, but a special responsibility. Civil religion is idolatrous because it substitutes temporal loyalties for eternal verities. Identifying the Judaeo-Christian posture with American nationalism is to lose the transcendent and absolute nature of the biblical faith. For both Jews and Christians, loyalty to God must transcend any earthly loyalty (Acts 5:28).

2. The crusade ethic is *foreign to the teachings of Jesus and contrary to a Christian commitment to the lordship of Christ.* God is the creator of all the people of the earth and wills the redemption of every nation. God sides exclusively with no country on the basis of ideology or national identity. It happens that some political systems are more influenced by the Christian tradition than others. But none perfectly embodies the will of God. To decide that America's enemies are God's enemies is to substitute nationalistic ideology for Christian theology and proclaim a pagan god over the nation who is not the God of all nations. Luke declared that God has made all nations (Acts 17:26), and Paul said that in Christ we are all one (Ephesians 2:11–18).

3. *The integrity of strategy and the moral acceptability of means* is as important as the desirability of certain goals or ends. Those who willingly distort the truth to pursue their moralistic objectives need to be reminded that "Satan is the father of all lies" (John 8:44) and that Jesus calls his followers to truth (John 16:13; 1 John 1:6). Bearing false witness violates a fundamental command of God (Exodus 20:6). We cannot be saved as long as we have no regard for the truth (Proverbs 6:17). The kingdom of God cannot be built on the shifting sands of deceit and falsehood; it is present only where there is

integrity. We are reminded of Reinhold Niebuhr's warning that "the temper and integrity with which the political fight is waged is more important for the health of the society than any particular policy."

4. *Lack of concern for justice.* The fundamentalist stress on such moralistic issues as abortion misses the great moral problems of the day, for example, racism, injustice, the threat of nuclear war, and world hunger. Christians are called to work for peace and justice (Matthew 5:9; Romans 14:17; John 14:27). They are to pray for enemies (Matthew 4:44–48), not attempt to destroy them.

Such political policies have been pursued by extremist political groups for years. Such groups have now been able to exploit the political influence of fundamentalists by appealing to their ardent nationalism and sense of morality. The minimal commitment to justice in the religious movement gives it no ethical posture by which to analyze its political alliances.

Abortion and the Providence of God

One of the most glaring weaknesses in the fundamentalists' theology regarding abortion is its doctrine of providence. What is at issue is the way in which God is related to the entire process of conception and birth or the processes of nature as such. For fundamentalists, God is the cause and power of all that is; God governs all natural processes. This is important for them in supporting the absolutism of their stance against abortion. Not only is the conceptus regarded as of equal value and personhood with the woman, conception is the consequence of the act of God. "What, therefore, God hath joined together, let no person put asunder" is, for fundamentalists, a biblical principle applicable to the abortion debate.

What is at stake in the fundamentalists' posture is a Calvinistic stress on the sovereignty of God. This stress combines theological notions of the power and activity of God with a type of law of nature, a combination similar to but without the sophistication of the natural-law theory in traditional Roman Catholic thought. The "causal connection between sexual intercourse and conception . . . is simply the means whereby God, the first cause of all things, gives his blessing."[8] In other words, however it happens in nature is the way God does it.

This view of providence poses profound theological problems. First, the goodness of God is compromised in favor of God's power. To argue seriously that God either causes or permits rape or incest and consequent pregnancy, or that God *causes* every hideous anomaly

180

is to say blasphemous and heretical things about God. Central to the teaching of Jesus was the idea that God is love and goodness. Jesus emphatically denounced and refuted the traditional theology that God caused evil things to happen. He drew a very simple test for deciding: "If you then, who are evil, know how to give good gifts to your children, how much more will your Father who is in heaven give good things to those who ask him? [Matt. 7:11]."

For fundamentalists, it is more acceptable to portray God as cruel than to suggest God may not be in total control. To blame evil on God is to risk confusing the work of Beelzebub with that of the Holy Spirit (Matthew 12:22–36; Luke 11:14–23). Jesus made it plain that an accounting would be made of those who attribute evil to God and good to evil.

One of the hidden agendas in Fundamentalism is its reactionary posture toward science. Regarding providence, for instance, it fears the scientific notions of chance and randomness that work in the creative process and thus reacts strongly to any notion that God is not totally in control.

A second problem posed by this notion of providence deals with the rôle of persons as stewards in the processes of nature and medical science. Fundamentalists portray people as the passive victims of whatever may befall. God only gives strength to bear the tragedy. It is unthinkable to argue that people, made in the image of God, may have to make some God-like decisions regarding our stewardship of procreative powers, as in abortion. This is forbidden territory for human intervention.

Notice the contradiction. People are simply to accept whatever hand of cards they are dealt genetically, but everything possible should be done to keep such persons alive. Although fundamentalists argue that nature's way is God's way, they also argue that doctors should intervene to keep nature from terminating a deformed fetus; they cannot have it both ways. To adopt the passive, noninterventionist posture is to undermine religious support for all of medical science.

Is it not more consistent to follow the clue given in the biblical doctrine of stewardship? As stewards, people work with God for the good of the entire created world—people, nature, and world alike. Our knowledge of the processes that hinder or help gives a divine mandate to make choices that help rather than hinder. We know mistakes are made in nature, that genetic codes can become terribly confused. Choice, not chance, becomes the divine mandate. We cannot be indifferent to the plight of persons who may be cursed by radical genetic deformity. We make decisions to abort as stewards of genetic knowledge and as guardians of the future.

The third problem with this view of providence concerns its limited and inadequate view of grace. Donald Shoemaker declares that God gives "sustaining grace" to those afflicted with pregnancy by rape or incest and to those bearing fetuses that are radically deformed. That God does provide sustaining grace in such situations we do not doubt. But does grace not also give permission to act in spite of ambiguity and with boldness lay hold of the promise of forgiveness?

Karl Barth understood the paradox in the command of God with regard to abortion. He set the subject in the context of "The Protection of Life" and explained "the great summons to halt issued by the command," forbidding the willful taking of human life.[9] Barth thundered God's No! to any such action.

But there is another side to God's command, said Barth. After hearing the No, we must be prepared "to stand by the truth that at some times or others, perhaps on the far frontier of all other possibilities, it may have to happen, in obedience to the commandment that man must be killed by man."[10] Certainly, the unborn cannot claim to be preserved in all circumstances. God may command the active participation of others in the killing of germinating life.[11] Where this occurs, it does not constitute murder.[12]

Although Barth is quoted by the fundamentalists to support their antiabortion stand, they never mention the fact that he also supported abortion.[13] Barth saw this paradox as the heart of the biblical message and as a necessary part of the meaning of the grace of God in the tragic circumstances of life.

Fundamentalists usually agree that the fetus may be terminated when the life of the woman is at stake. In such a case, it is a trade-off—a life for a life (Exodus 21:23), or a choice between an actual human being and a potential human being.[14] They also recognize that the command forbidding killing in the Old Testament is not an absolute. Most fundamentalists favor capital punishment, largely on biblical grounds. However, they draw back from applying this to abortion for at least two reasons. First, no injunction permitting abortion appears in the Bible. Biblical passages that provide rules about permissible behavior are favored. Second, fundamentalists argue the fetus is *innocent* human life and thus to be protected.[15] Those who have reached the age of accountability are held to be guilty sinners and thus may forfeit their right to life by committing capital crimes. Thus "capital punishment is commanded; self-defense is permitted," says Brown.[16]

The real reason lies in the fact that fundamentalists have developed a consensus that abortion violates an absolute moral rule based on the assumption that the fetus is a human being. This is a shaky argument at best, going beyond the biblical evidence.

The Fetus as Person

Supposedly, the teaching of the Bible is of central importance to the fundamentalists' position on abortion. Those who would ban abortion argue that the Bible teaches that (1) the fetus is a human being, and (2) that abortion is murder and thus should be legally forbidden. I am not at all certain that even an authoritative exposition of biblical teachings refuting the fundamentalist argument would be convincing to them. "Even though one appeared to them from the grave they would not believe." It is necessary to understand their interpretation of the Bible and respond on biblical grounds.

However, there are logical, moral, and biblical-theological reasons for not accepting the easy equation of fetus with person. Logically, no one can deny the continuum from fertilization to maturity and adulthood. This does not mean, however, that every step on the continuum has the same value or constitutes the same entity. The best analogy is that of a fertilized hen egg. Given the proper incubation environment, the egg becomes a chicken and the chicken grows to a hen or rooster. However, few of us are confused about the entity we are eating when we have eggs for breakfast. An egg—even a fertilized egg—is still an egg and not a chicken.

The genetic definition confuses potentialities with actualities. Potentialities are certainly important, but they do not have the same value as actualities. "An embryo is not a person but the possibility or the probability of there being a person many months or even years in the future," Charles Hartshorne has argued; "obviously possibilities are important, but to blur the distinction between them and actualities is to darken counsel."[17] The same point is made by John Stott, in saying that the decision to abort for reasons of maternal health is "a choice between an actual human being and a potential human being."[18]

The fallacy of this definition of person is also seen when the argument is reduced *ad absurdum*. Every body cell of a person contains one's deoxyribonucleic acid (DNA), or genetic code. This is why, theoretically at least, persons may be cloned or duplicated. If one uses the genetic definition of person, one would have to regard every body cell as a human being, because each cell has the potentiality for becoming another person through cloning. Think also of the implications of this definition for surgery or the excision of cancer cells from the body!

The fatal weakness of this argument is its radical reductionism. The easy equation of "person" with "fertilized ovum" (zygote) moves from a terribly complex entity to an irreducible minimum. A zygote is a cluster of cells but hardly complex or developed enough to qualify as person. A person or a human being has capacities of reflective choice, relational responses, social experience, moral perception, and self-awareness. Both the person and the zygote have life and are human, because they belong to Homo sapiens. But a zygote or a blastocyst does not fully embody the qualities that pertain to personhood. A great deal more complex development and growth is necessary before the attributes of person are acquired.

Morally speaking, the claim that a conceptus is a human being is to introduce what Sissela Bok has called "a premature ultimate."[19] People have an ultimate value in Western morality, but fetuses do not. Fetuses have value, but they are not of equal moral value with actual persons—in particular, the pregnant woman.

The Bible and the fetus. This distinction seems basic to the biblical story in Exodus 21:22–25—an important passage for fundamentalist perspectives—which is an account of a pregnant woman who becomes involved in a brawl between two men and has a miscarriage. A distinction is then made between the penalty that is to be exacted for the loss of the fetus and the penalty for any injury to the woman. For the fetus, a fine is paid as determined by the husband and the judges (v. 22). However, if the woman is injured or dies, *lex talionus* is applied: "You shall give life for life, eye for eye, tooth for tooth, hand for hand, foot for foot, burn for burn, wound for wound, stripe for stripe [vs. 23–25]."

The story has only limited application to the current abortion debate, because it deals with accidental, not willful, pregnancy termination. Even so, the distinction made between the protection accorded the woman and that accorded the fetus under covenant law is important. The woman has full standing as a person under the covenant; the fetus has only a relative standing, certainly inferior to that of the woman. This passage from Exodus gives no support to the parity argument that gives equal religious and moral worth to woman and fetus.

The Biblical View of Person

The biblical portrait of person does not begin with an explanation of conception, but with a portrayal of the creation of Adam and Eve. God created man as male and female. Three texts are of critical importance. Genesis 2:7 declares: "Then the Lord God formed man of dust from the ground, and breathed into his nostrils the breath of life; and man became a living being." The biological aspects of personhood are metaphorically portrayed in terms of dust or clay. God as the origin and giver of life is captured by breathing life into clay. The declaration "became a living being" designated the person as animated flesh. As the person is breathed into, so he or she breathes.

Another text distinguishes persons from animal creation. Genesis 1:27 declares that "God created man in his own image, in the image of God he created him." The biblical portrait of person centers in the notion of the image of God. This image is not a physical likeness, but a similarity of powers or abilities. These capacities or powers are spiritual, personal, relational, moral, and intellectual. Of all the creatures fashioned by God, only humans are able to relate to the creator in obedience or rebellion. Only they experience the God-like powers of self-transcendence and self-awareness. These creatures, like God, may be introspective, retrospective, and pro-spective. They may reflect on the past, anticipate the future, and discern the activity of God in their personal lives and histories.

The third text portrays the person as a moral decision-maker. In Genesis 3:22 God says, "Behold, the man has become like one of us, knowing good and evil." To be a person is to be a choice-maker, reflecting God's own ability to distinguish good from evil, right from wrong. This does not mean people have perfect knowledge of right and wrong as some intrinsic gift from birth. Decisions must be made on the basis of one's understanding of God's will. The fact people "ate of the tree of the knowledge of good and evil" indicates they are given the burden and responsibility of making decisions that reflect their unique place in God's creation.

The biblical portrait of person, therefore, is that of a complex, many-sided creature, with the God-like ability and responsibility to make choices. The fetus hardly meets these characteristics. At best, it begins to attain these biological basics necessary to show such capacities no earlier than the second half of gestation.

The one who unquestionably fits this portrayal is the woman, or mother, in question. Because the pregnancy is hers, so the decision is uniquely hers. Certainly, the entire circle of those most intimately involved with the abortion question are persons—reflecting on the meaning of this moment, considering the data, weighing the facts of the past, anticipating the future, and making some decision. The abortion question focuses the personhood of the woman, who in turn considers the potential personhood of the fetus in terms of the multiple dimensions of her own history and the future.

This is a God-like decision. Like the Creator, the woman reflects on what is good for the creation of which she is agent. As steward of these powers, she uses them for good and not ill for herself, the fetus, and the future of humankind. She is aware that God wills health and happiness for herself, for those she may bring into the world, and the future of the human race. Thus she is engaged in reflecting on her own well-being, the genetic health of the fetus, and the survival of the human race.

Still another relevant biblical passage pertains to the priesthood of all believers (1 Peter 2:9)—a New Testament extension of the Genesis statement on imago dei and moral knowledge. The person is one with direct access to God and the ability and responsibility to know and do God's will. No other persons may arrogate to themselves the right to stand between the person and God. Religious imperialism and moralistic authoritarianism are contradictory to this biblical principle. The woman has priestly powers—in her own conscientious obedience to the Creator-Redeemer; she bears God's image in making her decision.

This biblical portrait of person is the reason conservative fundamentalist scholars like W.A. Criswell have emphasized the woman, not the fetus. "I have always felt that it was only after a child was born and had life separate from its mother that it became an individual person," he said, "and it has always, therefore, seemed to me that what is best for the mother and for the future should be allowed."[20]

I believe this also helps to understand the absence of clear prohibitions against abortion in the Old Testament. This silence is amazing, considering the harsh prohibitions found in surrounding Middle Eastern cultures, such as Sumerian, Assyrian, Hittite, and Persian. Certainly the Hebrews knew of these codes that tacitly acknowledge abortion was practiced. The Assyrian Code (1500 B.C.) declared that "any woman who causes to fall what her womb holds—shall be tried, convicted and impaled upon a stake and shall not be buried."

Why, then, no prohibitions in the Old Testament? The absence may mean either that (1) no Hebrew woman ever aborted or that (2) the practice was accepted in their culture. Hebrew law gave a status to women that was unheard of in the ancient Near East (as compared to the Assyrian Code). It is reasonable to believe that the practice of pregnancy termination was not punishable by law, because it was left to the woman and her family to decide. The burden of this decision was best left to the family circle. It was not to be a matter of social regulation, except as specified in Exodus 21.

Conclusions

Theologically testing the fundamentalist antiabortion posture finds it lacking a biblical basis. The very Bible to which they claim such devotion refutes their position at every significant point. This helps to explain its resorting to heavy-handed tactics. Unable to persuade others on the basis of scripture or reason, fundamentalists have turned to political strategies to legislate their moralistic judgmentalism.

But their efforts must be resisted for the common good of this society and the personal well-being of those women who face tragic choices with regard to problem pregnancies. Their win-at-any-cost strategies need to be exposed as lacking integrity and as dealing maliciously with truth and persons.

Further, it will be necessary to counter the public image of the pro-choice posture at two important points. First, pro-choice advocates must be clear that there is a moral issue involved in pregnancy termination for nontherapeutic reasons. Too often pro-choicers are understood as portraying the decision in merely pragmatic terms. Those who argue that the fetus is little more than body tissue, and that abortion has no more a moral dimension than excising a hangnail or a wart, are enemies of the cause for free choice.

Second, it must be clear that free choice is not a camouflage for a calloused attitude toward abortion. Surely we can all agree that significant factors affecting the attitude of maternal or fetal health need to be present after viability of abortion to warrant abortion procedures. There may also be common ground on which antiabortion forces and pro-choice groups can meet in working to firm up regulations governing postviability abortions, for example.

At stake in the political arena of struggle is no less than the type of society we understand ourselves to be; are we an oppressive society that denies the personal rights of women, or a society that respects and protects various religious, moral, and personal points of view?

I believe the fundamentalist/New Right movement will come to the same end as the repressive politics of the McCarthy era. It will be exposed for what it is: A house built on the shifting sands of deception, falsehood, character assassination, willful distortion of the truth, power-crazed authoritarianism, a win-at-any-cost ethic, and a total disregard for personal values or religious freedom. It has already sown the seeds of its own destruction. Americans have periodically been stirred to frantic action by fears raised and exploited by misguided demagogues. The frenzy is usually short-lived, however. In the end a cooler, better wisdom prevails, and the American sense of justice and fair play returns to establish normalcy in domestic political affairs. The problem is—as it was during the Salem witchcraft hysteria and the McCarthy era—that many good people will be hurt before the scaffolding of this house without foundation begins to fall.

Let us resolve to resist the efforts of those who would force their wills on others and thereby undermine the principles of freedom and justice on which America was established.

Part VI

Critiques

James M. Gustafson
Beverly Wildung Harrison

A Protestant Ethical Approach

James M. Gustafson

IN THE ETHICS OF ABORTION, the differences of opinion surface not only on the substantial moral question of whether it is permissible but also on the question of what is the proper method of moral reflection. The two questions are not entirely independent of each other, as this essay demonstrates. Catholics and Protestants have been divided on the question of method, as well as on the substantial moral judgment.

Salient Aspects of Traditional Catholic Arguments

Any Protestant moralist writing about abortion is necessarily indebted to the work of Roman Catholic colleagues. Their work on this subject shows historical learning that is often absent among Protestants; it shows philosophical acumen exercised with great finesse once their starting principles are accepted; it shows command of the medical aspects of abortion beyond what one finds in cursory Protestant discussions; and it shows extraordinary seriousness about particular moral actions. Debt must also be acknowledged to the contemporary Protestant moralist who has learned most profoundly from the Catholics, namely, Paul Ramsey, for his voluminous writing about

Reprinted by permission of the publishers from *The Morality of Abortion*, edited by John T. Noonan Jr. (Cambridge, MA: Harvard University Press). © 1970 by the President and Fellows of Harvard College.

JAMES M. GUSTAFSON is professor of social ethics at the Divinity School of the University of Chicago, Chicago, Illinois.

problems of war and of medical ethics have introduced a note of intellectual rigor into Protestant ethics that was too often absent.[1]

Every moral argument, no matter who makes it and what is the issue at hand, must limit the factors that are brought into consideration. No one can handle all possible relevant bits of data, ranges of value, sources of insight, and pertinent principles in a manageable bit of discourse. What one admits to the statement of the moral issue in turn is crucial to the solutions given to it. The determination of which factors or principles are primary, or at least of greater importance than others, in the way one argues is also fairly decisive for the outcome of the argument. The traditional Catholic arguments about abortion can be characterized in part by the following delineations of the perspective from which they are made.[2]

First, the arguments are made by an *external judge*. They are written from the perspective of persons who claim the right to judge the past actions of others as morally right or wrong, or to tell others what future actions are morally right or wrong. To make the point differently, moral responsibility is ascribed to others for their actions, or it is prescribed or proscribed.

The perspective of the external judge can be distinguished from those of the persons who are more immediately involved in an abortion situation. It is clear, of course, that those involved, for example, physicians or mothers, might interpret their situations in terms that they have been taught by the external judges. Even if they do, the *position of personal responsibility* that physicians, mothers, and others have is different from that of the writer of a manual of moral theology, or of the priest who judges the moral rectitude of others and determines the penance that is to be required. To assume responsibility for an action is quite a different order of experience from ascribing responsibility to others for an action.[3] Physicians, mothers, and others are initiators of action, they are agents in the process of life who determine to a great extent what actually occurs. Their relationship to a situation involves their senses of accountability for consequences, their awareness of particular antecedents (for example, the conditions under which a pregnancy occurred), their sensibilities and emotions, their private past experiences and their private aspirations for the future, their personal commitments and loyalties.

Second, the arguments are made on a basically *juridical model*. The action is right or wrong depending on whether it conforms to or is contrary to a rule, a law, and the outcome of a moral argument. The rules or laws, of course, are defended on theological and philosophical grounds; they are not arbitrary fiats imposed by an authoritarian institution. Traditional authorities are cited; theological and philosophical principles are given to support the rules; the consequences of different possible courses of action are considered. The argument's principal terms and its logic, however, are directed toward the possibility of defining a morally right act and a morally wrong act. As with the civil law, there is a low tolerance for moral ambiguity. The advantages of this for those whose behavior conforms to the outcome of the authoritative argument is that they probably can act with a clear conscience and can justify their actions on the basis of authorities other than themselves. Their own responsibility for their actions, including its consequences, is decisively limited, for with reference to the juridical model of morality they have done what is determined by those whose authority they accept to be correct. If the primary agents of action—mothers and physicians, for example—do not judge themselves only in the light of the rules, if they exercise the virtue of prudence, and the virtue of *epikeia,* or equity in interpreting the law in a particular case, they are in a slightly different situation. Their own degree of responsibility is increased, and yet they have the advantage of the clarity of reflection that is given in the moral prescription.

The juridical model can be distinguished from others that view the justification for the moral rectitude of actions in different ways or that have different views of how moral judgments are to be made. Some persons have sought virtually to quantify the good and ill effects of courses of action, and as a result of this have suggested that action which assures the greatest good for the greatest number is right. Others have relied heavily on moral sentiment to be sensitive to the moral issues in a situation, and relied on compassion, the sense of altruism, or the sense of moral indignation to determine the act. Some have relied on insight and rational intuition to size up what is going on in a time and place and to discern what the proper human response ought to be. Or love has been asserted to have sufficient perspicacity and motivating power to enable one to perceive what is right in a situation. It has been cogently argued that morality develops out of experience, and that when laws become abstracted from experience, their informing and persuasive powers begin to evaporate.

Third, the traditional Catholic arguments largely confine the relevant data to *the physical.* The concern is with physical life, its sanctity and its preservation. Obviously, other aspects of human life depend on the biological basis of the human body, and thus the primacy of this concern is valid. But on the whole, the arguments have not been extended, to include concern for the emotional and spiritual well-being of the mother or the infant. The concern has been largely for the physical consequences of abortion.

Fourth, the arguments are limited by concerning themselves almost *exclusively with the physician and the patient* at the time of a particular pregnancy, isolating these two from the multiple relationships and responsibilities each has to and for others over long periods of time. The obvious basis for this is that physicians have to decide about abortions with individual patients as these patients come to them. But they also have responsibilities for the well-being of the whole of society, and for the spiritual and moral well-being of the patients' families. It could be argued that there is no dissonance between what would be decided in a particular relationship between two people and what is good for society, but this is not self-evident. The focus on the mother's physical condition, and on her as a statistical instance of a general and uniform category of mothers, makes it difficult to consider this particular mother, her particular relationships, and her past spiritual as well as physical history. For example, arguments pertaining to saving the life of the mother do not admit as important evidence such factors as whether she is the mother of six other children dependent on her, or no other children. In some other ways of discussing abortion such information might make a difference in the argument. I am suggesting that the time and space limits one uses to isolate what is "the case" have a considerable effect on the way one argues.

Fifth, the traditional Catholic arguments are *rationalistic*. Obviously, to make an argument one has to be rational, and to counter an argument one deems to be rationalistic one has to show what would be better reasons for arguing differently. What I refer to as rationalistic can be seen in the structure of many of the sections of the manuals of moral theology that deal with questions such as abortion, or the structure of manuals of medical ethics. One often finds brief assertions of fundamental truths that include definitions of terms used in these truths or in subsequent arguments. This might be followed by basic principles that will include distinctions between the kinds of law, principles pertaining to conscience, principles of action, a definition of the principle of double effect, and others. The principle of the sanctity of inviolability of human life is discussed at great length, since its application is primary to particular cases.

One must recognize that any argument about abortion will use principles. But the rationalistic character of the arguments seems to reduce spiritual and personal individuality to abstract cases. The learning from historical experiences with their personal nuances seems to be squeezed out of the timeless abstractions. The sense of human compassion for suffering and the profound tragedy that is built into any situation in which the taking of life is morally plausible are gone. Individual instances must be typified in order to find what rubric they come under in the manual. While it is eminently clear that any discussion must abstract facts and principles from the vitality and complexity of lived-experience, the degree of abstraction and the deductive reasoning of the traditional Catholic arguments remove the issues far from life. The alternative is not to wallow in feeling and visceral responses, nor is it to assume that one's deep involvement with the persons in a situation and one's awareness of the inexorable concreteness of their lives are sufficient to resolve the issues. But an approach that is more personal and experientially oriented is another possibility.

Sixth, the traditional perspective seeks to develop arguments that are based on *natural law,* and thus ought to be persuasive and binding on all people. Intentionally, the particular historical standpoint and substance of the Christian message is subordinated to the natural law in the arguments. To be sure, arguments can be given for the consistency between the natural law and particular Christian affirmation; also anyone who would begin with particular Christian affirmations would have to show their viability on moral questions to those who did not share his or her religious outlook and convictions. To indicate that arguments from natural law can be distinguished from arguments that place particular historical aspects of Christian thought at a different point in the discussion is not to assert that the answer to questions about abortion can be found in revelation, or that the use of human reason is less necessary. It is to suggest, however, that one's basic perspective toward life might be altered, and one's ordering of values might be different if the first-order affirmations dealt with God's will not only to preserve creation, but to redeem it. One's attitude toward the persons involved might well be more tolerant, patient, loving, and forgiving, rather than judgmental. One might look for consistency between one's principles and the great themes of the Christian faith at a more central place in the discussion than the traditional Catholic arguments do. To predict that the outcome of the argument would be greatly different in every case would be folly, although it might very well be in some cases. Since theologically based moral arguments, like all others, are arguments made by human beings, many other factors than commonly held convictions enter into them.

These six points are meant to provide a descriptive delineation of salient aspects of traditional Catholic arguments. I have sought to indicate that alternative ways of working are possible with regard to each of them. To claim them to be insufficient or invalid without providing an alternative would be presumptuous. As a way of suggesting and exploring an alternative, I shall describe a situation, and indicate how I would go about making and justifying my moral judgment pertaining to it. In its basic structure it is in accord with the situations of persons who have sought me out for counsel, although for various reasons I have made a composite description.

A Discussion of a Human Choice

The pregnant woman is in her early twenties. She is a lapsed Catholic, with no significant religious affiliation at the present time, although she expresses some need for a church. Her marriage was terminated by divorce; her husband was given custody of three children by this marriage. She had an affair with a man who befriended her, but there were no serious prospects for a marriage with him, and the affair has ended. Her family life was as disrupted and as tragic as that which is dramatically presented in Eugene O'Neill's *Long Day's Journey into Night*. Her alcoholic mother mistreated her children, coerced them into deceptive activity for her ends, and was given to periods of violence. Her father has been addicted to drugs, but has managed to continue in business, avoid incarceration, and provide a decent income for his family. The pregnant woman fled from home after high school to reside in a distant state and has no significant contact with her parents or siblings. She has two or three friends.

Her pregnancy occurred when she was raped by her former husband and three other men after she had agreed to meet him to talk about their children. The rapes can only be described as acts of sadistic vengeance. She is unwilling to prefer charges against the men, since she believes it would be a further detriment to her children. She has no steady job, partially because of periodic gastrointestinal illnesses, and has no other income. There are no known physiological difficulties that would jeopardize her life or that of the child. She is unusually intelligent and very articulate, and is not hysterical about her situation. Termination of the pregnancy is a live option for her as a way to cope with one of the many difficulties she faces.

The Christian moralist's responsible relationship. In indicating that the position of writers of moral argument about abortion in traditional Catholicism is that of an external judge, I did not wish to suggest that priests are not compassionate, understanding, and loving in their relationships to physicians and to mothers, nor did I intend to suggest that they overrule the liberty of conscience of others through authoritarian ecclesiastical sanctions. No doubt some have acted more like rigorous judges than loving pastors, but many have been patient, tolerant, loving, and aware of the limitations of any human authority.

(This is not the place to raise the difficult problem of the magisterial authority of the Church, which logically could be raised here, an authority still used to threaten, coerce, and suspend dissident voices.) I do wish to suggest, however, that I believe the responsible relation of a Christian moralist to other persons precludes the primacy of the judgmental posture, either in the way we write or in the way we converse with others.

The moralist responding to this woman can establish one of a number of ways of relating to her in conversation. The two extremes are obvious. On the one hand, the moralist could determine that no physiological difficulties seem to be present in the pregnancy, and thus seek to enforce the woman's compliance with the standard rule against abortions. The manuals would decide what right conduct is; her predicament would be defined so that factors that are important for others who respond to her are not pertinent to the decision about abortion. Both the moralist and the woman could defer futher moral responsibility to the textbooks. On the other hand, the moralist could take a highly permissive approach to the conversation. In reliance on a theory of morality that would minimize the objective moral considerations, and affirm that what a person feels is best is morally right, the moralist could affirm consistently what the woman's own dominant disposition seemed to be, and let this determine the decision.

Somewhere between these is what I would delineate as a more responsible relationship than either of the two extremes. It would recognize that moralists and women are in an interpersonal relationship; this is to say that as human beings they need to be open to one another, to have a high measure of confidence in one another, to have empathy for one another. Obviously, moralists, like any other counselors, are in a position to have more disclosed to them than they disclose of themselves to the other, and they have professional competence that enables them to be relatively objective within the intersubjectivity of the relationship. But as Christian moralists, their obligation is first to be open and to understand the other, not to judge and to prescribe. They will recognize that their judgment and that of others who have informed them, while learned, mature, and hopefully sound, remains the judgment of finite beings, with all the limitations of their perspective. They will, in a situation like this, acknowledge the liberty of a woman's conscience, and will not immediately offer an authoritative answer to her question; indeed, the context of her question, and its nuances might make it a subtly different question than the one the textbooks answer. All this is not to say that moralists have nothing to contribute to the conversation. As moralists they are to help her to objectify her situation, to see it from other perspectives than the one she comes with. They are to call to her attention not only

197

alternative courses of action with some of the potential consequences of each (including the violation of civil law), but also the value of life and those values that would have to be higher in order to warrant the taking of life. They are to help her to understand her past, not as a way of excusing anything in the present, but as a way of gaining some objectivity toward the present. They are to find what constitutes her moral integrity and convictions, her desires and ends. They may find themselves bringing these into the light of other ends which they deem to be important, or they may find themselves inquiring whether potential courses of action are more or less in accord with the values and convictions she has. It is their obligation as Christian moralists to bring the predicament into the light of as many subjective and objective considerations as their competence permits, including concerns for the wider moral order of the human community of which she is a part as this is sustained in civil laws.

Salient facts in one Christian moralist's interpretation. The relationship of moralists to a person who seeks conversation with them is by no means simple. Thus it is not easy to isolate what the salient facts of the predicament are, and to give a ready valence to each of them. Efforts at this analytical task are incumbent on them, but they also *perceive* the person and the situation in some patterns or in a single whole pattern that already establish in their perceptions some of the relationships between the factors. They never confront the salient facts as isolates, or as discrete entities that can be added arithmetically into a sum. The person confronts them not as isolable elements, and her experiences are not detached moments only chronologically related to each other. They do not respond to her any more than they respond to a portrait first of all as a series of colors, or a series of lines. They can in reflection discriminate between the colors and talk about the lines, but even then these are in particular relationships to each other in the portrait, and in their perceptions of it. They do not perceive the woman in pure objectivity, nor as she perceives her own predicament, although obviously they seek to have their own perception informed by the actual predicament insofar as possible. Even in this however, their perspective conditions how they see and feel the relationships between factors that can be abstracted and isolated. This preface to a statement of salient facts is important, for it precludes both oversimplification and dogmatic analytical authority. They can never say to another person, "In comparable situations find out the answers to the following factual questions, and you will have an accurate picture of the predicament."

In the personal situation under discussion, it is clear that if medical factors alone were to be considered grounds for an abortion, none

198

would be morally permissible. The woman had three pregnancies that came to full term, and the children were healthy. To the best of her knowledge there are no medical problems at the present time. Periodic gastrointestinal illnesses, which might be relieved with better medical care, would not be sufficient medical grounds. Although the present pregnancy is disturbing for many reasons, including both the occasion on which the pregnancy occurred and the future social prospects for the woman and the child, in the judgment of the moralist the woman is able to cope with her situation without serious threat to her mental health. The medical factors insofar as the moralist can grasp them would not warrant a therapeutic abortion.

Legal factors potentially involved in this situation are serious. First, and most obvious, the woman resides in a state where abortion of pregnancies due to sexual crimes is not at present legally permissible. Since there are not sufficient grounds for a therapeutic abortion, a request to a physician would put the physician in legal jeopardy. Even if abortion was permissible because of the rapes, this woman was unwilling to report the rapes to the police since it involved her former husband and had potential implications for the care of her children. To report the rapes would involve the woman in court procedures that seem also to require time and energy she needs to support herself financially. To seek an abortion on conscientious moral grounds would be to violate the law, and to implicate others in the violation. Not to press charges against the rapists is to protect them from prosecution. Disclosure of the rapes would make the abortion morally justifiable in the eyes of many, but it might lead to implications for her children. The legal factors are snarled and are complicated by social factors.

The moralist has to reckon with the financial plight of the woman. She is self-supporting, but her income is irregular. There are no savings. Application for welfare support might lead to the disclosure of matters she wishes to keep in confidence. If a legal abortion was possible, the physician would receive little or no remuneration from the patient. There are no funds in sight to finance an illegal abortion, and the medical risks involved in securing a quack rule that out as a viable prospect. The child, if not aborted, could be let out for adoption, and means might be found to give minimum support for the mother during pregnancy. If she should choose to keep the child, which is her moral right to do, there are no prospects for sufficient financial support, although with the recovery of her health the woman could join the work force and probably with her intelligence earn a modest income.

The spiritual and emotional factors involved are more difficult to assess. While the moralist is impressed with the relative calm with which the woman converses about her predicament, he is aware that this ability is probably the result of learning to cope with previous inhumane treatment and with events that led to no happy ending. Socially, she is sustained only by two or three friends, and these friendships could readily be disrupted by geographical mobility. She has no significant, explicit religious faith, and as a lapsed Catholic who views the Church and its priests as harsh taskmasters, she is unwilling to turn to it for spiritual and moral sustenance. She has a profound desire not merely to achieve a situation of equanimity, of absence of suffering and conflict, but also to achieve positive goals. Her mind is active, and she has read fairly widely; she expresses the aspiration to go to college, to become a teacher, or to engage in some other professional work, both for the sake of her self-fulfillment and for the contribution she can make to others. She has not been defeated by her past. She can articulate the possibility of keeping the child, and see the child as part of the world in which there would be some realization of goals, especially since she has been deprived of her other children. She has confidence, she has hope, and she seems to be able to love, although she wonders what else could happen to make her life any more difficult than it is. She carries something of a guilt load; the courts gave custody of her three children to the husband because of adultery charges against her. Yet, her interpretation of this marriage in her youth was that it freed her from her parental home, but that the marriage itself was a prison. She responds to the rapes more in horror than in hatred but is too close to this experience to know its long-range impact on her.

The more readily identifiable moral factors are three, although in the ethical perspective of this essay, this constitutes an oversimple limitation of the moral and of the nature of moral responsibility. One is the inviolability of life, the sanctity of life. My opinion is that since the genotype is formed at conception, all the genetic potentialities of personal existence are there. Thus it is to be preserved unless reasons can be given that make an exception morally justifiable. A second is rape—not only a crime, but a morally evil deed. The sexual relations from which the pregnancy came were not only engaged in against the woman's will, but were in her judgment acts of retaliation and vengeance. The third is the relation of morality to the civil law. If abortion were considered to be morally justifiable, to have it done would be to break the civil law. It would be an act of conscientious objection to existing laws, and susceptible to scrutiny by the moral arguments that pertain to this subject in itself.

All of these factors in isolated listing, and others that could be enumerated, do not add up to a moral decision. They are related to one another in particular ways, and the woman is related to her own ends, values, and to other beings. And the moralist's relationship is not that of a systems analyst sorting out and computing. His relationship is one of respect and concern for the person; it is colored by his perspective. It is necessary, then, to state what seem to be the factors that are present in the perspective of the moralist that influence his interpretation and judgment.

Salient aspects of the moralist's perspective. The perception and the interpretation of the moralist are not a simple matter to discuss. It would be simpler if the author could reduce his perspective to (1) theological and philosophical principles, (2) moral inferences drawn from these, and (3) rational application of these principles to a narrowly defined case. But more than belief, principles, and logic are involved in the moral decision. A basic perspective toward life accents certain values and shadows others. Attitudes, affections, and feelings of indignation against evil, compassion for suffering, and desire for restoration of wholeness color one's interpretation and judgment. Imagination, sensitivity, and empathy are all involved. For Christians, and many others presumably, love is at work, not merely as a word to be defined, and as a subject of propositions so that inferences can be drawn from it, but love as a human relationship, which can both move and inform the other virtues, including prudence and equity (to make a reference to Thomas Aquinas). All of this does not mean a moral judgment is a total mystery, it does not mean it is without objectivity.

The perspective of the Christian moralist is informed and directed by his fundamentalist trust that the forces of life seek the human good, that God is good, is love. This is a matter of trust and confidence, and not merely a matter of believing certain propositions to be true. (I believe certain statements about my wife to be true, including the statement that she wills and seeks my good, but the reasons for my trust in her cannot be described simply by such a statement.) Yet the way I state my convictions about this trust defines in part my moral perspective and my fundamental intentionality. (What I know *about* my wife sustains my trust in her, and in part sets the direction of our marriage.) Life, and particularly human life, is given to humans by God's love: physical being dependent on genetic continuity; the capacity of the human spirit for self-awareness, responsiveness, knowledge, and creativity; life together in human communities, in which we live and care for others and others live and care for us.

God wills the creation, preservation, reconciliation, and redemption of human life. Thus, one can infer, it is better to give and preserve life than to take it away; it is better to prevent its coming into being than to destroy it when it has come into being. But the purposes of God for life pertain to more than physical existence: there are conditions for human life that need delineation—physical health, possibilities for future good and meaning that engender and sustain hope, relationships of trust and love, freedom to respond and initiate and achieve, and many others. The love of God, and in response to it, the loves of human beings, are particularly sensitive to "the widow, the orphan, and the stranger in your midst," to the oppressed and the weak.

These brief and cryptic statements are the grounds for moral biases: life is to be preserved, the weak and the helpless are to be cared for especially, the moral requisites of trust, hope, love, freedom, justice, and others are to be met so that human life can be meaningful. The bias gives a direction, a fundamental intention that does not in itself resolve the darknesses beyond the reach of its light, the ambiguities of particular cases. It begins to order what preferences one would have under ideal conditions and under real conditions. One would prefer not to induce an abortion in this instance. There is consistency between this preference and the Christian moralist's faith and convictions. But one would prefer for conception to arise within love rather than hate, and one would prefer that there would be indications that the unknowable future were more favorably disposed to the human well-being of the mother and the child.

The perspective of the Christian moralist is informed and directed by his or her understanding of the nature of human life, as well as convictions about God. Abbreviated statements of some convictions are sufficient here. These would be first, that moral life is a life of action, in which intentions, judgments, the exercise of bodily power and other forms of power and influence give direction to our responses to past events, and direction to future events themselves. Persons are active, responsive, creative, reflective, self-aware, initiating. The second would be that we can discern something of the order of relationships and activity that sustains, preserves, and develops our humanity. The child conceived in love, within a marriage (an order of love), within an order of society that maintains justice, is more likely to have a higher quality of life than one who is conceived in other conditions. The decision to seek an abortion is human, the act of abortion would be human, the relationships before, during, and after the abortion are human. The consequences are not fully predictable beyond the physical, and yet the human is more than perpetuation of the body. A moral order was violated in rape; are the human conditions present that would sustain and heal the humanity of the child and the mother in the future? The answer to this question is a

202

finite, human answer, and how it will be answered by the mother and others deeply affects a most decisive act.

A third pertinent affirmation about human life is important: to be a creature is to be limited, and the good and the right are found within the conditions of limitation. Present acts respond to the conditions of past actions, conditions that are usually irrevocable, unalterable. Their consequences will be projected into the future and quickly become part of other actions and responses so that the actors in the present cannot fully know or determine the future. The limitations of knowledge, both of potentially verifiable facts and of good and evil, while no excuse for not knowing what can be known, nonetheless are present. Thus not only physical risk, but moral risk is fundamental to human action, and this risk in the life of this woman involves potential tragedy, suffering, and anguish. But her condition itself is the fruit both of events beyond her control (for example, the rapes) and events that have occurred because of choices (for example, earlier adultery). What many people find out about the dark side of existence through novels and dramas, she has experienced. Action is required within the limits; the good or the evil that is involved will be concrete, actual. Thus there is no abstract standard of conduct that can predetermine without moral ambiguity what the right action is in this predicament. Since predicaments like this have emerged before, however, one's conscientious moral interpretation can use those generalizations that have emerged out of the past for illumination, and for direction. They may present values or principles so universally valid that the present decision, if contrary to them, must be justified as a clear exception. Since action is specific, either the following of established rules, or the finding of exceptions to them refers to specifics. Specificity of good and evil is the human condition (I never know either in the abstract); choices are agonizingly specific. The moralist has the obligation conscientiously to assess the specific in the light of principles and arguments that pertain to it; the woman is entitled to see her predicament and potential courses of action in the light of as much distilled wisdom and experience as she can handle. Indeed, the principle of double effect (preferably multiple effects none of which are totally evil, and none of which are totally good) might assist in the reflection. But the choice remains in the realm of the finite, the limited, and the potentially wrong as well as right.

Pertinent principles that can be stipulated for reflection. Neither the moralist nor the woman comes to a situation without some convictions and beliefs that begin to dissolve some of the complexity of the particularities into manageable terms. Perhaps the traditional Catholic arguments simply assume that one can begin with these convictions

203

and principles, and need not immerse oneself in the tragic concreteness. The pertinent ones in this case have already been alluded to, but here they can be reduced to a simpler scheme.

1. Life is to be preserved rather than destroyed.
2. Those who cannot assert their own rights to life are especially to be protected.
3. There are exceptions to these rules.

Possible exceptions are:

a. medical indications that make therapeutic abortion morally viable. Conditions not present here.
b. the pregnancy has occurred as a result of sexual crime. (I would grant this as a viable possible exception in every instance for reasons imbedded in the above discussion, if the woman herself were convinced that it was right. In other than detached academic discussions I would never dispatch an inquiry with a ready granting of the exception. If the woman sees the exception as valid, she has a right to more than a potentially legal justification for her decision; as a person she has the right to understand why it is an exception in her dreadful plight.)
c. the social and emotional conditions do not appear to be beneficial for the well-being of the mother and the child. (In particular circumstances, this may appear to be a justification, but I would not resort to it until possibilities for financial, social, and spiritual help have been explored.)

In the shorthand of principles this can be reduced to an inconsistency between on the one hand the first and second, and on the other hand 3.b. and perhaps 3.c. While I am called on to give as many reasons for a decision between these two as I can, the choice can never be fully rationalized.

The decision of the moralist. My own decision is: (1) if I were in the woman's human predicament I believe I could morally justify an abortion, and thus: (2) I would affirm its moral propriety in this instance. Clearly, logic alone is not the process by which a defense of this particular judgment can be given; clearly, the facts of the matter do not add up to a justification of abortion so that one can say "the situation determines everything." Nor is it a matter of some inspiration of the Spirit. It is a human decision, made in freedom, informed and governed by beliefs and values, as well as by attitudes and a fundamental perspective. It is a discernment of compassion for the woman, as well as of objective moral reflection. It may not be morally right in the eyes of others, and although we could indicate where the matters of dispute between us are in discourse, and perhaps even close the gap between opinions to some extent, argument about it would probably not be persuasive. The judgment is made with a sense of its limitations, which include the limitations of the one who decides (which might well result from lack of courage, from pride, slothfulness in thinking, and other perversities).[4]

Continuing responsibilities of the moralist. The responsibilities of the moralist, like the consequences for the woman, do not end at the moment a decision might be made in favor of an abortion. Some of them can be briefly indicated, since they have already been alluded to in the discussion. Since the moralist concurs in the decision, and since the decision was made in a relationship in which he accepts limited but real responsibility for the woman, he is obligated to continue his responsible relationship to her in ways consistent with the decision, and with her well-being. He cannot dismiss her to engage in subsequent implications of the decision on her own and to accept the consequences of such implications on her own. First, he is obligated to assist, if necessary, in finding competent medical care. In such a situation as the one described, with abortion laws as they now stand in most states, this is not necessarily an easy matter and not a trivial one. Second, financial resources are needed. To put her on her own in this regard would be to resign responsibility prematurely for a course of action in which the moralist concurred, and might jeopardize the woman's health and welfare. Third, the woman needs continuing social and moral support in her efforts to achieve her aspirations for relief from anguish and for a better human future. To deny continued support in this case is comparable to denying continued care and concern for the well-being of those who have large families as a result of a moral doctrine prohibiting contraception, or for children born out of wedlock, both reprehensible limitations of responsibility in my judgment. Fourth, the moralist is under obligation, if he is convinced of the propriety in this human situation of an abortion, to seek reform of abortion legislation that would remove the unjust legal barrier to what he believes to be morally appropriate. Other considerations must be brought to bear on the discussion of legal reform, such as the crucial matter of the legal and moral rights of the defenseless unborn persons, but it is consistent with the moral judgment in this case that the laws permit an action which is deemed to be morally approvable. To judge an action to be morally appropriate, and not to seek the alteration of legislation that would make such an action possible without penalties would be a serious inconsistency in the moralist's thinking and action. It would be comparable to approving conscientious objection to specific wars on moral grounds and not seeking to make such objection a legal possibility.

These points are made to indicate that the time and space limits of a moral issue extend beyond the focal point of a particular act. Indeed, the focal point has not been the abortion, but the well-being of the woman over a long range of time. If such a delineation of the situation is made, the responsibility of the moralist must be consonant in its dimensions with that. These points are made to reiterate an earlier one, then, namely, that the delimitation which a moral issue receives from its discussants is a crucial factor in determining what data are significant and what the extent of responsibilities is.

The Location of This Discussion on the Current Map of Moral Theology

This essay began with a description of salient aspects of the traditional Catholic arguments. With reference to each of these, I have emphasized a different way of working. This essay does not provide a totally different way of thinking about the matter; indeed, the concerns of traditional moral theology are brought into it.

In place of the external judge, the position of the persons who must assume responsibility for the decision has been stressed. This requires empathy with the woman and the physician who might become involved. But the moralist himself is responsible for his decision: if he offers recommendations he is responsible to all who accept and act on them. If an abortion is induced, he shares moral responsibility for it. Moral decisions, however, are not made wallowing in sympathy and empathy. The element of disinterested objectivity is a necessity, something of the stance of the external judge or observer is involved. In a process of conversation with one who has the serious moral choice, however, the interpersonal relationship not only establishes the possibilities of open communication, but provides insight and understanding, and sensitizes the affections.

In place of the determination of an action as right or wrong by its conformity to a rule and its application, I have stressed the primacy of the person and human relationships and the concreteness of the choice within limited possibilities. There can be no guarantee of an objectively right action in the situation I have discussed, since there are several values that are objectively important, but that do not resolve themselves into a harmonious relation to one another. Since there is not a single overriding determination of what constitutes a right action, there can be no unambiguously right act.

206

Whereas the moral theology manuals generally limit discussion to the physical aspects of the human situation, I have set these in a wider context of human values, responsibilities, and aspirations. While this does not make the physical less serious, it sets it in relation to other matters of a morally serious nature, and thus qualifies the way one decides by complicating the values and factors to be taken into account.

I find it difficult in discussing possible abortions to limit the personal relationships as exclusively to the physician and the patient as do the manual discussions, and to limit the time span of experience to the fact of pregnancy and action pertaining to it alone. Most significantly in the instance discussed, the conditions under which the pregnancy occurred modify the discussion of the abortion.

The role of compassion and indignation, of attitudes and affections in the process of making a decision is affirmed in my discussion to a degree not admitted in traditional moral theology. Indeed, I indicated the importance of one's basic perspective, and the way in which one's perception of a situation is conditioned by this perspective. Situations cannot be reduced to discrete facts; one's response to them is determined in part by one's faith, basic intentions, and dispositions, as well as by analysis and the rational application of principles.

Although I have only sketched most briefly the theological convictions that inform the perspective, they perhaps have a more central place in the ways in which I proceed than is the case in traditional moral theology. I wish not to suggest there is a deposit of revelation, supernaturally given, which I accept on authority as a basis of moral perspective; such a position is not the alternative to natural law. Ampler elaboration of this, however, is beyond the bounds of this paper.

Although the structure I have used as a model differs from the model used by the Roman Catholic manuals of moral theology, in a specific instance a Catholic moralist might reach a conclusion not strikingly dissimilar from my own in counseling the woman. He could do so by means of the classic Catholic doctrine of good faith. As expounded by Alphonsus Liguori, a confessor is not to disturb the good faith of the penitent if he believes that telling the penitent he is committing a sin will not deter him from his course of action, but will merely put him in "bad faith," that is, in a state of mind where he is aware that what he is doing is opposed to the will of God. There are exceptions to this doctrine, where the penitent must be informed of what is necessary to salvation, or where the common good is endangered by the proposed actions. These exceptions, however, do not seem applicable to the special kind of case I have outlined. Consequently, a Catholic moralist faced with a woman who believes she is doing what is right in seeking an abortion, and who in all probability would not be deterred by advice to the contrary, might well conclude that his responsibility was not to put the woman in bad faith.[5]

This Catholic approach to a particular case accords with mine in recognizing a principle of personal responsibility that the moralist must honor. He cannot coerce the person; in some sense each person must decide for herself or himself. This approach differs from mine, however, in the analysis of the act of abortion, which is treated in a special sense as a sin. Elucidation of this difference would require extensive discussion of the relation of religion and morality in the two approaches, in the uses of the concept of sin, and other matters too large to be developed here. This Catholic approach also differs from mine in the limits it would impose on cooperation with the act by the counselor.

A Catholic moral theologian, if he approved of the outcome of the discussion presented here, might compliment it by indicating that it is an example of prudence informed by charity at work, or that it is an exercise in the virtue of *epikeia,* applying principles to particular cases. If such generosity were shown, I would not be averse to being pleased, for it would indicate that some of the polarizations of contemporary moral theology between ethics of law and situational ethics are excessively drawn. I would also suggest that there is a different valence given to prudence and equity, indeed, to the moral virtues, in the order of ethical analysis here than is the case in the treatises on medical ethics. There is a sense in which the present discussion subordinates law to virtue as points of reliance in making moral decisions.

Since there is no fixed position called situation ethics, it would be futile to distinguish the approach taken here from what cannot be readily defined. I would say in general that in comparison with Paul Lehmann's ethics of the theonomous conscience,[6] with its confidence in a renewed sensitivity and imagination to perceive what God is doing in the world to make and keep human life human, the approach of this essay is more complex, and ultimately less certain about its answer. Further, the weight of responsibility for reflection and for action rests heavily on the actor, since no perceptive powers I have enable me to overcome the distance between God and the action I respond to. I cannot claim to perceive what *God* is doing. The polemical force with which Lehmann attacks "absolutist ethics" is foreign to this approach;[7] while I clearly believe that abstract principles and logic alone do not contain the dynamics of suffering and evil, or of love and good, their utility in bringing clarity to discussion is much treasured.

208

As the morally conscientious soldier fighting in a particular war is convinced that life can and ought to be taken justly but also mournfully,[8] so the moralist can be convinced that the life of the defenseless fetus can be taken less justly but more mournfully.

20

Theology of Pro-choice: A Feminist Perspective

Beverly Wildung Harrison

Much discussion of abortion betrays the heavy hand of misogyny or the hatred of women. We all have a responsibility to recognize this bias—sometimes subtle—when ancient negative attitudes toward women intrude into the abortion debate. It is morally incumbent on us to convert the Christian position to a teaching more respectful of women's concrete history and experience.

My professional peers who are my opponents on this question feel they own the Christian tradition in this matter and recognize no need to rethink their positions in the light of this claim. As a feminist, I cannot sit in silence when women's right to shape the use of our own procreative power is denied. Women's competence as moral decision-makers is once again challenged by the State, even before the moral basis of women's right to procreative choice has been fully elaborated

This essay has been adapted from an address delivered at the Symposium on the Theology of Pro-Choice in the Abortion, sponsored by Religious Leaders for a Free Choice, and the Religious Coalition on Abortion Rights, which took place at the Stephen Wise Free Synagogue, New York, New York on October 9, 1980. Reprinted with permission from the July and September 1981 issues of *The Witness*, P.O. Box 359, Ambler, PA 19002. Revised by the author for this volume.

BEVERLY WILDUNG HARRISON is professor of Christian ethics, Union Theological Seminary, New York, New York.

and recognized. Those who deny women control of procreative power claim that they do so in defense of moral sensibility, in the name of the sanctity of human life. We have a long way to go before the sanctity of human life will include genuine regard and concern for every female already born, and no social policy discussion that obscures this fact deserves to be called moral.

Although some Protestants wrongly claim scriptural warrant for antiabortion teaching, it is, in fact, the assumptions about women and sexuality imbedded in ancient natural-law reasoning that have shaped abortion teaching in Christianity.[1] Unfortunately, all major strands of natural-law reflection have been every bit as awful as Protestant Biblicism on any matter involving human sexuality, including discussion of women's nature and women's divine vocation in relation to procreative power.

As a result, Protestants who oppose procreative choice[2] either tend to follow official Catholic moral theology on these matters or ground their positions in Biblicist anti-intellectualism, claiming that God's word requires no justification other than their claim that it (God's word) says what it says. Against such irrationalism, no rational objections have a chance. But when Protestant fundamentalists give clear reasons why they believe abortion is evil, they, too, invariably revert to traditional natural-law assumptions about women, sex, and procreation. Therefore, it is from the claims of traditional Catholic natural-law thinking on the subject of sexuality, procreation, and women's power of rational choice that misogyny stems and to which direct objection must be registered.

A treatment of any moral problem is inadequate if it fails to analyze the morality of a given act in a way that represents the concrete experience of the agent who faces a decision with respect to this act. Misogyny in Christian discussions of abortion is evidenced clearly in that the abortion decision is never treated in the way it arises as part of the female agent's life process. The decision at issue when the dilemma of choice arises for women is whether or not to be pregnant. In most discussions of the morality of abortion it is treated as an abstract act,[3] rather than as a possible way we deal with a pregnancy, which, frequently, is the result of circumstances beyond the woman's control. In any pregnancy a woman's life is deeply, irrevocably affected. Those who uphold the unexceptional immorality of abortion are probably wise to obscure the fact that an unwanted pregnancy always involves a life-shaping consequence for a woman, because suppressing the identity of the moral agent and the reality of her dilemma greatly reduces the ability to recognize the moral complexity of abortion. When the question of abortion arises it is usually because a woman finds herself facing an *unwanted* pregnancy. Consider the

211

actual circumstances that may precipitate this. One is the situation in which a woman did not intend to be sexually active or did not enter into a sexual act voluntarily. Since women are frequently victims of sexual violence, numerous cases of this type arise because of rape, incest, or forced marital coitus. Many morally sensitive opponents of abortion concede that in such cases abortion *may* be morally justifiable. I insist that in such cases it is a moral *good,* because it is not rational to treat a newly fertilized ovum as though it had the same value as the existent, pregnant, female person, and because it is morally wrong to make the victim of sexual violence suffer the further agonies of unwanted pregnancy and childbearing against her will. Enforced pregnancy would be viewed as a morally reprehensible violation of bodily integrity if women were recognized as fully human moral agents.

Another more frequent case results when a woman—or usually a young girl—participates in heterosexual activity without clear knowledge of how pregnancy occurs and without intention to conceive a child. A girl who became pregnant in this manner would, by traditional natural-law morality, be held to be in a state of invincible ignorance and therefore not morally culpable. One scholarly Roman Catholic nun I met argued—quite appropriately, I believe—that her Church should not consider the abortions of young Catholic girls as morally culpable because the Church overly protected them, which contributed to their lack of understanding procreation or to their inability to cope with the sexual pressures girls experience in contemporary society.

A related type of pregnancy happens when a woman runs risks by not using contraceptives, perhaps because taking precaution in romantic affairs is not perceived as ladylike or requires her to be too unspontaneous about sex. However, when pregnancies occur because women are skirting the edges of responsibility and running risks out of immaturity, is enforced motherhood a desirable solution? Such pregnancies could be minimized only by challenging precisely those childish myths of female socialization embedded in natural-law teaching about female sexuality.

In likelihood, most decisions about abortion arise because mature women who are sexually active with men and who understand the risk of pregnancy nevertheless experience contraceptive failure. Misogynist schizophrenia in this matter is exhibited in that many believe women have more responsibility than men to practice contraception, and that family planning is always a moral good, but even so rule out abortion altogether. Such a split consciousness ignores the fact no inexorable biological line exists between prevention of conception

212

and abortion.[4] More important, such reasoning ignores the genuine risks involved in female contraceptive methods. Some women are at higher risk than others in terms of using the most reliable means of birth control. Furthermore, the reason we do not have more concern for safer contraceptive methods for men and women is that matters relating to women's health and well-being are never urgent in this society. Moreover, many contraceptive failures are due to the irresponsibility of the producers of contraceptives rather than to bad luck.[5] Given these facts, should a woman who actively attempts to avoid pregnancy be punished for contraceptive failure when it occurs?

Misogyny in Theological Argument

In the history of Christian theology, a central metaphor for understanding life, including human life, is as a gift of God. Creation itself has always been seen primarily under this metaphor. It follows that in this creational context procreation itself took on special significance as the central image for divine blessing, the more so within patriarchal societies where it is the male's power that is enhanced by this divine gift. To this day males tend to romanticize procreation as *the* central metaphor for divine blessing.

Throughout history, however, women's power of procreation stands in definite tension with male social control. In fact, what we feminists call patriarchy, i.e. patterned or institutionalized legitimations of male superiority, derives from the need of men, through male-dominated political institutions, such as tribes, states, and religious systems, to control women's power to procreate the species. One with critical consciousness should begin by assuming, then, that many of these efforts at social control of procreation—including some church teaching on contraception and abortion—were part of this institutional system. The perpetuation of patriarchal control itself depended on wresting the power of procreation from women and shaping women's lives accordingly. Natural-law teaching about women's nature is itself part of this system of control.

In the past four centuries the entire Christian story has had to undergo dramatic accommodation to new and emergent world conditions and to the scientific revolution. As the older theological metaphors for creation encountered the rising power of science, a new self-understanding including our human capacity to affect nature had to be incorporated into Christian theology or its central theological story would have become obscurantist. Human agency had to be introjected into a dialectical understanding of creation.

213

The range of human freedom to shape and enhance creation is now celebrated theologically, but only up to the point of changes in our understanding of what is natural for women. Here a barrier has been drawn that declares, No Radical Freedom! The only difference between mainline Protestant and Roman Catholic theologians on these matters is at the point of contraception, which Protestants more readily accept. However, Protestants like Karl Barth and Helmut Thielicke exhibit a subtle shift of mood when they turn to discussing issues regarding women. They exhibit the typical Protestant pattern; they have accepted contraception or family planning as part of the new freedom, granted by God, but both draw back from the idea that abortion could be morally acceptable. In the *Ethics of Sex,* Thielicke offers a romantic, ecstatic celebration of family planning on one page and a total denunciation of abortion as unthinkable on the next.[6] Most Christian *theological* opinion draws the line between contraception and abortion, whereas the *official* Catholic teaching still anathematizes contraception.

The problem, then, is that Christian theology celebrates the power of human freedom to shape and determine the quality of human life except when the issue of procreative choice arises. Abortion is anathema, and widespread sterilization abuse is hardly mentioned! The power of *man* to shape creation radically is never rejected. When one stops to consider the awesome power over nature that males take for granted and celebrate, including the power to alter the conditions of human life in myriad ways, the suspicion dawns that the near hysteria that prevails about the immorality of women's right to choose abortion derives its forces from misogyny rather than from any passion for the sacredness of human life. The refusal of male theologians to incorporate the full range of human power to shape creation into their theological world view when this power relates to the quality of women's lives and women's freedom and women's role as full moral agents, is an index of the continuing misogyny in Christian tradition.

By contrast, a feminist theological approach recognizes that *nothing* is more urgent, in light of the changing circumstances of human beings on planet Earth, than to recognize that the entire natural-historical context of human procreative power has shifted.[7] We desperately need a desacralization of our *biological* power to reproduce,[8] and at the same time a real concern for human dignity and the social conditions for personhood and the values of human relationship.[9] And note that desacralization does not mean complete devaluation of the worth of procreation. It means we must shift away from the notion that the central metaphors for divine blessing are expressed at the biological level to the recognition that

214

our social relations bear the image of what is most holy. The best statement I know on this point comes from Marie Augusta Neal, a Roman Catholic feminist who is also a distinguished sociologist of religion:

> As long as the central human need called for was continued motivation to propagate the race, it was essential that religious symbols idealize that process above all others. Given the vicissitudes of life in a hostile environment, women had to be encouraged to bear children and men to support them; childbearing was central to the struggle for existence. Today, however, the size of the base population, together with knowledge already accumulated about artificial insemination, sperm banking, cloning, make more certain a peopled world.
>
> The more serious human problems now are who will live, who will die and who will decide.[10]

Misogyny in Interpretations of the History of Christian Abortion Teaching

Between persons who oppose all abortions on moral grounds and those who believe abortion is sometimes or frequently morally justifiable, *there is no difference of moral principle.* Pro-choice advocates and antiabortion advocates share the ethical principle of respect for human life, which is probably why the debate is so acrimonious. I have already indicated that one major source of disagreement is the way in which the theological story is appropriated in relation to the changing circumstances of history. In addition, we should recognize that whenever strong moral disagreement is encountered, we simultaneously confront different readings of the history of a moral issue. The way we interpret the past is already laden with and shaped by our present sense of what the moral problem is.

For example, professional male Christian ethicists tend to assume the history of the morality of abortion can best be traced by studying the teaching of the now best-remembered theologians. Looking at the matter this way, one can find plenty of proof-texts to show that *some* of the church fathers (as we call them) condemned abortion and equated abortion with either homicide or murder. Whenever a "leading" churchman equated abortion with homicide or murder, he also *and simultaneously* equated *contraception* with homicide or murder as well. This reflects both male chauvinist biology and the then almost hysterical antisexual bias of the Christian tradition. Claims that one can separate abortion teaching into an ethic of killing separate from an antisexual and antifemale ethic in the history of Christianity do not stand critical scrutiny.[11]

This antisexual, antiabortion tradition is *not* universal, even among

215

theologians and canon lawyers. On the subject of sexuality and its abuse many well-known theologians had nothing to say; abortion was not even mentioned in most moral theology. An important, untold chapter in Christian history is the great struggle that took place in the medieval period, when clerical celibacy came to be *imposed* and the rules of sexual behavior rigidified.

My thesis is that there is a relative disinterest in the question of abortion overall in Christian history. Occasionally, Christian theologians picked up the issue, *especially when these theologians were state-related theologians,* i.e., articulating policy not only for the church, but for the political authority. Demographer Jean Meyer, himself a Catholic, insists that the Christian tradition took over "expansion by population growth" from the Roman empire.[12] Christians only opposed abortion strongly when Christianity was closely identified with imperial state policy or when theologians were inveighing against women and any sexuality except that expressed in the reluctant service of procreation.

The Holy Crusade quality of present teaching on abortion is quite new in Christianity, and is related to cultural shifts that are requiring the Christian tradition to choose sides in the present ideological struggle, under pressure to rethink its entire attitude to women and sexuality. No Protestant clergy or theologian gave early support for proposed nineteenth-century laws banning abortion in the United States. It is my impression that Protestant clergy, usually married and often poor, were aware that romanticizing nature's bounty with respect to procreation resulted in a great deal of human suffering. The Protestant clergy who finally did join the antiabortion crusade were racist, classist, white clergy, who feared America's strength was being threatened because white, middle-class, respectable women had a lower birthrate than black and ethnic women. Such arguments are still with us.

One other point must be stressed. Until the late nineteenth century the natural-law tradition, and Biblicism following it, tended to define the act of abortion as interruption of pregnancy after ensoulment, which was understood to be the point at which the breath of God entered the fetus. The point at which ensoulment was said to occur varied, but most typically it was marked by quickening, when fetal movement began. Knowledge about embryology was primitive until the past half-century, so this commonsense understanding prevailed. As a result, when abortion was condemned in earlier Christian teaching it was understood to refer to the termination of a pregnancy well into the process of this pregnancy, after ensoulment. Until the late nineteenth century, then, abortion in ecclesiastical teaching

216

applied only to termination of prenatal life in more advanced stages of pregnancy.

Another distortion in the male-generated history of this issue derives from failure to note that, until the development of safe, surgical, elective abortion, the act of abortion commonly referred to something done to the woman, with or without her consent (see Exodus 22), either as a wrong done a husband or for the better moral reason that abortion was an act of violence against *both* a pregnant woman and fetal life. In recent discussion it is the woman who does the wrongful act. No one would deny that abortion, if it terminates a pregnancy against the woman's wishes, is morally wrong. And until recent decades abortion endangered the woman's life as much as it did the prenatal life in her womb. No one has a right to discuss the morality of abortion today without recognizing that one of the traditional and appropriate moral reasons for objecting to abortion —concern for women's well-being—now inheres in the pro-choice side of the debate.

Beyond all this the deepest moral flaw in the pro-life position's historical view is that none of its proponents has attempted to reconstruct the all but desperate struggle by sexually active women to gain some proximate control over nature's profligacy in conception. Under the most adverse conditions women have had to try to control their fertility—everywhere, always. As noted, women's relationship to procreation irrevocably marks and shapes our lives, even those who have sought to avoid sexual contact with males, through celibacy or through lesbian love, have been potential, even probable, victims of male sexual violence or have had to bear heavy social stigma for refusing the centrality of dependence on men and of procreation in their lives. Infertile women, too, have their lives shaped by procreative expectation. Women's lack of social power, in all recorded history, has made this struggle to control procreation a life-bending, often life-destroying one.

So most women have had to do whatever they could to prevent too numerous pregnancies. In societies and cultures, except the most patriarchal, the processes of procreation have been transmitted through women's culture. Birth control techniques have been widely practiced, and some primitive ones have proven effective. Increasingly, anthropologists are gaining hints of how procreative control occurred in some premodern societies. Women often have had to choose to risk their lives in order not to have that extra child which would destroy the family's ability to cope or that would bring about an unmanageable crisis in their lives.

We have to concede that modern medicine, for all its misogyny, has replaced some dangerous contraceptive practices still widely used where surgical abortion is unavailable. In light of these gains more privileged Western women must not lose the ability to imagine the real-life pressures that lead women in other cultures to resort to ground-glass douches, reeds inserted in the uterus, and so on, to induce labor. The radical nature of methods women use bespeaks the desperation involved in unwanted pregnancy.

Nor should we suppress the fact that a major means of birth control now is as it was in earlier times, *infanticide*. And let no one imagine that women made decisions to expose or kill newborn infants casually. Women understand what many men cannot seem to grasp —that the birth of a child requires that some person must be prepared to care, without interruption, for this infant, provide material resources and energy-draining amounts of time and attention for it. The human infant is the most needy and dependent of all newborn creatures. It seems to me that men, especially celibate men, romanticize this total and uncompromising dependency of the infant on the already existing human community. Women bear the brunt of this reality and know its full implications. And this dependency is even greater in a fragmented, centralized urban-industrial modern culture than in a rural culture, where another pair of hands often increased an extended family unit's productive power. No historical interpretation of abortion as a moral issue that ignores these matters deserves moral standing in the present debate.

In drawing this section to a close, I want to stress that if present efforts to criminalize abortion succeed, we will need a State apparatus of massive proportions to enforce compulsory childbearing. In addition, withdrawal of legal abortion will create one more massively profitable underworld economy in which the Mafia and other sections of quasi-legal capitalism may and will profitably invest. The radical Right promises to get the State out of regulation of people's lives, but what they really mean is that they will let economic activity go unrestrained. What their agenda signifies for the personal lives of women is quite another matter.

An adequate historical perspective on abortion recognizes the long struggle women have waged for some degree of control over fertility and their efforts to regain control of procreative power from patriarchal and State-imperial culture and institutions. Such a perspective also takes into account that more nearly adequate contraceptive methods and the existence of safe, surgical, elective abortion represent positive historic steps toward full human freedom and dignity for women. While the same gains in medical knowledge also open the way to new forms of sterilization abuse and to social

218

pressures against some women's use of their power of procreation, I know of no women who would choose to return to a state of lesser knowledge about these matters.

There has been an objective gain in the quality of women's lives for those fortunate enough to have access to procreative choice. That millions upon millions of women as yet do not possess even the rudimentary conditions—moral or physical—for such choice is obvious. Our goal morally should be to struggle against those real barriers—poverty, racism, and antifemale cultural oppression—that prevent authentic choice from being a reality for every woman. In this process we will be able to minimize the need for abortions only insofar as we place the abortion debate in the real lived-world context of women's lives.

Misogynist Moral Factors in the Debate

The greatest *strategic* problem of pro-choice advocates is the widespread assumption that pro-lifers have a monopoly on the moral factors that ought to enter into decisions about abortion. Moral legitimacy seems to adhere to *their* position in part because traditionalists have an array of religiomoral terminology at their command that the sometimes more secular proponents of choice lack. But those who would displace women's power of choice by the power of the State and/or the medical profession do not deserve the aura of moral sanctity. We must do our homework if we are to dispel this myth of moral superiority. A major way in which Christian moral theologians and moral philosophers contribute to this monopoly of moral sanctity is by equating fetal or prenatal life with human personhood in a simplistic way, and by failing to acknowledge changes regarding this issue in the history of Christianity.

We need to remember that even in Roman Catholic teaching the definition of the status of fetal life has shifted over time and that the status of prenatal life involves a moral judgment, not a scientific one. The question is properly posed this way: What status are we morally wise to predicate to prenatal human life, given that the fetus is not yet a fully existent human being? Those constrained under Catholic teaching have been required for the past ninety years to believe a human being exists from conception, when the ovum and sperm merge.[13] This answer from *one* tradition has had far wider impact on our culture than most people recognize. Other Christians come from traditions that do not offer (and could not offer, given their conception of the structure of the church as moral community) a definitive answer to this question.

Even so, some contemporary Protestant medical ethicists, fascinated by the recent discoveries in genetics—deoxyribonucleic acid (DNA), for example—have all but sacralized the moment in which the genetic code is implanted as the moment of humanization, which leaves them close to the traditional Roman position. Protestant male theologians have long let their enthrallment with science lead to a sacralization of specific exciting scientific discoveries, usually to the detriment of theological and moral clarity. (*Moral* here is defined as that which makes for the self-respect and well-being of human persons and their environment.) In any case, I would like to make two responses to the claim that the fetus in early stages of development is a human life or, more dubiously, a human person.

1. Whatever one's judgment about the moral status of the fetus, it cannot be argued that it deserves greater moral standing in analysis than does the pregnant woman. This matter of assessing the value of prenatal life is where morally sensitive people make differing judgments. What I cannot believe is that any morally sensitive person would fail to value the woman's full existent life less than they value early fetal life. Most women can become pregnant and carry fetal life to term many, many times in their lifetimes. The distinctly human power is not our biologic capacity to bear children, but our power actively to love, to nurture, to care for one another and to shape one another's existence in cultural and social interaction.[14] To equate a biologic process with full normative humanity is crass biologic reductionism, and such reductionism is never practiced in religious ethics except where women's lives and well-being are involved.

2. A second point is that even though prenatal life, as it moves toward biologic individuation of human form, has value, the equation of abortion with murder is dubious. And the equation of abortion with homicide—the taking of human life—should be carefully weighed. We should also remember that we live in a world where men extend other men wide moral range in relationship to justifiable homicide. For example, the just war tradition has legitimated widespread forms of killing in war, and Christian ethicists have often extended great latitude to rulers and those in power in making choices about killing human beings.[15] Would that such moralists would extend equal benefit of a doubt to any woman facing life-crushing psychological and politico-economic resources to support her childbearing! Men, daily, make life-determining decisions concerning nuclear power or chemical use in the environment, for example, that affect the well-being of fetuses, and our society expresses no significant opposition, even when such decisions do widespread genetic damage. When we argue for the appropriateness of legal abortion, moral outrage rises.

The so-called pro-life position also gains support by involving the general principle of respect for human life as foundational to its morality in a way that suggests that the pro-choice advocates are unprincipled. I have already noted that pro-choice advocates have every right to claim the same moral principle, and that this debate, like most debates that are morally acrimonious, is in no sense about basic moral principles. I do not believe there is any clear-cut conflict of principle in this very deep, very bitter controversy.

It needs to be stressed that we all have an absolute obligation to honor any moral principle that seems, after rational deliberation, to be sound. This is the one absolutism appropriate to ethics. There are often several moral principles relevant to a decision and many ways to relate a given principle to a decisional context. For most right-to-lifers only one principle has moral standing in this argument. Admitting only one principle to one's process of moral reasoning means that a range of other moral values is slighted. Right-to-lifers are also moral absolutists in the sense that they admit only one possible meaning or application of the principle they invoke. Both these types of absolutism obscure moral debate and lead to less, not more, rational deliberation. The principle of respect for human life is one we should all honor, but we must also recognize that this principle often comes into conflict with other valid moral principles in the process of making real, lived-world decisions. Understood in an adequate way, this principle can be restated to mean we should treat what falls under a reasonable definition of human life as having sanctity or intrinsic moral value. But even when this is clear, other principles are needed to help us choose between two intrinsic values, i.e., between the prenatal life and the pregnant woman's life.

Another general moral principle from which we cannot exempt our actions is the principle of justice, or right relations between persons and between groups of persons and communities. Another relevant principle is respect for all that supports human life, i.e., the natural environment. As any person knows who thinks deeply about morality, genuine moral conflicts, as often as not, are due not to ignoring moral principles, but to the fact that different principles lead to conflicting implications for action or are selectively related to decisions.

One further proviso on this issue of principles in moral reasoning: There are several distinct theories among religious ethicists and moral philosophers as to what the function of principles ought to be. One group believes moral principles are for the purpose of terminating the process of moral reasoning. Hence, if this sort of moralist tells you always to honor the principle of respect for human life, what he or she means is for you to stop reflection and act in a certain way—in this case to accept one's pregnancy regardless of consequences. By contrast, others believe that principles (broad, generalized moral criteria) or rules (narrower, specific moral prescriptions) should function to *open up processes of reasoning* rather than closing them off. The principle of respect for life, on this reading, is not invoked to prescribe action, but to help locate and weigh values, to illuminate a range of values that always inhere in significant human decisions. A major difference in the moral debate on abortion, then, is that some believe that to invoke the principle of respect for human life settles the matter, stops debate, and precludes the single, simple act of abortion. By contrast, many of us believe the breadth of the principle opens us up to reconsider what the essential moral quality of human life is all about and to increase moral seriousness about choosing whether or when to bear children.

Two other concerns related to our efforts to make a strong moral case for women's right to procreative choice need to be touched on.

The first has to do with the problems our Christian tradition creates for any attempt to make clear why women's right to control our bodies is an urgent and substantive moral claim. One of Christianity's greatest weaknesses is its spiritualizing neglect of respect for the physical body and physical well-being. Tragically, women, more than men, are expected in Christian teaching never to take their own well-being as a moral consideration. I want to stress, then, that we have no moral tradition in Christianity which starts with body-space, or body-right, as a basic condition of moral relations. Hence, many Christian ethicists simply do not get the point when we speak of women's right to bodily integrity. They seem to think such talk is a disguise for women to plead self-indulgence.

We must articulate our view that body-right is a basic moral claim and also remind our hearers that there is no analogy among other human activities to women's procreative power. Pregnancy is a unique human experience. In any social relation, body-space must be respected or nothing deeply human or moral can be created. The social institutions most similar to compulsory pregnancy in their moral violations of body-space are chattel slavery or peonage. These institutions distort the moral relations of the community and deform this community over time. (Witness racism in the United States.) Coercion of women, through enforced sterilization or enforced pregnancy legitimates unjust power in the intimate human relationships, and cuts to the heart of our capacity for moral social relations. As we should recognize, given our violence-prone society, people learn violence at home and at an early age when women's lives are violated!

Even so, we must be careful when we make the case for our right to bodily integrity, not to confuse moral rights with mere liberties. To claim that we have a moral right to procreative choice does not mean we believe women can exercise this right free of all moral claims from the community. For example, we need to teach girl children that childbearing is not a purely capricious, individualistic matter, and we need to challenge the assumption that a woman who enjoys motherhood should have as many children as she and her mate wish, regardless of its effects on others.[16] Population self-control is a moral issue, although more so in high-consuming, affluent societies like our own than in nations where a modest, simple, and less wasteful life-style obtains.

A final point that needs to be mentioned is the need, as we work politically for a pro-choice social policy, to avoid the use of morally objectionable arguments to mobilize support for our side of the issue. One can get a lot of political mileage in U.S. society by using covert racist and classist appeals ("abortion lowers the cost of welfare roles or reduces illegitimacy," or "paying for abortions saves the taxpayers money in the long run"). Sometimes it is argued that good politics is more important than good morality and that one should use whatever arguments work to gain political support. I do not believe these crassly utilitarian[17] arguments turn out, in the long run, to be good politics—for they are costly to our sense of polis and of community. But even if they were effective in the short run, I am doubly sure that on the issue of the right to choose abortion, good morality doth a good political struggle make. I believe, deeply, that moral right is on the side of the struggle for the freedom and self-respect of women, especially poor and nonwhite women, and on the side of developing social policy which assures that every child born can be certain to be a wanted child. Issues of justice are those that deserve the deepest moral caretaking as we develop a political strategy.

Only when people see that they cannot prohibit safe, legal, elective surgical abortion without violating the conditions of well-being for the vast majority of women—especially those most socially vulnerable because of historic patterns of oppression—will the effort to impose a selective, abstract morality of the sanctity of human life on all of us cease. This is a moral battle par excellence, and whenever we forget that we make it harder to reach the group most important to the cause of procreative choice—those women who have never suffered from childbearing pressures, who have not yet put this issue into a larger historical context, and who reverence women's historical commitment to childbearing. We will surely not reach them with pragmatic appeals to the taxpayer's wallet! To be sure, we cannot let such women go unchallenged as they support ruling-class ideology that the State should control procreation. But they will not change their politics until they see that pro-choice is grounded in a deeper, tougher, more caring moral vision than the political option they now endorse.

Social Policy Dimensions of the Debate

Most people fail to understand that in ethics we need, provisionally, to separate our reflection on the morality of specific acts from questions about how we express our moral values within our social institutions and systems (i.e., social policy). When we do this, the morality of abortion appears in a different light. Focusing attention away from the single act of abortion to the larger historical context enables us to make clear where we most differ from the pro-lifers, i.e., in our total skepticism that a State-enforced antiabortion policy could ever have the intended pro-life consequences they claim.

We must always insist that the objective social conditions that make women, and children already born, highly vulnerable can only be worsened by a social policy of compulsory pregnancy. However one judges the moral quality of the individual act of abortion (and here, differences among us do exist that are morally justifiable) it is still necessary to distinguish between how one judges the act of abortion morally and what one believes a society-wide policy on abortion should be. We must not let those who have moral scruples against the personal act ignore the fact that a just social policy must also include active concern for enhancement of women's well-being and for policies that would in fact make abortions less necessary. To anathematize abortion when the social and material conditions for control of procreation do not exist is to blame the victim, not to address the deep dilemmas of female existence in this society.

Even so, there is no reason for those of us who celebrate procreative choice as a great moral good to pretend that resort to abortion is ever a desirable means of expressing this choice. I know of no one on the pro-choice side who has confused the desirability of the availability of abortion with the celebration of this act itself. We all have every reason to hope that safer, more reliable means of contraception may be found and that violence against women will be reduced. Furthermore, we should be emphatic that our social policy demands include opposition to sterilization abuse, insistence on higher standards of health care for women and children, better prenatal care, reduction of unnecessary surgery on women's reproductive systems, increased research to improve contraception, etc. Nor should we draw back from criticizing a health-care delivery system that exploits women. An

224

abortion industry thrives on the profitability of abortion, but women are not to blame.

A feminist pro-life position is a position which demands social conditions that support women's full, self-respecting right to procreative choice, including the right not to be sterilized against their wills, the right to choose abortion as a birth control means of last resort, and the right to a prenatal and postnatal health-care system that will reduce infant mortality and infant and maternal illness, and that will also reduce the now widespread trauma of having to deliver one's babies in a rigid, impersonal, health-care system.

Pro-lifers do best politically when we allow them to keep the discussion narrowly focused on the morality of the act of abortion and on the moral value of the fetus. We do best politically when we make the deep-level connections between the full context of this issue in women's lives, including this society's systemic or patterned injustice toward women.

It is well to remember that it has been traditional Catholic natural-law ethics that most clarified and stressed this distinction between the morality of an individual act, on the one hand, and the policies that produce the optional social morality, on the other. This tradition is probably reflected in the fact that even now most polls show that slightly more Catholics than Protestants believe it unwise for the State to attempt to regulate abortion. In the past, Catholics, more than Protestants, have been wary of using the State as an instrument of moral crusade. Tragically, by taking their present approach to abortion, the Roman Catholic hierarchy may be risking the loss of the deepest wisdom of its own ethical tradition. By failing to acknowledge a distinction between the Church's moral teaching on the act of abortion and the question of what is a desirable social policy to minimize abortion, as well as by overemphasis on this issue to the neglect of (other) social justice concerns, the Roman Catholic Church may well be dissipating the best of its moral tradition.[18]

If we are to be a society genuinely concerned to enhance women's well-being and to minimize the necessity of abortions, thereby avoiding the danger over time of becoming an abortion culture,[19] what kind of a society must we become? It is here that the moral clarity of the feminist analysis becomes most obvious.

How may we reduce the number of abortions due to contraceptive failure? By placing greater emphasis on medical research in this area, by requiring producers of contraceptives to behave more responsibly, and by developing patterns of institutional life that place as much emphasis on male responsibility for procreation and long-term care and nurturance of children as on female responsibility.

How may we reduce the number of abortions due to childish ignorance about sexuality among girl children or adult women and their mates? By adopting a widespread program of sex education, and by supporting institutional policies that teach male and female children alike that a girl is as fully capable as a boy of enjoying sex and that both must share moral responsibility for preventing pregnancy except when they have decided, as a deliberative moral act, to have a child.

How would we reduce the necessity of abortion due to sexual violence against women in and out of marriage? By challenging vicious male-generated myths that women exist primarily to meet the sexual needs of men; that women are, by nature, those who are really fulfilled only through their procreative powers. We would teach feminist history, as the truthful history of the race, stressing that historic patterns of patriarchy were morally wrong and that a humane or moral society would be a fully nonsexist society.

Technological developments that may reduce the need for abortions are not entirely within our control, but the sociomoral ethos that makes abortion common is within our power to change. And we would begin to create such conditions by adopting a thoroughgoing feminist program for society. Nothing less, I submit, expresses genuine respect for *all* human life.

Notes

Abstract

Abbreviations

AAS   *Acta Apostolicae Sedis, commentarium officiale;* Rome: 1909f.

ES   *Enchiridion Symbolorum Definitionum de Rebus Fidei et Morum,* H. Denzinger, A. Schonmetzer, et al., editors (32nd. ed.: Barcelona: Herder, 1963).

ThE   Helmut Thielicke, *Theological Ethics.*

ST   *Summa Theologica.*

TS   *Theological Studies.*

Chapter 3. The Woman's Right of Privacy

1. Larry Bumpass and Charles F. Westoff, "The Perfect Contraceptive Population," *Science,* Vol. 169, No. 3951 (September 18, 1970), pp. 1177, 1180.
2. "The association of people is not mentioned in the Constitution nor in the Bill of Rights. The right to educate a child in a school of the parents' choice—whether public or private or parochial—is also not mentioned. Nor is the right to study any particular subject or any foreign language. Yet the first Amendment has been construed to include certain of those rights." *Griswold v. Connecticut,* 381 U.S. 479, 482 (1965).
3. *Loving v. Commonwealth,* 388 U.S. 1, 12 (1967) (alternate ground of decision).
4. *Skinner v. Oklahoma,* 316 U.S. 535, 536 (1942).
5. *Griswold v. Connecticut,* 381 U.S. 479 (1965).
6. *Pierce v. Society of Sisters,* 268 U.S. 510 (1925).
7. *United States v. Guest,* 383 U.S. 745 (1966).
8. *California v. Belous,* 71 Cal. 2d 954, 458 P.2d 194, 199, 80 Cal. Rptr. 354 (1969), cert. denied, 397 U.S. 915 (1970).
9. *Doe v. Bolton,* 319 F. Supp. 1048, 1055 (N.D. Ga. 1970) (per curiam).
10. *Doe v. Scott,* 321 F. Supp. 1385, 1389–90 (N.D. Ill.) appeal docketed sub nom. *Hanrahan v. Doe,* 39 U.S.L.W. 3438 (U.S. Mar. 29, 1971) (No. 70–105, 1971 Term).

11. *California v. Belous,* 80 Cal. Rptr. 354, 359 (1969) cert. denied, 397 U.S. 915 (1970).
12. Christopher Tietze, "Legal Abortion In Eastern Europe," *Journal of the American Medical Association,* April 1961.
13. *Studies in Family Planning* (New York: Population Council), Vol. 34 (September 1969), pp. 6–8.
14. CGST 31–236(5), *Janello v. Administrator, Unemployment Compensation Act,* 178 A.2d 282, 23 Conn. Supp. 155 (1961).
15. *Lukienchuk v. Administrator, Unemp. Comp. Act,* 176 A.2d 892, 23 Conn. Sup. 85 (Super. Ct., 1961).
16. *Lenz v. Administrator, Unemp. Comp. Act,* 17 Conn. Sup. 315 (Super. Ct., 1951).
17. *Phillips v. Martin Marietta Corp.,* 411 F.2d 1 (5th Cir., 1969).
18. *American Women,* Report of the President's Commission on the Status of Women (1963), p. 11.

Chapter 4. Rules for Abortion Debate

1. "Call to Concern," *Christianity and Crisis,* Vol. XXXVII (1977), p. 222.
2. James Burtchaell, "A Call and a Reply," *Christianity and Crisis,* Vol. XXXVII (1977), pp. 221–22.
3. Pope Paul VI, "Pourquoi l'église ne peut accepter l'avortement," *Documentation Catholique,* Vol. LXX (1973), pp. 4–5.
4. Daniel Callahan, "Abortion: Thinking and Experiencing," *Christianity and Crisis,* Vol. XXXII (1973), pp. 295–98.
5. *The New York Times,* January 23, 1973, editorial.
6. Roger L. Shinn, "Personal Decisions and Social Policies in a Pluralist Society," *Perkins Journal,* Vol. XXVII (1973), pp. 58–63. (See chapter 17 in this book.)
7. This statement is cited in Franz Scholz, "Durch ethische Grentzsituationem aufworfene Normenprobleme," *Theologisch-praktische Quartalschrift,* Vol. CXXIII (1975), p. 342.
8. "Déclaration des évêques belges sur l'avortement," *Documentation Catholique,* Vol. LXX (1973), pp. 432–38.
9. Vatican Council II, "Pastoral Constitution on the Church in the Modern World (*Gaudium et spes*), translated from the Latin and reprinted in Walter M. Abbott, ed., *The Documents of Vatican II* (New York: Herder & Herder/Association Press, 1966), pp. 199–308, No. 62.
10. Bernard Häring, *Medical Ethics* (Notre Dame, IN: Fides, 1973), p. 89.
11. Martin I. Silverman, *Sh'ma,* January 20, 1978.
12. Linda Bird Francke, *The Ambivalence of Abortion* (New York: Random House, 1978).

Chapter 8. The Roman Catholic Position

1. James M. Gustafson, "A Christian Approach to the Ethics of Abortion," *The Dublin Review,* No. 514 (Winter 1967–68), pp. 347–50.
2. See, for instance, Bernard Häring, *The Law of Christ* (Westminster, MD: Newman Press, 1966), Vol. III, p. 209: "God alone is the author of life and death. No physician may pass and execute the sentence of death on one who is innocent. . . . If despite all his sincere efforts . . . he is not successful, then God Himself has rendered the decision and passed the verdict on a human life." Fr. Charles McFadden, in line with many other

Catholic moralists, argues that only those who are theists can understand this kind of point (*Medical Ethics* [3d. ed.; Philadelphia, F.A. Davis Co., 1955], p. 165).

3. Thomas J. O'Donnell, "Abortion, II (Moral Aspect)," *New Catholic Encyclopedia* (New York: McGraw-Hill, 1967), Vol. I, p. 29.

4. I. Aertnys et al., *Theologiae Moralis* (17th ed.; Turin: Marietti, 1956), pp. 547–49.

5. Richard A. McCormick, "Morality of War," *New Catholic Encyclopedia* (New York: McGraw-Hill, 1967), Vol. XIV, p. 805; see Jonathan Bennett, "Whatever the Consequences," *Analysis*, January 1966, pp. 83–102.

6. Cf. John P. Kenny, *Principles of Medical Ethics* (Westminster, MD: Newman Press, 1952), p. 131; Giuseppe Bosio, "Animazione," *Enciclopedia Cattolica* (Rome: Citta del Vaticano, 1948), cols. 1352–54; H. Noldin et al., *Summa Theologica Moralis*, Vol. II (34th ed.; Innsbruck: F. Rauch, 1963), p. 313; Rudolph Joseph Gerber, "When Is the Human Soul Infused?," *Laval Théologique et Philosophique*, Vol. XXII (1966), pp. 234–47.

7. *Ethical and Religious Directives for Catholic Hospitals* (St. Louis: The Catholic Hospital Association of the United States and Canada, 1965), p. 4; see also Karl Rahner, *Schriften zur Theologie* (Einsiedeln: Benziger Verlag, 1966), p. 317, where the unborn child is called a human being.

8. Robert F. Drinan, "The Inviolability of the Right to be Born," *Abortion and the Law*, edited by David T. Smith (Cleveland: Western Reserve University Press, 1967), p. 107.

9. John T. Noonan Jr., "Abortion and the Catholic Church: A Summary History," *Natural Law Forum*, Vol. XII (1967), p. 125.

10. See David Granfield, *The Abortion Decision* (New York: Doubleday, 1969), chapter 1, "The Scientific Background," pp. 15–41.

11. Josef Fuchs, *Natural Law*, translated by H. Reckter and J.A. Dowling (New York: Sheed & Ward, 1965), p. 123. A standard manual of moral theology that argues in the same fashion is E. Genicot, J. Salsmans, A. Gortebecke, J. Beyer, *Institutiones Theologiae Moralis*, Vol. I (17th ed.; [Beyer] Louvain: Desclee de Brouwer, 1964), pp. 304–5.

12. Granfield, *The Abortion Decision*, op. cit., p. 144.

13. Robert F. Drinan, "The Right of the Foetus to be Born," *The Dublin Review*, No. 514 (Winter 1967–68), p. 377.

14. O'Donnell, "Abortion, II," op. cit., p. 219.

15. Häring, *The Law of Christ*, op. cit., p. 209.

16. Noonan, "Abortion and the Catholic Church," op. cit., p. 131.

17. I. Aertnys et al., *Theologiae Moralis*, op. cit., p. 547.

18. John Marshall, *The Ethics of Medical Practice* (London: Darton, Longman & Todd, 1960), p. 103.

19. Richard A. McCormick, *America*, Vol. CXVII (December 9, 1967), p. 717.

20. *S.T.*, IIa-IIae. q. 64, art. 7.

21. This set of specifications has been taken from Noldin et al., *Summa Theologica Moralis*, op. cit., pp. 84ff.; for an application to abortion decisions, see A. Vermeersch, *Theologiae Moralis*, Vol. I (4th ed.; Rome: Gregorian University Press, 1967), pp. 105–7; F. Hurth, *De Statibus* (Rome: Gregorian University Press, 1946), p. 325; E. Genicot et al., *Institutiones Theologiae Moralis*, op. cit., pp. 305–6; "Aborto," *Enciclopedia Cattolica* (Rome: Città del Vaticano, 1948), col. 107.

22. A. Bouscaren, *Ethics of Ectopic Operations* (2d ed.; Milwaukee: Bruce, 1943), pp. 1–2. Bouscaren's book remains the most thorough treatment of the subject of ectopic operations. See also, Gerard Kelly, *Medico-Moral*

Problems (St. Louis: The Catholic Hospital Association, 1958), p. 26; Joseph J. Farraher, "Notes on Moral Theology," *TS,* Vol. XXII (December 1961), p. 622; John J. Lynch, "Ectopic Pregnancy: A Theological Review," *TS,* Vol. XXVIII (February 1961), p. 12.

23. See Noldin et al., *Summa Theologica Moralis,* op. cit., pp. 340ff.
24. Granfield, *The Abortion Decision,* op. cit., p. 139.
25. Noonan, "Abortion and the Catholic Church," op. cit., p. 130.
26. Fuchs, *Natural Law,* op. cit., p. 131.
27. Granfield, *The Abortion Decision,* op. cit., p. 143.
28. Noonan, "Abortion and the Catholic Church," op. cit., p. 130.

Chapter 9. The Morality of Abortion

1. In order to take care of the case of identical twins (and also to account for the special ways in which our already unique combination of genetic determiners develops over a lifetime), it is necessary, of course, to bring in the modern version of creationism to which I have referred. Identical twins have the same genotype. They arise from the same informational speck. Yet each is and knows he or she is a unique, unrepeatable human person, something that never was by virtue of genes. He or she became something, at some time and in some manner, that was not already, from the fission following original conception. It is the environment who is the maker of all twin differences and the creator of a twin person's unsharable individual being; after they were born the environment "infused" this into these two blobs of identical hereditary material, which contained not only an incalculable number of powers distinguishing them as human blobs but also an incalculable number of the features of the individual beings each is to spend a whole lifetime becoming and exhibiting.

   The case of identical twins does suggest a significant modification of any proof from genotype. If we are seeking to locate a moment in the development of nascent life subsequent to impregnation and prior to birth (or graduation from Princeton) at which it would be reasonable to believe that an individual life *begins* to be inviolate, it is at least *arguable* that this takes place at the stage of *blastocyst.* In the blastocyst there appears a primitive streak across the hollow cluster of developing cells that signals the separation of the same genotype into identical twins. This segmentation is completed by about the time of implantation, i.e., on the seventh or eighth day after ovulation. It might be asserted that at blastocyst—not earlier, not later—these two products of human generation become animate, each a unique individual soul. This is *not* to say that any credit is to be given to those self-serving arguments that implantation is the first moment of life having claims on our respect. These are, in the worst sense of the word, mere rationalizations currently offered for the purpose of rejecting out of hand the proofs that intrauterine devices (IUDs) are abortifacient, and that the morning-after or retroactive pill (which will be available soon) will directly abort a human life. Still, blastocyst (which, as it happens, is roughly coincident with implantation) affords serious moralists a fact concerning nascent life (and not only concerning its location) that may and must be taken into account when dealing with the morality of using IUDs or a retroactive contraceptive pill. This may have bearing on whether the question raised by these scientific applications is one of abortion or contraception only, or of an attack on prehuman organic matter.

2. Many of the themes and distinctions in the text above are exhibited in the remarks of a much-used commentary on the Code of Canon Law of 1917, specifically on Canon 985, in reference to actions that after baptism would incur for a person "irregularity by delict" and render this person unworthy of entering the clerical state or of exercising the orders already received. The paragraph is as follows: "Those who perform an abortion on a human being incur irregularity, provided, of course, the act is committed, not accidentally or unawares, but intentionally or through grievous culpability, even though by accident. The aborted fetus must be a *fetus humanus,* and is generally added, *animatus,* i.e., a living human fetus. We were surprised to see no reference, among Card. Gasparri's quotations, to the Constitution of Gregory XIV, "*Sedes Apostolica,*" of May 31, 1591, which restricted irregularity and penalties to the *fetus animatus,* as the old law had it. However, said Constitution is quoted under can. 2350, 1. We believe that the unanimous teaching of the school should not be set aside, especially since the wording *fetus humanus* can only signify a living fetus. Animation, as stated before, takes place within the first week after conception. Theologians as well as canonists admit that the old theory concerning animation may still be held as far as the incurring of penalties and irregularities is concerned. This theory is that between the conception and the animation of a male fetus forty days, and of a female fetus, eighty days elapse. As long as no authentic declaration has been issued, the strict interpretation applied to penal laws may be followed here, and the period of forty, respectively eighty days be admitted. At any rate, we cannot scientifically speak of a human fetus before the lapse of six days after conception." (Roger John Huser, *The Crime of Abortion in Canon Law* [Washington, DC: Catholic University of America, 1942], quoted by Eugene Quay, "Justifiable Abortion," *Georgetown Law Journal,* Vol. XLIX, No. 3 [Spring, 1961], p. 438.)
3. That is, on the assumption that the morality of abortion is—at least to some degree—a science-based issue. After attributing to the present writer the view that "the biological and genetic criteria are the only practical way of resolving the problem," Charles E. Curran goes on to point out (with a degree of approval) that "the problem exists precisely because some people will not accept the biological and genetic criteria for *establishing* the beginning of human life" ["Natural Law and Contemporary Moral Theology," in Charles E. Curran, ed., *Contraception: Authority and Dissent* (New York: Herder & Herder, 1969), p. 164 and n. 24, italics added]. It is in place here simply to point out that one cannot arbitrarily have it both ways. One cannot appeal to those paper popes—medical and socioscientific research papers, or scientific findings in general—when in agreement with them in some matters and then disavow the relevance of biological data when one wants to mount a moral argument loosed from such considerations.
4. Glanville Williams, *The Sanctity of Life and the Criminal Law* (New York: Knopf, 1957), p. 231. On the assumption that men are *rational* animals even when they are discussing controversial moral questions and controverted public questions such as abortion, we can demand a degree of consistency between their views of when a human life begins and when a human life ends. If electroencephophalography is to determine the moment of death, electroencephalography should be decisive in determining the moment of life's beginning. If spontaneous heartbeat still counts as a vital sign for the terminal patient, it would seem also to be a

good candidate for inclusion among the vital signs of when the fetus becomes alive among us. If respiration should ever be dismissed as an indication that a brain-damaged patient is still alive, why then should respiration at birth be given such importance? If the achievement of brain and heart and lung function are all to be counted at the first of life as necessary for an individual to qualify as a being deserving respect and protection, why should not the cessation of all three be required before we cease to protect this same individual when she or he comes to the end of life?

5. Tertullian, *Apologia,* Vol. IX, pp. 6–7.
6. Karl Barth, *Church Dogmatics* (Edinburgh: T & T Clark, 1961), pt. III/4, para. 55, p. 335. All parenthetical references in the text are to this work.
7. Ibid., p. 338.
8. Ibid., p. 339.
9. Ibid., p. 344.
10. Ibid., pp. 415–16.
11. Ibid., p. 416.
12. Ibid., p. 418.
13. Ibid., p. 425.
14. No less an authority than Thomas Aquinas can be cited in support of this analysis of an act of justifiable killing, in his original formulation of the rule of double effect (*S.T.,* IIa-IIae, q. 64, art. 7). After much derision of Catholic moral analysis, Williams makes this same point in *The Sanctity of Life,* op. cit., p. 204.
15. See Richard A. McCormick, "Past Church Teaching on Abortion," *Proceedings of the Catholic Theological Society of America,* Vol. XXIII (1968), pp. 131–51, especially pp. 137–40.
16. "Abortion and the Law," *CBS Reports,* April 5, 1965.
17. Note that I say, "lead to less evil being done than is *done,*" not "to less evil *happening* than now occurs." This is to say that a primary legislative purpose of law and of the reform of law in this area should remain a moral one. The goal of law is the regulation of human *conduct,* and not only the prevention of certain consequences.
18. Williams, *The Sanctity of Life,* op. cit., p. 242.
19. There are sometimes, of course, serious effects from having German measles. Still, it is arguable that these effects would be far less serious than the destruction of both damaged and undamaged nascent lives which, it is said, ought now systematically to be inflicted while we await the perfection and widespread use of a vaccine.

Chapter 10. The Protection of Life

1. *E.S.,* No. 2242f.
2. *Swiss Penal Code,* §34.
3. Ibid., §120.

Chapter 12. Abortion: Mediate vs. Immediate Animation

1. *ES.,* No. 481.
2. H. de Dorlodot, "A Vindication of the Mediate Animation Theory," *Theology and Evolution,* edited by E.C. Messenger (London: Sands, 1949), p. 260.

Chapter 13. Abortion: Its Moral Aspects

1. *A.A.S.*, Vol. LX (1968), p. 490.
2. *A.A.S.*, Vol. XLIII (1951), p. 857.
3. John T. Noonan Jr., "Abortion and the Catholic Church: A Summary History," *Natural Law Forum*, Vol. XII (1967), pp. 85–131.
4. H.M. Hering, "De tempore animationis foetus humani," *Angelicum*, Vol. XXVIII (1951), p. 19.
5. John Canon McCarthy, *Problems in Theology*, Vol. I: *The Sacraments* (Westminster, MD: Newman Press, 1956), pp. 15–21.
6. *A.A.S.*, Vol. XLIII (1951), p. 859.
7. Ibid., p. 838.
8. Richard A. McCormick, "Past Church Teaching on Abortion," *Proceedings of the Catholic Theological Society of America*, Vol. XXIII (1968), pp. 133–37.
9. *A.A.S.*, Vol. LX (1968), p. 490.
10. Noonan, "Abortion and the Catholic Church," op. cit. Note that in my judgment Noonan misinterprets the position of Thomas Sanchez and of Arthur Vermeersch. Germain G. Grisez, in *Abortion: The Myths, The Realities and the Arguments* (New York: Corpus Books, 1970), pp. 117–84, also misinterprets Sanchez, for he holds like Noonan that Sanchez would allow the abortion of an inanimate fetus to save the life of the mother that might be threatened if it were known she had conceived through sinful intercourse. On p. 168 Grisez maintains about Sanchez that apparently he alone in the Catholic tradition holds such an opinion. Although Sanchez did not hold such an opinion, in the next paragraph in the text I mention some Catholic theologians who did hold such a position.
11. John of Naples is cited by both Antoninus of Florence and Sylvester da Prieras in the places referred to in the next two notes.
12. S. Antoninus, *Summa Theologica* (Verona, 1760), Pars III, Tit. VII, Cap. III.
13. Sylvester Prierate, *Summa Sylvestrina* (Antwerp, 1569), Medicus, n. 4.
14. Martinus Azpilcueta, *Enchiridion sive Manuale Confessoriorum et Poenitentium* (Venice, 1593), c. XXV, n. 60–64.
15. Franciscus Torreblanca, *Epitome Delictorum sive De Magia* (Lyons, 1678), Lib. II, Cap. XLIII, n. 10.
16. Leo Zambellus, *Reportorium Morale Resolutorium Casum Conscientiae* (Venice, 1640), Medicus, n. 11.
17. Joannes Baptista de Lezana, *Summa Questionum Regularium seu de Casibus Conscientiae* (Venice, 1646), Tom. III, Abortus, n. 5.
18. Joannes Aegidius Trullenchus, *Opus Morale* (Barcelona, 1701), Tom. II, Lib. V, Cap. I, Dub. 4.
19. Gabriellus a S. Vincentio, *De Sacramentis*, Pars IV, De Matrimonio, Disp. VII, Q. V, n. 42.
20. The following theologians cite the opinion proposed by Torreblanca but do not follow it: Zanardus, Amicus, Franciscus Bonae Spei, Azor, Diana, Sporer.
21. *E.S.*, No. 2134.
22. John R. Connery, "Grisez on Abortion," *TS*, Vol. XXXI (1970), p. 173.
23. John T. Noonan Jr., *Contraception: A History of Its Treatment by the Catholic Theologians and Canonists* (Cambridge, MA: Harvard University Press, 1965).

24. The understanding of the value of the historical tradition as expressed in this sentence is similar to the opinion expressed in a roundtable discussion by René Simon, *Avortement et respect de la vie humaine,* p. 233.
25. Joseph A. Komonchak, "Ordinary Papal Magisterium and Religious Assent," *Contraception: Authority and Dissent,* edited by Charles E. Curran (New York: Herder & Herder, 1969), pp. 101–26.
26. For a summary of these, see D. Mongillo et al., "L'Aborto," *Rivista de Teologia Morale,* Vol. IV (1972), pp. 374–77.
27. Daniel Callahan, *Abortion: Law, Choice and Morality* (New York: Macmillan, 1970), pp. 409–47.
28. Ibid., pp. 378–401.
29. Bruno Ribes, "Recherche philosophique et théologique," *Avortement et respect de la vie humaine,* p. 200.
30. Bernard Quelquejeu, "La volonté de procréer," *Lumière et Vie,* Vol. XXI, n. 109 (Aout-Octobre, 1972), p. 67.
31. Jacques-Marie Pohier, "Réflexions théologiques sur la position de l'église Catholique," *Lumière et Vie,* Vol. XXI, n. 109 (Août-Octobre, 1972), p. 84.
32. Louis Beinart, "L'avortement est-il infanticide?," *Études,* Vol. CCCXXXIII (1970), p. 522.
33. Pohier, *Avortement et respect de la vie humaine,* p. 179.
34. Ribes, *Avortement et respect de la vie humaine,* p. 202.
35. Quelquejeu, "La volonté de procréer," op. cit., pp. 57–62.
36. Joseph F. Donceel, "Abortion: Mediate vs. Immediate Animation," *Continuum,* Vol. V (1967), pp. 167–71 (see chapter 12 in this book). Cf. Donceel, "A Liberal Catholic View," *Abortion in a Changing World,* edited by Robert E. Hall (New York: Columbia University Press, 1970), Vol. I, pp. 39–45; see also Donceel, "Immediate Animation and Delayed Hominization," *TS,* Vol. XXXI (1970), pp. 76–105.
37. Joseph F. Donceel, *TS,* Vol. XXXI (1970), pp. 83, 101.
38. John F. Dedek, *Human Life: Some Moral Issues* (New York: Sheed & Ward, 1972), pp. 88–89.
39. Wilfried Ruff, "Das embryoale Werden des Individuums," *Stimmen der Zeit,* Vol. CLXXXI (1968), pp. 107–19; Ruff, "Das embryoale Werden des Menschen," *Stimmen der Zeit,* Vol. CLXXXI (1968), pp. 327–37; Ruff, "Individualität und Personalität in embryoanalen Werden," *Theologie et Philosophie,* Vol. XLV (1970), pp. 24–59.
40. Andre E. Hellegers, "Fetal Development," *TS,* Vol. XXXI (1970), pp. 4–6.
41. Edouard Pousset, "Etre humain déjà," *Études,* Vol. CCCXXXIII (1970), pp. 512–13; Roger Troisfontaines, "Faut-it légaliser l'avortement?" *Nouvelle Revue Théologique,* Vol. CIII (1971), p. 491.
42. Grisez, *Abortion,* op. cit., pp. 333–46.
43. For a perceptive summary of recent debate on this question, see Richard A. McCormick, "Notes on Moral Theology," *TS,* Vol. XXXII (1971), pp. 80–97; Cf. *TS,* Vol. XXXIII (1972), pp. 68–86.
44. *A New Look at Christian Morality* (Notre Dame, IN: Fides, 1968), p. 243.
45. Richard A. McCormick, *Ambiguity in Moral Choice* (Milwaukee: Marquette University, 1973).
46. Marcellinus Zalba, *Theologiae Moralis Summa,* Vol. II: *Theologia Moralis Specialis* (Madrid: Biblioteca de Autores Christianos, 1953), pp. 276–77.

Chapter 14. The Interruption of Pregnancy

1. We have analyzed this case in detail as a particularly significant model of the borderline situation and here refer the reader especially to the section on "The Conflict Between Life and Life," in Helmut Thielicke, *Theological Ethics*, edited by William H. Lazareth (Philadelphia: Fortress Press, 1969), Vol. II, 1, par. 739ff., especially the footnotes to par. 744, and also the bibliographical references given there.
2. Cf. ibid., Vol. I, par. 1330ff.
3. Cf. on the problem of casuistry, ibid., Vol. II, 1, pp. 3ff.; Vol. II, 2, par. 4354ff. (Cf. "The Freedom of Decision: The Impossibility of Casuistry in Ethical Christianity," in Helmut Thielicke, *The Freedom of the Christian Man* [New York: Harper & Row, 1963], pp. 148ff.)
4. The fact that this does not relegate the eschatalogical and protological demands to the status of Platonic marginal phenomena of the ethos, but rather possesses an enormous historical immediacy, we have set forth in the "ethics of politics"; cf. Thielicke, *Theological Ethics*, op. cit., Vol. II, 2, index, "Bergpredigt," especially par. 562ff., pp. 665–68.
5. Cf. the discussion of this under the theme of how this transposition of the original "natural law" is to be made in the circumstances of this aeon in ibid., Vol. I, par. 2054ff.
6. Cf. ibid., Vol. I, par. 1001, especially 1014.
7. Cf. ibid., Vol. I, par. 2010ff.
8. Cf. ibid., Vol. I, par. 2144ff.
9. Cf. *ES*, No. 2243.
10. Cf., e.g., Thielicke, *Theological Ethics*, op. cit., Vol. II, 1, par. 2222ff., 2234ff.
11. Cf. Helmut Thielicke, *Tod und Leben* (3 ed.), p. 213. E.T.: *Death and Life*, translated by Edward H. Schroeder (Philadelphia: Fortress Press, 1970).
12. Cf. Thielicke, *Theological Ethics*, op. cit., Vol. I, par. 991ff., 1366ff.
13. However, even here certain changes are not entirely lacking when the norms of the order of creation are applied to this world. Here too a distinction is made between absolute and relative natural law. Nevertheless the break between the original state and the fallen world is viewed in a way completely different from that of Reformation theology. Cf. ibid., Vol. I, par. 2016ff.
14. The more precise reasons for this are set forth in our doctrine of sin, which we have developed in constant discussion with Catholic theology, Cf. ibid., Vol. I, index.

Chapter 16. Civil Law and Christian Morality: Abortion and the Churches

1. Patrick Devlin, *The Enforcement of Morals* (London: Oxford University Press, 1968), p. 9.
2. Basil Mitchell, *Law, Morality and Religion in a Secular Society* (London: Oxford University Press, 1967), pp. 131–36.
3. Pius Augustine, *Religious Freedom in Church and State* (Baltimore: Helicon, 1966); Richard J. Regan, *Conflict and Consensus: Religious Freedom and the Second Vatican Council* (New York: Macmillan, 1967).
4. Norman St. John-Stevas, *Birth Control and Public Policy* (Santa Barbara,

CA: Center for the Study of Democratic Institutions, 1960), pp. 57–58. St. John-Stevas wrote extensively on this question in the 1960s and also reasoned that private homosexual acts between consenting adults should not be legally prohibited. His reasoning is not quite the same as the approach to be developed in this essay. For his most systematic study of the question, see Norman St. John-Stevas, *Life, Death and the Law: Law and Christian Morals in England and the United States* (Bloomington, IN: Indiana University Press, 1961).

5. Aaron I. Abell, *American Catholicism and Social Action 1865–1950* (Notre Dame, IN: University of Notre Dame Press, 1963), pp. 199–205.
6. Thomas Aquinas, *De Regimine Principum*, Caput 14.
7. Aquinas: *Selected Political Writings*, ed. with an introduction by A.P. D'Entreves (Oxford: Basil Blackwell, 1954), pp. xxi–xxiv.
8. *S.T.*, IIa-IIae, q. 10, art. 9.
9. *S.T.*, a.11. For a further development of the teaching of Thomas Aquinas from the viewpoint of the rights of conscience of individuals in questions of religion, see Eric D'Arcy, *Conscience and its Right to Freedom* (New York: Sheed & Ward, 1961), pp. 87–180.
10. For a general overview of the question, see John Coleman Bennett, *Christians and the State* (New York: Charles Scribner's Sons, 1958). For a Lutheran approach, see Helmut Thielicke, *Theological Ethics*, Vol. II: *Politics*, edited by William H. Lazareth (Philadelphia: Fortress Press, 1969).
11. In what follows I am heavily indebted to R.A. Markus, "Two Conceptions of Political Authority: Augustine, *De Civitate Dei*, Vol. XIX, pp. 14–15, and "Some Thirteenth Century Interpretations," *The Journal of Theological Studies*, Vol. XVI (1965), pp. 69–100. For an authoritative study of Augustine's thought with emphasis on the more negative aspects of the state, see Herbert A Deane, *The Political and Social Ideas of St. Augustine* (New York: Columbia University Press, 1963). A contrary view is expressed by Etienne Gilson in St. Augustine, *The City of God,* foreword by Etienne Gilson (Garden City, NY: Doubleday Image Books, 1958), pp. 13–35.
12. *In Sent.* II, D. 44, q. 1, art. 3.
13. Ibid.
14. Ia, q. 96, art. 4.
15. *S.T.* For a development of Aquinas' teaching on dominion as a natural condition, see Thomas Gilby, *The Political Thought of Thomas Aquinas* (Chicago: University of Chicago Press, 1958), pp. 146–58.
16. Markus, *The Journal of Theological Studies*, Vol. XVI (1965), pp. 88–100.
17. *S.T.*, Ia–IIae, q. 90, art. 4.
18. *S.T.*, Ia–IIae, q. 95, art. 2.
19. *S.T.*, Ia–IIae, q. 96, art. 3.
20. *S.T.*, Ia–IIae, q. 96, art. 2.
21. *S.T.*, IIa–IIae, q. 10, art. 11.
22. Franz Böckle, *Fundamental Concepts of Moral Theology* (New York: Paulist Press, 1967), pp. 45–46, 63–64. Note the date of this work, which might no longer express the author's view of these questions, but such teaching is typical of the manualist approach.
23. St. John-Stevas, *Life, Death and the Law,* op. cit., p. 88. St. John-Stevas himself rejects this argument.
24. William J. Kenealy, "Contraception: A Violation of God's Law," *Catholic Mind*, Vol. XLVI (1948), pp. 552–64.

25. William J. Kenealy, "Law and Morals," *The Catholic Lawyer,* Vol. IX (1963), pp. 200–10.

26. *The Tablet,* Vol. CCX (1957), p. 523. The previous Archbishop of Westminster established a committee to make suggestions to the Wolfenden Committee in the course of its work. This committee concluded there should be no law against homosexual acts in private between consenting adults. For their report, see *The Dublin Review,* Vol. CCXXX (1956), pp. 60–65.

27. Declaration on Religious Freedom, n. 2.

28. Pope Pius XII, "*Ci riesce,*" *A.A.S.,* XLV (1953), p. 799.

29. D'Arcy, p. 259.

30. John Courtney Murray, *The Problem of Religious Freedom* (Westminster, MD: Newman Press, 1965), pp. 19–22; John Courtney Murray, "The Declaration on Religious Freedom: A Moment in its Legislative History," in *Religious Liberty: An End and A Beginning* (New York: Macmillan, 1966), pp. 15–42.

31. Murray, *The Problem of Religious Freedom,* op. cit., pp. 28–31.

32. Richard J. Regan, *Conflict and Consensus: Religious Freedom and the Second Vatican Council* (New York: Macmillan, 1967), p. 124.

33. Pope John XXIII, *Mater et Magistra,* n. 59–66.

34. Declaration on Religious Freedom, *The Documents of Vatican II,* edited by Walter M. Abbott (New York: Guild Press, 1966), p. 687, fn. 21. This is not an official footnote of the text of the document but rather a comment made by Murray.

35. Murray, *The Problem of Freedom,* op. cit., pp. 47–84.

36. *Mater et Magistra,* n. 226.

37. *Pacem in Terris,* n. 35.

38. Murray, *The Problem of Religious Freedom,* op. cit., pp. 29–30.

39. Declaration on Religious Freedom, n. 7.

40. *Documents of Vatican II,* p. 686, fn. 20. Again, this is an unofficial footnote expressing Murray's view of public order.

41. "Declaration on Procured Abortion," Sacred Congregation for the Doctrine of the Faith (Vatican City: Vatican Polyglot Press, 1974).

42. "Déclaration du conseil permanent de l'épiscopat français sur l'avortement," *La Documentation Catholique,* Vol. LV (1973), p. 677.

43. Ibid. For diverse comments on this declaration, see, "Les évêques français experiment un point de vue nuancé sur l'avortement," *Informations Catholiques Internationales,* n. 436 (July 15, 1973), pp. 10–11.

44. "Abortion: Law and Morality in Contemporary Catholic Theology," *The Jurist,* Vol. XXXII (1973), pp. 162–83. The same essay appears in *New Perspectives in Moral Theology* (Notre Dame, IN: Fides, 1974), pp. 163–93 (see Chapter 13 in this book).

45. Supreme Court of the United States, *Roe et al. v. Wade,* decided January 22, 1973 (Slip Opinion); *Roe et al. v. Bolton,* decided January 22, 1973 (Slip Opinion).

46. For a summary of the debate on the Supreme Court decisions in particular and the abortion question in general, see Richard A. McCormick, "Notes on Moral Theology: The Abortion Dossier," *T.S.,* Vol. XXXV (1974), pp. 312–59.

47. *Roe,* VI, p. 15; IX, p. 44.

48. *Roe,* VI, p. 19.

49. *Roe,* IX, p. 44.

50. *Roe,* Mr. Chief Justice Burger concurring, p. 2.
51. Declaration on Religious Freedom, n. 7.

Chapter 17. Personal Decisions and Social Policies in a Pluralist Society

1. William L. O'Neill in a book review in the *New Republic,* September 9, 1972, p. 26.
2. Walter Lippmann, *New York Post,* May 18, 1968.
3. Leon R. Kass, "New Beginnings in Life," *New Genetics and the Future of Man,* edited by Michael Hamilton (Grand Rapids, MI: Eerdmans, 1972), p. 35, n. 27.
4. Landrum B. Shettles, Letter to the Editor, *The New York Times,* February 14, 1973.
5. *The New York Times,* editorial, "Respect for Privacy," January 24, 1973.

Chapter 18. A Theological Response to Fundamentalism on the Abortion Issue

1. See *Newsweek,* "A Tide of Born-Again Politics," Vol. XCV (September 15, 1980), pp. 28–36.
2. See *Conservative Digest,* "Born Again Christians: A New Political Force," August 1979.
3. See Harold O.J. Brown, "Abortion on Demand," Brochure of Christian Action Council, Washington, DC.
4. *The Christian Century,* Vol. XCVII, No. 1 (July 30–August 6, 1980), p. 748.
5. Quoted by Stan Hastey in "Right Religion, Right Politics," *Missions,* September–October 1980, p. 68.
6. Roland Hegstad in *Liberty,* quoted by James Wall, in *loc. cit.*
7. Roland Bainton, *Christian Attitudes Toward War and Peace* (New York: Abingdon Press, 1969), p. 148.
8. Bruce Waltke, "Reflections from the Old Testament on Abortion," Presidential address at the December 29, 1975, meeting of the Evangelical Theological Society, p. 11.
9. Karl Barth, *Church Dogmatics* III/4 (Edinburgh: T. & T. Clark, 1961), p. 416. (See chapter 10 in this book.)
10. Ibid.
11. Ibid., p. 420.
12. Ibid., p. 421.
13. Harold O.J. Brown, *Death Before Life* (Nashville: Thomas Nelson, 1977), p. 127.
14. See John R.S. Stott, "Reverence for Human Life," *Christianity Today,* Vol. XVI, No. 18 (June 9, 1972), p. 12.
15. Not all fundamentalists agree on this. Waltke, for instance, uses the notion of the biological transmission of sin to argue that the fetus is a sinner by conception and thus a person. See "Reflections from the Old Testament on Abortion," op. cit., p. 12.
16. Brown, *Death Before Life,* op. cit., p. 118, note 1.
17. Charles Hartshorne, "Ethics and the Process of Living," Conference on Religion, Ethics and the Life Process, Institute of Religion and Human Development. Texas Medical Center, March 18–19, 1974.
18. Stott, "Reverence for Human Life," op. cit., p. 10.

19. Sissela Bok, "Who Shall Count as a Human Being?" in *Abortion: Pro and Con,* edited by Robert C. Perkins (Cambridge, MA: Schenkman Press, 1974), p. 91.
20. W.A. Criswell, quoted in *Christianity and Today,* February 16, 1973.

Chapter 19. A Protestant Ethical Approach

1. See, for example, his essay in this book (chapter 9).
2. The generalizations do not do injustice to the treatment of abortion in at least the following books: Thomas J. O'Donnell, S.J., *Morals in Medicine* (2d ed.; Westminster, MD: Newman Press, 1960); Charles J. McFadden, O.S.A., *Medical Ethics* (5th ed.; Philadelphia: F.A. Davis Co., 1961); John P. Kenny, O.P., *Principles of Medical Ethics* (2d ed.; Westminster, MD: Newman Press, 1962); Gerald Kelly, S.J., *Medico-Moral Problems* (St. Louis: The Catholic Hospital Association, 1958); Allen Keenan, O.F.M., and John Ryan, F.R.C.S.E., *Marriage: A Medical and Sacramental Study* (New York: Sheed & Ward, 1955). They apply also to manuals of moral theology that are more comprehensive than these which focus on medical care.
3. Albert Jonsen, S.J., *Responsibility in Modern Religious Ethics* (Washington, DC: Corpus Books, 1968), demonstrates the importance of the distinction made here. See pp. 36ff.
4. This procedure can be applied to cases other than pregnancy due to rape, obviously, and *might* lead to similar conclusions in instances of unwed girls, or older married women with large families, etc.
5. See Bernard Häring, "A Theological Evaluation" in *The Morality of Abortion,* edited by John T. Noonan Jr. (Cambridge, MA: Harvard University Press, 1970), pp. 123–45.
6. Paul Lehmann, *Ethics in a Christian Context* (New York: Harper & Row, 1964).
7. Ibid., pp. 124–32.
8. See Roland H. Bainton's discussions of the mournful mood of the just war theorists in *Christian Attitudes toward War and Peace* (New York: Abingdon Press, 1960), pp. 98, 112, 139, 145, 221–22.

Chapter 20. Theology of Pro-choice: A Feminist Perspective

1. The Christian natural-law tradition developed because many Christians understood that the power of moral reason inhered in human beings *qua* human beings, not merely in the understanding that comes from being Christian. Those who follow natural-law methods address moral issues from the standpoint of what options appear rationally compelling, given present reflection, rather than from theological claims alone. My own moral theological method is congenial to certain of these natural-law assumptions. Roman Catholic natural-law teaching, however, has become internally incoherent by insisting that in some matters of morality the *teaching authority* of the hierarchy must be taken as the proper definition of what is rational. This replacement of reasoned reflection by ecclesial authority seems to this Protestant to offend against what we must mean by moral reasoning on best understanding. I would argue that a moral theology cannot forfeit final judgment or even penultimate judgment on

moral matters to anything except *fully deliberated contemporary communal consensus.* On the abortion issue, this of course would mean women would be consulted in a degree that reflects their numbers in the Catholic Church. No a priori claims to authoritative moral reason are ever possible and if those affected are not consulted, the teaching *cannot* claim rationality.

2. See Paul D. Simmons' essay, chapter 18 in this book.

3. H. Richard Niebuhr often warned his theological compatriots about abstracting acts from the life-project in which they are imbedded, but this warning is much neglected in the writings of Christian moralists. Cf. "The Christian Church in the World Crises," *Christianity and Society,* Vol. VI, 1941.

4. We know now that the birth control pill does not always work by preventing fertilization of the ova by the sperm. Frequently, the pill causes the wall of the uterus to expel the newly fertilized ova. The point here is that, from a biological point of view, there is no point in a procreative process that can be taken as a clear dividing line on which to pin neat moral distinctions.

5. The most conspicuous example of corporate involvement in contraceptive failure was the famous Dalkan Shield scandal. Note also that the manufacturer of the Dalkan Shield is still dumping its dangerous and ineffective product on family-planning programs of so-called Third World (over-exploited) countries.

6. Helmut Thielicke, *The Ethics of Sex* (New York: Harper & Row, 1964), pp. 199–247. Compare pp. 210 and 226ff. Barth's position on abortion is a bit more complicated than I can elaborate here, which is why one will find him quoted on both sides of the debate. Barth's method allows him to argue that any given radical human act could turn out to be "the will of God" in a given context or setting. We may at any time be given "permission" by God's radical freedom to do what was not before permissible. My point here is that Barth exposits this possible exception in such a traditional, prohibitory context that I do not believe it appropriate to cite him on the pro-choice side of the debate. In my opinion, no woman could ever accept the convoluted way in which Barth's biblical exegesis opens the door (a slight crack) to woman's full humanity. His reasoning on these questions simply demonstrates what deep difficulty the Christian tradition's exegetical tradition is in with respect to the full humanity and moral agency of women. (See chapter 10 in this book.)

7. Cf. my "When Fruitfulness and Blessedness Diverge," *Religion and Life,* 1972. (My views on the seriousness of misogyny as an historical force have deepened since I wrote this essay.)

8. Marie Augusta Neal, "Sociology and Sexuality: A Feminist Perspective," *Christianity and Crisis,* Vol. 39, No. 8 (May 14, 1979).

9. For a feminist theology of relationship, see Carter Heyward, *Toward the Redemption of God: A Theology of Mutual Relation* (Washington, DC: University Press of America, 1982).

10. Neal, "Sociology and Sexuality," op. cit. This article is of critical importance in discussions of the theology and morality of abortion.

11. Susan Teft Nicholson, *Abortion and the Roman Catholic Church. JRE* studies in Religious Ethics II, the University of Tennessee (Knoxville TN: Religious Ethics, Inc., 1978). This carefully crafted study assumes that there has been a clear "anti-killing" ethic separable from any antisexual

ethic in Christianity. This is an assumption that my historical research does not sustain.

12. Jean Meyer, "Toward a Non-Malthusian Population Policy" in Daniel Callahan, ed., *The American Population Debate* (Garden City, NY: Doubleday, 1971).

13. I am well aware that Catholic moral theology opens up several ways for faithful Catholics to challenge the teaching office of the Church on moral questions. However, I remain unsatisfied that these qualifications of inerrancy in moral matters stand up in situations of moral controversy. If freedom of conscience does not function de jure, should it be claimed as existent in principle?

14. I elaborate this point in greater detail in "Anger As a Work of Love: Christian Ethics for Women and Other Strangers," *Union Seminary Quarterly Review,* January 1981.

15. For example, Paul Ramsey gave unqualified support to U.S. military involvement in Southeast Asia in light of just war considerations but finds abortion to be an unexceptional moral wrong.

16. One of the reasons why abortion-on-demand rhetoric—even when it is politically effective in the immediate moment—has had a backlash effect is because it seems to many to imply a lack of reciprocity between women's needs and society's needs. While I would not deny, in principle, a possible conflict of interest between women's well-being and community's needs for reproduction, there is little or no historical evidence that suggests women are less responsible to well-being-of-the-community considerations than are men! We need not fall into a liberal, individualistic trap in arguing the central importance of procreative choice to issues of women's well-being in society. The right in question is body-right or freedom from coercion in childbearing. It is careless to say that the right in question is the right to an abortion. Morally, the right is bodily self-determination, a fundamental condition of personhood and a foundational moral right.

17. A theory is crassly utilitarian only if it fails to grant equal moral worth to all persons in the calculation of social consequences—as, for example, when some people's financial well-being is weighted more than someone else's basic physical existence. I do *not* mean to criticize any type of utilitarian moral theory that weighs the actual consequences of actions. In fact, I believe no moral theory is adequate if it does not have a strong utilitarian component.

18. For a perceptive discussion of this danger by a distinguished Catholic priest, read George C. Higgins "The Prolife Movement and the New Right," *America,* September 13, 1980, pp. 107–10.

19. I believe the single most valid concern raised by opponents of abortion is that the frequent practice of abortion, over time, creates an ethos which may contribute to a general cultural insensitivity to the value of human life. I hope all the foregoing makes clear my adamant objection to letting this insight justify yet more violence against women in this society. However, I do believe we should be very clear that we stand ready to support—emphatically—any social policies which would lessen the need for abortion *without* jeopardizing women's right to control our procreative power.

Selected Bibliography

Aquinas, Thomas. *Summa Theologica.*

Aristotle. *De Anima.*

Athenagoras. *Embassy for the Christians.*

Augustine. *De Anima.*

———. *De Nuptiis et Concupiscentia.*

———. *Enchiridion.*

———. *Epistola.*

Barth, Karl. *Church Dogmatics.* Pt. III/4. Edinburgh: T. & T. Clark, 1961.

Basil of Cappadocia. *Letters.*

Baum, Gregory. "Abortion: An Ecumenical Dilemma," *Commonweal,* Vol. 99, No. 9 (November 30, 1973), pp. 231–35.

Bleich, David. "Abortion in Halakhic Literature," *Tradition,* Vol. 10 (1968), pp. 70–120.

Bok, Sissela. "Ethical Problems of Abortion," *Hastings Center Studies,* Vol. 2 (1974), pp. 33–52.

Bonhoeffer, Dietrich. *Ethics.* Translated by Neville Horton Smith. Edited by Eberhard Bethge. London: S.C.M. Press, 1955.

Brody, Baruch. "Abortion and the Sanctity of Human Life," *American Philosophical Quarterly,* Vol. 10 (April 1973), pp. 133–40.

Callahan, Daniel. *Abortion: Law, Choice and Morality.* New York: Macmillan, 1977.

———. "Abortion: Thinking and Experiencing," *Christianity and Crisis,* Vol. 32 (January 8, 1973), pp. 295–98.

———. "Rights of Fetus Uncertain," *National Catholic Reporter,* Vol. 13, No. 32 (February 18, 1977).

Church of England, Board of Social Responsibility. *Abortion: An Ethical Discussion.* London: Church Information Office, 1965.

Clement of Alexandria. *Pedagogus.*

Connery, John. *Abortion: The Development of the Roman Catholic Perspective.* Chicago: Loyola University Press, 1977.

Curran, Charles E. "Abortion: Ethical Aspects," *Encyclopedia of Bioethics.* Edited by Warren T. Reich. New York: Free Press, 1978, Vol. 1, pp. 17–25.

———. "Civil Law and Christian Morality," *Clergy Review,* Vol. 62, No. 6 (June 1977), pp. 227–42.

———. *Contemporary Problems in Moral Theology.* Notre Dame, IN: Fides, 1970.

———. *Issues in Sexual and Medical Ethics.* Notre Dame, IN: University of Notre Dame Press, 1978.

———. *New Perspectives in Moral Theology.* Notre Dame, IN: Fides, 1974, pp. 163–93.

———. *Transition and Tradition in Moral Theology.* Notre Dame, IN: University of Notre Dame Press, 1979.

Cyprian. *Epistle* 52.

Dedek, John. "Abortion: A Theological Judgement," *Chicago Studies*, Vol. 101 (Fall 1971), pp. 313–33.

———. *Some Moral Issues.* New York: Sheed & Ward, 1972.

Degnan, D. "Laws, Morals and Abortion," *Commonweal*, Vol. 100, No. 13, (May 31, 1974), pp. 305–8.

Didache, The.

Donceel, Joseph F., S.J. "Abortion: Mediate vs. Immediate Animation," *Continuum*, Vol. 5, No. 1 (Spring 1967), pp. 167–71.

———. "Immediate Animation and Delayed Hominization," *Theological Studies*, Vol. 31, No. 1 (March 1970), pp. 76–105.

———. "Why Is Abortion Wrong?" *America*, Vol. 133, No. 4 (August 16, 1975), pp. 65–67.

Drinan, Robert F., S.J. "Abortions on Medicaid," *Commonweal*, Vol. 97, No. 19, (February 16, 1973), pp. 438–40.

———. "Catholic Moral Teaching and Abortion Laws in America," *Catholic Theological Society of America Proceedings*, Vol. 23 (1968), pp. 118–30.

———. "Contemporary Protestant Thinking," *America*, Vol. 117, No. 24 (December 9, 1967), p. 713.

———. "Jurisprudential Options," *Theological Studies*, Vol. 31, No. 1 (March 1970), pp. 149–69.

———. "The Right of the Fetus to Be Born," *Dublin Review*, No. 514 (Winter 1967–68), pp. 365–81.

Dupre, L.K. "New Approach to Abortion Question," *Theological Studies*, Vol. 38, (September 1973), pp. 481–88.

Epistle of Barnabas.

Epistle to Diognetus.

Feldman, David M. *Birth Control and Jewish Law.* New York: New York University Press, 1968.

Fletcher, Joseph F. "Abortion and the True Believer," *Christian Century*, Vol. 91, No. 41 (November 27, 1974), pp. 1126–27.

———. *Humanhood: Essays in Biomedical Ethics.* Buffalo: Prometheus Books, 1979.

———. *Situation Ethics.* Philadelphia: Westminster Press, 1966.

Gratian. *Decretum.*

Greenburg, Blu. "Abortion: A Challenge to Halakhah," *Judaism*, Vol. 25, No. 2. (Spring 1976), pp. 436–40.

Grisez, Germain. *Abortion: Myths, the Realities, and the Arguments.* New York: Corpus Books, 1970.

Gustafson, James M. "A Christian Approach to the Ethics of Abortion, *Dublin Review*, No. 514 (Winter 1967–68), pp. 346–64.

———. "A Protestant Ethical Approach," *The Morality of Abortion.* Edited by John T. Noonan Jr. Cambridge, MA: Harvard University Press, 1970, pp. 101–22.

Häring, Bernard. *Faithful and Free in Christ*, Vol. I. New York: Seabury Press, 1978.

————. *Faithful and Free in Christ,* Vol. II. New York: Seabury Press, 1979.

————. *Medical Ethics.* Edited by Gabrielle L. Jean. Notre Dame, IN: Fides, 1973, pp. 94–119.

————. "New Dimensions of Responsible Parenthood," *Theological Studies,* Vol. 37, No. 1 (March 1976), pp. 120–32.

————. "A Theological Evaluation," *The Morality of Abortion.* Edited by John T. Noonan Jr. Cambridge, MA: Harvard University Press, 1970, pp. 123–45.

Harrison, Beverly Wildung. "Theology of Pro-Choice: A Feminist Perspective," *The Witness,* Vol. 64, Nos. 7 and 8 (July and September 1981).

Hauerwas, Stanley. "Abortion and Normative Ethics," *Cross Currents,* Vol. 21, No. 4 (Fall 1971), pp. 399–414.

————. "Abortion: The Agent's Perspective," *American Ecclesiastical Review,* Vol. 167, No. 2 (February 1973), pp. 102–20.

————. *Vision and Virtue.* Notre Dame, IN: University of Notre Dame Press, 1981.

Jakobowitz, Isaac. *Jewish Medical Ethics,* 2d ed. New York: Block Publishing Company, 1975, pp. 170–91.

Jerome. *Epistle* 22.

Klein, Isaac. "Abortion: A Jewish View," *Dublin Review,* No. 514 (Winter 1967–68), pp. 382–90.

Kraus, James E. "Is Abortion Absolutely Prohibited?," *Continuum,* Vol. 6, No. 3 (Fall 1968), pp. 436–40.

McCormick, Richard A. "Aspects of the Moral Question," *America,* Vol. 117, No. 24 (December 9, 1967), pp. 716–19.

————. "A Changing Morality and Policy," *Hospital Progress,* Vol. 60 (February 1979), pp. 36–44.

————. *How Brave A New World?* Garden City, NY: Doubleday, 1981.

————. "Notes on Moral Theology: The Abortion Dossier," *Theological Studies,* Vol. 35 (June 1974), pp. 312–59.

————. "Past Church Teaching on Abortion," *Catholic Theological Society of America Proceedings,* Vol. 23 (1968), pp. 131–51.

————. "Rules for Debate," *America,* Vol. 139, No. 2 (July 15–22, 1978), pp. 26–30.

McDonagh, Edna. "Ethical Problems of Abortion," *Irish Theological Quarterly,* Vol. 35 (July 1968), pp. 268–97.

Mead, Margaret, "Rights to Life," *Christianity and Crisis,* Vol. 32 (January 8, 1973) pp. 288–92.

Milhaven, John G. "The Abortion Debate: An Epistemological Interpretation," *Theological Studies,* Vol. 31, No. 1 (March 1970), pp. 106–24.

————. *Towards a New Catholic Morality.* Garden City, NY: Doubleday, 1970.

National Council of Churches in the U.S.A., Faith and Order Commission. *Guidelines for Ecumenical Debate on Homosexuality and Abortion.* New York: National Council of Churches, 1979.

Nelson, J. Robert. "What Does Theology Say About Abortion?" *Christian Century,* Vol. 90, No. 5 (January 31, 1973), pp. 124–28.

Nelson, James B. "Abortion: Protestant Perspectives," *Encyclopedia of Bioethics,* edited by Warren T. Reich. New York: The Free Press, 1978, pp. 13–17.

Neuhaus, Richard J. "The Dangerous Assumption," *Commonweal,* Vol. 86, No. 15. (June 30, 1967), pp. 408–13.

Newton, Lisa. "Is Abortion a Religious Issue?," *Hastings Center Report,* Vol. 8, No. 4 (August 1978), pp. 16–17.

Noonan, John T., Jr. "Abortion and the Catholic Church: A Summary History," *Natural Law Forum*, Vol. 12 (1967), pp. 85–131.

———. "An Almost Absolute Value in History," *The Morality of Abortion*, edited by John T. Noonan Jr. Cambridge, MA: Harvard University Press, 1970.

Noonan, John T., Jr. et al. *Abortion*. Cambridge, MA: Harvard University Press, 1968.

Ramsey, Paul. "Abortion: A Review Article," *The Thomist*, Vol. 37, No. 1 (January 1973), pp. 174–226.

———. "Feticide/Infanticide upon Request," *Religion in Life*, Vol. 39 (Summer 1970), pp. 170–86.

———. "The Morality of Abortion," *Life or Death: Ethics and Options*, edited by Daniel H. Labby. Seattle: University of Washington Press, 1968, pp. 60–93.

———. "The Morality of Abortion," *Moral Problems: A Collection of Philosophical Essays*, edited by James Rachels. New York: Harper & Row, 1971, pp. 4–27.

———. "Protecting the Unborn," *Commonweal*, Vol. 100, No. 13 (May 31, 1974), pp. 308–14.

———. "Reference Points in Deciding About Abortion," *The Morality of Abortion*, edited by John T. Noonan Jr. Cambridge, MA: Harvard University Press, 1970.

———. "The Sanctity of Life." *Dublin Review*, Vol. 241 (Spring 1967), pp. 3–23.

Shinn, Roger L. "Personal Decisions and Social Policies," *Perkins Journal*, Vol. 27, No. 1 (Fall 1973), pp. 58–63.

Simmons, Paul D. "A Theological Response to Fundamentalism on the Abortion Issue," *Church and Society*, Vol. 71, No. 4 (March–April 1981), pp. 22–35.

Tertullian, *De Anima*.

Thielicke, Helmut. *The Ethics of Sex*, translated by John W. Doberstein. New York: Harper & Row, 1964, pp. 226–47.

Wassner, Thomas. "Contemporary Attitudes of the Roman Catholic Church Toward Abortion," *Journal of Religion and Health*, Vol. 7, No. 4 (October 1968), pp. 311–23.

Weddington, Sarah Ragle. "The Woman's Right of Privacy," *Perkins Journal*, Vol. 27, No. 1 (Fall 1973), pp. 35–41.

Williams, George H. "Religious Residues and Presuppositions in the American Debate on Abortion," *Theological Studies*, Vol. 31, No. 1 (March 1970), pp. 10–75.

———. "The Sacred Condominium," *The Morality of Abortion*, edited by John T. Noonan Jr. Cambridge, MA: Harvard University Press, 1970, pp. 146–71.